Homeric Misdirection

MICHIGAN MONOGRAPHS IN CLASSICAL ANTIQUITY

The Play of Fictions: Studies in Ovid's *Metamorphoses* Book 2
   A. M. Keith

Homeric Misdirection: False Predictions in the *Iliad*
   James V. Morrison

Homeric Misdirection

False Predictions in the *Iliad*

James V. Morrison

Ann Arbor
THE UNIVERSITY OF MICHIGAN PRESS

Copyright © by the University of Michigan 1992
All rights reserved
Published in the United States of America by
The University of Michigan Press
Manufactured in the United States of America

1995   1994   1993   1992   4   3   2   1

Library of Congress Cataloging-in-Publication Data

Morrison, James V., 1956–
   Homeric misdirection : false predictions in the Iliad / James
V. Morrison.
     p.   cm. — (Michigan monographs in classical antiquity)
  Includes bibliographical references and indexes.
  ISBN 0-472-10352-0 (alk. paper)
   1. Homer. Iliad.   2. Achilles (Greek mythology) in literature.
3. Truthfulness and falsehood in literature.   4. Authors and
readers—Greece.   5. Trojan War in literature.   6. Prophecies in
literature.   7. Deception in literature.   8. Narration (Rhetoric).
9. Rhetoric, Ancient.   10. Homer—Technique.   I. Title.
II. Series.
PA4037.M73   1992
883'.01—dc20   92-27449
                                                                   CIP

To my wife, Ruth

ἀλλ' οὐ Ζεὺς ἀνδρεσσι νοήματα πάντα τελευτᾷ.
But Zeus does not bring to fulfillment all thoughts in the minds of men.
—(*Iliad* 18.328)

Ὣς ἔφατ', οἱ δ' ἄρα πάντες ἀκὴν ἐγένοντο σιωπῇ
κηληθμῷ δ' ἔσχοντο κατὰ μέγαρα σκιόεντα.
Thus he spoke, and they were all struck with silence,
held by the spell of his words in the shadowy halls.
—(*Odyssey* 11.333-34 = 13.1-2)

Acknowledgments

I would like to take this opportunity to thank the many people who have offered help, encouragement, and valuable suggestions. Tony Edwards, Jim Porter, and Jim White offered critical comments and thoughtful reflections upon the larger significance of misdirection in Homer, when I was first developing my argument. I have benefited enormously from the advice of Bill Slater, Catherine Connors, and Louise Pratt, who read this manuscript at various states of completion. I am aware of the many hours these readers have spent on earlier versions and wish to offer my appreciation for their criticisms, both substantive and for those numerous passages in which I might have expressed myself better. Their advice has vastly improved my overall project.

I owe much to my conversations with Vicki Pedrick, who is a wise reader of Homer. Tom Rosenthal, who combines musical skill with an interest in literature and classics, provided a critical perspective to my thinking on the role of the artist working within a tradition.

I thank Ellen Bauerle of the University of Michigan Press for allowing me enough freedom to improve this manuscript and for the encouragement I needed to persevere, and Christina Milton for her assistance with editing the manuscript. I also wish to thank the two anonymous readers for their invariably constructive criticism.

I am especially grateful to Ruth Scodel. This project began as her idea. Her valuable responses and timely encouragement not only improved my work but helped to make this entire enterprise worthwhile and enjoyable. I feel fortunate to have had the opportunity to work with her.

Contents

1. Misdirection as a Poetic Strategy   1
2. A Narrative Analysis of the *Iliad*   11
3. *Iliad* 1 and Alternatives to the Epic Tradition   23
4. Misdirection 1: False Anticipation   35
5. Misdirection 2: Epic Suspense   51
6. Misdirection 3: Thematic Misdirection   73
7. The *Iliad* and the Audience: Mortal Miscalculation   95
8. Homer and the Tradition   109

Appendix: The Myth of Meleager and Homeric Misdirection   119

Notes   125

Bibliography   149

Index of Passages   157

General Index   165

Text and Abbreviations

I have used Allen's text of Homer. Unless the *Odyssey* is specified, all Homeric passages are from the *Iliad*. The reading of the scholia follows Erbse 1969–83. Translation of the Homeric passages is based upon Lattimore 1951. At times I have modified his wording. The translations of the scholia are my own. Modern scholarship is cited by the last name of the author and the date of publication.

Chapter 1

Misdirection as a Poetic Strategy

False predictions in the *Iliad* of Homer have puzzled readers for over two thousand years. In this study, I argue that such misleading statements are part of a deliberate effort to upset the expectations of the audience. The poet introduces false predictions in order to promote suspense and uncertainty, as he presents his version of the traditional story of the Trojan War. This chapter begins with an example of a false prediction, a representative instance of Homeric misdirection in which the poet misleads his audience. After a brief review of previous explanations, I offer my own approach and close with a preliminary sketch of the advantages of this new interpretation.

On the third day of fighting in the *Iliad*, Agamemnon leads the Greeks into battle. When the Greek leader is on the point of reaching Troy, Zeus sends Iris to Hector with a message advising Hector not to challenge Agamemnon (11.181–209). Zeus' message closes with these words:

"αὐτὰρ ἐπεί ['Αγαμέμνων] κ' ἢ δουρὶ τυπεὶς ἢ βλήμενος ἰῷ
εἰς ἵππους ἅλεται, τότε οἱ ["Εκτορι] κράτος ἐγγυαλίξω
κτείνειν, εἰς ὅ κε νῆας ἐυσσέλμους ἀφίκηται
δύῃ τ' ἠέλιος καὶ ἐπὶ κνέφας ἱερὸν ἔλθῃ."

"But when, either struck with a spear or hit by an arrow,
[Agamemnon] springs up behind his horses, then I guarantee
   power to [Hector]
to kill men, till he makes his way to the strong-benched vessels,
until the sun goes down and the blessed darkness comes over."
(11.191–94 ≈ 11.206–9)

The god promises that, after Agamemnon receives a wound and leaves the battlefield, Hector will enjoy success until sundown. In response, Hector withdraws, while the poet describes Agamemnon's final moments of success. The Greek leader is soon wounded and returns to his camp. Hector recalls Zeus' assurance and leads his men into battle (11.284–98). Thus far Zeus' announcement has proven accurate. Now that Agamemnon has withdrawn, Hector—and the audience—anticipate a Trojan victory led by Hector.[1] The poet heightens the audience's expectation by asking:

Ἔνθα τίνα πρῶτον, τίνα δ' ὕστατον ἐξενάριξεν
Ἕκτωρ Πριαμίδης, ὅτε οἱ Ζεὺς κῦδος ἔδωκεν;

Whom then was the first, and whom the last that he slaughtered,
Hector, Priam's son, now that Zeus granted him glory?
(11.299–300)

Contrary to expectation, however, when Hector begins to force a Greek retreat, he soon encounters Diomedes and Odysseus, who drive him to his knees (cf. esp. 11.354–56).[2] After blacking out, Hector himself retreats from the battlefront and is virtually unheard of for over five hundred lines of the epic.[3]

Zeus has guaranteed a Trojan victory early in the epic (cf. 1.508–30). On the second day of fighting, the Trojans do not yet drive the Greeks to their ships, but that evening, Zeus predicts that no one will stop Hector until Achilles acts (8.470–77). Zeus' promise that Hector will be victorious until sundown (11.191–94) appears to indicate that, after Agamemnon is injured, Hector will advance without further obstacle. The audience anticipates that this is the moment for Hector's victory, only to be disappointed in that expectation. After such apparently unambiguous announcements, how are we to understand Hector's unanticipated removal from battle in book 11?[4]

This is only one instance of a scene in the *Iliad* that contradicts expectations generated earlier in the epic. Similar unanticipated episodes occur elsewhere. In book 3, every indication has been given that battle will begin, when Paris proposes a duel with Menelaus. Not only are the Greeks and Trojans shocked (cf. 3.95), but again the audience has every reason to believe the armies are to meet in battle. Once battle begins in earnest, a Greek defeat appears inevitable—yet the Trojans are in such desperate straits they must send Hector back to Troy to seek divine aid (6.73-76). When the Greek ships are threatened, Zeus says that Achilles will send Patroclus to battle after Hector reaches the Myrmidons' camp (15.60-65). In fact, Achilles acts long before his own ships are threatened. Hector's unexpected withdrawal in book 11—contradicting earlier predictions—is not a unique occurrence in this epic.

Scholars have attempted to explain why plans, promises, and prophecies are often inconsistent with what later transpires in the *Iliad*. These accounts employ diverse methods of criticism. The Alexandrian editors "athetized"—or marked as problematic—false predictions, questioning their authenticity. In more recent times, the analysts viewed the *Iliad* as a conglomeration of separate songs by distinct poets, joined together by a less than ingenious editor. Seeing false predictions as evidence of multiple authorship, they regarded the inconsistencies as a result of the *Iliad*'s patchwork genesis. A third view follows from the recognition that Homeric epic derives from an oral tradition. This theory maintains that the oral poet and his eighth-century B.C. audience did not value consistency as highly as their literate counterparts today. The concerns of the singer were purely momentary: he would concentrate upon each scene only during its presentation, while the audience would not notice lack of harmony between an early prediction and a scene presented several hours (or days) later.[5] These approaches are diverse, yet underlying them all is the common assumption that the poet is a reliable guide. By accurately preparing the audience for later events, the poet's goal is that foreshadowing be consistent with the subsequent narrative—at least to the extent that the poet notices such things.[6] Thus false predictions have been viewed negatively; they are seen as having no positive function within the narrative itself.

I propose another way to understand the discrepancy between predictions and the succeeding narrative in the *Iliad*. I maintain that Homer frequently raises the audience's anticipations for a particular scene only to upset such anticipations. False predictions may function positively if the poet introduces them in order to mislead the audience. Zeus' misleading guarantee in book 11 is not a fault to be removed or an incidental lapse to be explained away; the unexpected blow to Hector is paradigmatic for the epic as a whole. The poet is in complete control of these false signals, with the deliberate goal—in book 11 and elsewhere—of disappointing the audience's expectations. Indeed, false predictions play an integral role in the poet's presentation of the story of the *Iliad*. When the poet structures the narrative in such a way as to upset or disappoint the audience's expectations in some way, I call this *misdirection*.[7]

Several perspectives on the *Iliad* have led me to this interpretation. As scholarship of the past sixty years has shown, the *Iliad* is a sophisticated narrative. Its intricate design has been demonstrated at the levels of structure, theme, and image. In *Homer and the Heroic Tradition,* Whitman has shown how geometric patterns furnish the epic with a compositional framework. One instance he notes is the neat correspondence between books 1 and 24. The sequence of episodes in book 1—supplication, burial, message to Zeus, and divine quarrel—correspond in mirror image to the closing book of the epic.[8] In addition, recent work has emphasized the carefully developed sequence of supplication scenes providing an anchor for the entire work.[9] Besides formal design and theme, we find that earlier paradigmatic images are recalled at later critical junctures in the narrative. For example, the singular simile of a "dark-water spring" is used to describe Agamemnon in tears before he sends the embassy to Achilles and is echoed when Patroclus approaches Achilles (9.14-15, 16.3-4).[10] These patterns of balance, development, and recall express the careful arrangement of a single poet.

It is reasonable also to expect such carefully crafted composition with regard to predictions in the epic, and in general, this is what we find. Homer often gives clear indications of what will happen. For example, the poet unambiguously foreshadows the deaths of Sarpedon, Patroclus, and Hector. Even Achilles' death—which is not presented within the *Iliad*—is anticipated for the audience in extensive detail.[11] Formulaic language or rapid composition do not prevent the poet from giving clear indications of what will follow, if he decides to do so.

If the *Iliad* is a carefully constructed narrative, and this care may be seen in the foreshadowing of heroes' deaths, for example, I think it unwise to dismiss out of hand predictions that are ambiguous or misleading. An effort should be made first to recover the effect of such passages upon the audience and second to seek possible motivations on the part of the poet for structuring his story as he does. A vague or deceptive prediction has the potential to unsettle the audience's preconception of how the story will proceed. We might contrast the utter clarity of predictions that Patroclus will die with the anticipations of Achilles' return to battle. Zeus refers to the death of Patroclus (8.473-76). The poet later explicitly tells us that Patroclus is seeking his own death (16.46-47). The audience has no doubt concerning the outcome of Patroclus' meeting with Hector. Such clarity, however, does not attend the predictions regarding Achilles' reentry into battle. Early in the epic, we learn that Achilles will return to battle (2.694), yet the circumstances of that return are left vague. It is unclear whether Achilles will wait until his own ships are threatened (cf. 9.649-55, 15.61-65) or until after Patroclus' death (cf. 8.473-76). Again the signals conflict on the related issue of Hector's triumph in Achilles' absence. Can anyone other than Achilles slow Hector's advance (cf. 8.473-77, 9.649-55)? Later, after Achilles slays him, the fate of Hector's corpse consumes our attention, yet there is no clear resolution until the final book of the epic. These episodes—Achilles' return, Hector's victory, the burial of Hector's corpse—are of central importance to the epic as a whole, yet Homer does not furnish the audience in advance with a clear picture of what will transpire. The poet manipulates the audience throughout the epic, and as the effect of such false and misleading predictions, the audience experiences suspense and surprise.

Yet in a traditional work such as the *Iliad,* what type of uncertainty could the audience experience? Let me briefly recapitulate the scholarly consensus regarding suspense and surprise in Homeric epic (a view I wish to modify). By general agreement, the *Iliad* is not the sort of work that strives for surprise. Because the story of the *Iliad* derives from an oral tradition that over many generations told of an earlier age when the Greeks sailed to Troy, Homer should be viewed as only one of many poets who had sung about the Trojan War. The ancient audience knew the epic tradition and was familiar with the heroes, the gods, and the general story line. Such an audience would not value unexpected twists in the plot. Delight in invention and outright surprise, according to the consensus, is a modern taste better suited to novels and detective stories. The oral poet does all he can to keep the audience aware of impending events, so that the only suspense felt would be an animated interest in how or when the anticipated events would occur. The events themselves are conspicuously anticipated by earlier predictions. G.E.D. Duckworth expresses this view in his book *Foreshadowing and Suspense in the Epics of Homer, Vergil, and Apollonius*:

> In the first part of each of the Homeric poems there is a gradual development in the reader's foreknowledge; when approximately two-thirds of the narrative have been set forth, the remainder of the action is forecast in detail. This knowledge of the later action does not remove

the suspense experienced by the reader, however. He still feels a deep interest in the manner and time of the fulfillment of each foreshadowed event, an interest which the poet heightens by the repetition of the announcement and by the retardation of the expected event.[12]

Duckworth and others believe that the only uncertainty at work in the *Iliad* concerns the time and manner of the fulfillment of previously anticipated events.[13]

This view is correct in part. The audience is familiar with the epic tradition and knows how the story is likely to come out. The *Iliad* is not like a modern novel: it presupposes a knowledgeable audience, well-versed in epic tales.[14] And it is true that foreshadowing prepares the audience for later episodes, reinforcing the audience's presumption that it knows what to expect. But this is not the whole story. The consensus view of the *Iliad* is colored, I believe, by our reactions as readers and rereaders. For us, the *Iliad* has become an essentially fixed text; we do not doubt how the story will end. Yet if we can look at the *Iliad* afresh, we see that misdirection—the deliberate disappointment of the audience's expectations—is a complement to the better recognized phenomenon of foreshadowing. While foreshadowing offers the audience an omniscient, "divine" perspective upon the events at Troy, misdirection has the effect of undermining the audience's confidence in its ability to anticipate how the story of Achilles' anger will actually turn out. A poet singing a traditional song can mislead a knowledgeable audience by exploiting the audience's assumption that it is in a privileged position of superior knowledge. False predictions and untraditional episodes—alternating with accurate predictions and familiar scenes—force the audience to negotiate between everything it knows (based on knowledge of the tradition and expectations generated early in the epic) and an uncertainty as to how and whether the story will indeed turn out as expected. In a sense, the audience knows that the Greeks will win the war, yet even this basic assumption is at times thrown into doubt. Misdirection—the careful creation and disappointment of expectations—is the poet's means for promoting uncertainty. Even for a reading and rereading audience, the effects of misdirection are experienced, if perhaps in a different, more subtle way. In recent times, only W. Schadewaldt has viewed the raising of false expectations as a deliberate ploy on the part of the poet. Beginning with the scene in book 11, his analysis in *Iliasstudien* demonstrates the audience's disappointment in its expectation of Hector's victory.

Schadewaldt remarks that in the *Iliad* "the unexpected belongs to the telling."[15] I shall build upon his careful analysis to present a more systematic overview of Homer's narrative strategy of misdirection.

After a survey of the techniques of false and misleading predictions and the audience's response, we will be in a position to consider the underlying significance of repeatedly manipulating the audience's expectations and the poet's possible motivations for doing so. For now, I briefly sketch out these conclusions in advance. At times, we find that the false clues and signals about the direction the narrative is to take are relatively trivial: they simply pique the audience's sense of anticipation about the outcome of a sequence of episodes. The poet may prepare the audience for a particular event, only to delay the presentation of that scene. In book 20, the audience anticipates Achilles' meeting with Hector. The poet brings the two heroes into proximity but repeatedly postpones their final meeting. The audience's expectations are eventually realized—Achilles slays Hector in book 22—but the fulfillment comes later than anticipated. While the poet misleads the audience concerning the occasion or timing of this particular event, the anticipated event, nevertheless, does take place. Such "retardation" has been noted by Duckworth and others. At some level, the explanation of this relatively simple type of misdirection may lie in the circumstances surrounding the original performance of this work. By misleading his audience, the singer has the purely pragmatic goal of keeping the audience interested in his telling of a traditional song. If the audience is enticed and wishes to hear more, the singer secures a livelihood beyond the singing of that episode on one particular occasion.[16]

Misdirection may also be quite broad-ranging and thematically central to the epic, compelling the audience to ponder much more significant issues. Could key heroes die unexpectedly (i.e., untraditionally)? Could the war itself end differently? If Paris and Menelaus fight a duel to resolve their conflict, would Troy still be vanquished? Could the Greeks succeed if Achilles sails home? Would the Greeks be stranded if Hector destroys their fleet? Misdirection is Homer's means of testing the limits of his tradition by exploring possibilities outside the standard myth. He indicates how he could violate the familiar story, although he never actually does so. Far from denying the force of the tradition, Homeric misdirection actually depends upon the story being well known. Because the audience is familiar with the basic outline of the story and brings definite assumptions to each performance (or reading), it expects certain episodes to occur and others to be impossible. The poet raises expectations for later events within the epic: the audience anticipates a Greek defeat, the death of Patroclus, and Achilles' return and vengeance. Yet the poet manipulates the audience's perspective on these events by introducing alternatives to such expectations. As Homer uses false predictions to raise the possibility of events that would contradict the plot of the *Iliad* or the larger tradition underlying it, the audience must reexamine its own assumptions. At each stage of the *Iliad*'s narrative, the audience is led to compare what it knows will happen with contradictory movements and unsettling predictions. Without actually surprising his audience in an absolute sense, the poet furnishes a new perspective on this traditional subject.[17]

Homer not only leads the audience to reflect upon what happened and what might have happened on the plain of Troy but sets up a dynamic between the audience and the characters within the epic. Ultimately Homer uses misdirection to draw the audience closer to the central problem faced by characters in the *Iliad*: mortal expectation and miscalculation. Just as Achilles or Hector assume they have a good idea about what is likely to happen on the battlefield, the audience presumes a clear view of how the story will proceed. If the poet withholds crucial information or actively misleads, the audience is brought to the realization that its own perspective on the story can be nearly as limited as that of any character within the story. The audience is thereby reminded of the purely human scope of its own knowledge. This affinity with mortal characters—rather than with the narrator or the omniscient gods—produces on the part of the audience more sympathy for those characters.

Throughout this study, I analyze the narrative from the audience's point of view, using its expectations as the standard to gauge the effect of false and misleading predictions. Misdirection, I believe, can best be judged from this perspective. Due to my focus upon the audience and its expectations, I have drawn upon the work of W. Iser and G. Genette. Because both critics primarily analyze the experience of readers of novels, their insights must be adapted to the peculiarities of Homeric epic. The idea of approaching literature from the reader's point of view has already led to valuable interpretations of ancient texts. J. Winkler's narratological study of Apuleius' *Golden Ass* and I. de Jong's *Narrators and Focalizers: The Presentation of the Story in the Iliad* have provided models for my work.[18] In addition to these works—and Schadewaldt's—

I have found that the ancient commentators on Homer, now excerpted and surviving for us as scholia, were sensitive to the techniques of foreshadowing and surprise. With their rhetorical brand of literary criticism, the Alexandrian scholars interpreted the *Iliad* as a dramatic work, noting subtleties in terms of both the poet's formulations and the audience's response.[19] I have drawn on both ancient and modern methodologies and commentaries in reconstructing the audience's response to Homer's narrative.[20]

I give a full account of my approach in chapter 2. This entails explaining my method of narrative analysis with definitions of the essential categories of poet, narrator, audience, foreshadowing, and misdirection. The dynamic relationship between misdirection and foreshadowing is also examined. Chapter 3 shows how the poet's presentation of the sequence of events in the first book of the *Iliad* contrasts in a number of ways with the larger epic tradition. Chapters 4, 5, and 6 examine three types of misdirection: false anticipation, epic suspense, and thematic misdirection. Throughout 4, 5, and 6, I examine representative portions of the narrative, giving careful attention to what the audience has learned in preceding sections of the poem.

I conclude with two chapters on the significance of misdirection from the perspectives of the audience and the poet. In chapter 7, the implications of the theme of miscalculation that links audience and character are further developed. I also consider the effects of misdirection not only upon an implied first-time audience but upon a modern audience that rereads this poem. Chapter 8 examines the significance of misdirection from the poet's perspective in terms of his attitude toward the tradition out of which he has come. From this analysis, we learn something about Homer's attitude toward the past. Any traditional poet faces a problem: how can he examine or question the tradition within which he is working? The quest for a theory of Homeric poetics usually leads scholars to the *Odyssey,* where Phemius, Demodocus, and Odysseus sing a variety of tales. The *Iliad* itself offers the tales of Bellerophon and Meleager, as well as Nestor's frequent recounting of his glorious younger days. This approach of looking at internal narratives to uncover Homeric poetics, however enlightening, ignores the central story of the wrath of Achilles. Our poet has chosen to set his tale alongside many other possible story lines, and, in doing so, tells an old story in a new way. Homer responds rhetorically to the poets of the past by posing alternatives to the *Iliad*'s plot and the epic tradition as a whole. In promoting other possibilities for consideration, he demonstrates that he might very well have presented another story. Although never ultimately deviating from the tradition, Homer is able to assert his independence from the past by calling the tradition into question.

Chapter 2

A Narrative Analysis of the *Iliad*

This chapter sets forth my method of analyzing misdirection in the *Iliad*. I begin by defining the poet, narrator, and audience with respect to the narrative itself. Once these categories are explained, the definition of misdirection can be restated more precisely, in terms of narrator and audience. The mechanisms of both foreshadowing and misdirection—and their effects—are then explored. Foreshadowing bolsters the audience's confidence that it knows what will happen; misdirection, by contrast, undermines that confidence. In the *Iliad,* the narrator creates a precarious position for the audience, which finds itself negotiating between knowledge gained by foreshadowing and familiarity with the tradition and ignorance about how this particular narrative will proceed.

My starting point is the epic poem the *Iliad*. In this study, I base my analysis upon the text as it stands: a written document. I do not wish to ignore this work's genesis. Over a period of several hundred years, an oral tradition evolved, as singers performed songs about Greek heroes fighting in Troy. Although the story of the Trojan War became a staple of oral performance, singers would not sing a wholly preconceived poem, at least not in detail. Each performance was flexible, being influenced by various factors: for example, the singer's own disposition, the audience's attentiveness, or the presence of potential patrons in the audience. These songs resulted not only from preparation and experience but from an inspired spontaneity. The idea of a fixed text was alien to both singer and audience. No song could be reproduced verbatim according to our way of thinking. And yet what has survived—an inflexible, written text—is in many ways at variance with the culture out of which it arose. Although the text of the *Iliad* bears many features of an oral tradition, we as modern readers gain access to this early Greek art form by reading the texts of the *Iliad* and *Odyssey.* These works represent the end of a tradition, whose development is a subject on which we can only speculate.[1] Because we have the *Iliad* in written form, Homer's poem is not an oral work for us. Though many of its features can only be explained on the ground that it was originally produced for a listening audience in a very different culture, we must analyze it as a written text.[2]

My focus in analyzing misdirection in the *Iliad* is the narrator's presentation and the audience's reception of this narrative. The terms *narrator* and *audience* refer to entities implied by the narrative, for the text itself allows us to reconstruct a narrator and an audience. Before discussing how the narrator manipulates the expectations of his implied audience, we should consider the characteristics that the text conveys of narrator and audience.

The text implies the characteristics of the narrator. While the narrator is the source of narration, he is a fictional entity internal to the text just as surely as the gods and mortal characters are. The narrator may be omniscient or deficient, reliable or manipulative. We should keep the poet of the *Iliad* distinct from the narrator of the *Iliad*'s narrative. The poet refers to the composer, a real person. In a strictly narrative analysis, it is impossible to learn much about the historical author, but the text does allow us to reconstruct the narrator as the figure presenting the story. The poet might be said to orchestrate the presentation of the narrator, but the narrator is the immediate voice offering the narrative.[3] It is possible to speak of the narrator—internal to the text—"addressing" Patroclus, a character within the story (e.g., 16.692-93). Such direct address is impossible for the actual author: Patroclus is a fictional character, accessible only to the narrator. The narrator acts as a delegate created by the poet and presents the story, guides the audience, and anticipates later action.[4] The narrator—normally reliable—chooses to prepare the audience for later scenes. Because the audience comes to share the narrator's point of view (in a sense, it has no other choice), the poet may manipulate the audience's perspective by creating a manipulative narrator. In discussing misdirection, I refer to the false and misleading signals of such a narrator.

The term *audience* means the recipient of the narrator's story.[5] Again this is an idealized entity that is internal to the text and quite distinct from a historical audience. We may use the text of the *Iliad* to reconstruct the audience, for the narrative assigns it certain attributes. Two features of the audience are particularly relevant to this study: (1) it is familiar with the epic tradition, and (2) it is a first-time audience that has not previously heard (or read) the *Iliad*.⁶ Evidence supporting the construction of such an audience is readily found. It is evident that the implied audience of the *Iliad*'s narrative is expected to be familiar with the traditional story of a Greek sack of Troy. Set in the tenth year of the war, the narrative offers brief glimpses into the past and future, which need supplementing by the audience. The spareness of the allusions to the past predictions of the seer Calchas (1.106-8) or the Judgment of Paris (24.27-30) imply that the narrator demands a familiarity with the general outline of the story.⁷ Menelaus' condemnation of Paris (3.351- 54, cf. 13.620-27) can only be understood by an audience that knows the story of Helen's abduction. The narrator merely alludes to the inevitable victory of the Greeks, because the results of the war are part of the audience's working knowledge (cf. 12.10-18). If little supplemental information is supplied, the audience must be expected to fill in the gaps. The *Iliad* presupposes a knowledgeable audience, familiar with the gods and heroes and with the basic outline of the story of the Trojan War: the abduction of Helen, the ten-year Greek siege, and the sack of Troy.⁸

The audience implied by the *Iliad*'s text is a first-time audience that has no previous exposure to the *Iliad*. Thus, in spite of its familiarity with the epic tradition, the audience is in need of guidance as it hears the story of Achilles' wrath. Only the presupposition that the audience has not previously experienced the *Iliad* can explain the extensive system of foreshadowing found in this epic. For example, the narrator informs the audience that Achilles will soon return to battle (2.694) and that Patroclus was asking for his own death (16.46-47). If the implied audience knew how this particular narrative were about to unfold, these narrative hints and signals would be superfluous. The presence of numerous and detailed predictions in the *Iliad* leads to the conclusion that the audience does not know the development of this epic, ending, as it does, with the ransom and burial of Hector's corpse.

The audience's experience therefore is influenced by two types of expectations. It brings its own set of expectations to the performance of the *Iliad* based on a familiarity with the epic tradition. It also adopts new, specific expectations that are generated within the course of the narrative. Misdirection, as we shall see, undermines the audience's confidence in both sets of expectations, as the narrator challenges the audience's preconceptions about how such a story might unfold and calls into question the reliability of his own predictions. Homeric misdirection can now be restated more precisely as the narrator misleading the implied first-time audience of the *Iliad.*

In order to explore possible motivations for a poet to introduce an unreliable narrator, the effects of misdirection on an actual listening audience must be considered. After the phenomenon of misdirection has been analyzed, I will turn to the relationship of the implied audience to real (i.e., historical) audiences. The experience of the modern reading and rereading audience differs in certain respects from that of an ancient listening audience and from the implied audience internal to the text. In chapters 7 and 8, I turn to the underlying significance of misdirection in terms of both implied and actual audiences and to the possible motivations of the oral poet himself. At that time, we shall see that an implied audience whose reactions are engineered by the narrator instructs us as readers in our attempt to recover meaning from this narrative. Not only is the modern rereader in a position to appreciate how the narrator has manipulated the internal audience's expectations, but even a reading audience is affected by misdirection—perhaps less immediately, but still profoundly. The unique dynamics of an oral performance must be taken into account if we are to recover the singer's motivation. For now, I postpone speculation on how the circumstances of an actual performance may have led the poet to have extensive recourse to both foreshadowing and misdirection. In chapters 3-6, I limit my focus to the narrator—grounded in the text—and his implied audience. It is necessary to carry out this more narrowly defined investigation before turning to the question of real audiences and the historical poet.

Misdirection occurs when the narrative is structured in such a way that the audience's expectations are upset. In order to describe the mechanism of misdirection, we must see how the narrator generates expectations in preparing the audience for later scenes. While this happens in a number of ways, our focus here is on the most frequent means by which the narrator raises the audience's expectations: predictions.[9] In this study, I define a prediction as any statement that refers to what may take place in the subsequent narrative. I use it as a broad, inclusive term, referring to statements occurring in the mouths of characters within the story as well as anticipatory remarks by the narrator. Prophecy, prayer, request, threat, suggestion, and the narrator's foreshadowing are all future-directed statements, that is, predictions. In the *Iliad,* the narrator announces the death of Patroclus (16.692-93), Zeus guarantees a Trojan victory (1.522-30), and Achilles threatens to mutilate Hector's corpse (22.335-36, 22.352-54). All of these are predictions, as I employ the term, looking forward to possible later action. I use *anticipate* and *anticipation* as precise equivalents for *predict* and *prediction*.[10] "The narrator predicts the death of Patroclus" and "The narrator anticipates the death of Patroclus" are to be viewed as synonymous. I employ *foreshadowing* as a general term to describe the introduction of true predictions, that is, predictions that are fulfilled. When predictions are inaccurate in some respect and raise false expectations, I label this *misdirection*. In the rest of this chapter, I introduce a method for determining which predictions function as instances of foreshadowing and which function as instances of misdirection.

To be systematic in examining the function of predictions, we might first consider the narrator's options. At each point of the narrative, the narrator makes several choices. (1) He may either introduce or not introduce a prediction. Naturally there are countless points in the narrative without future-oriented statements, but the narrator always has the option to introduce one. (2) If the narrator chooses to present a prediction, the prediction may or may not be persuasive. Only persuasive predictions generate expectations. (3) If the narrator introduces a persuasive prediction, that prediction may be accurate or inaccurate (true or false) with respect to the later narrative. These three choices are continually made by the narrator. We might speak of him following a strategy of alternatives: to predict or not to predict, to persuade or not to persuade, to be accurate or not to be accurate.

The effect of these decisions by the narrator may be examined from the audience's perspective. My goal throughout is to see how predictions (or their absence) anticipate action or mislead the audience. The narrator may give information about later events by introducing a prediction. For example, after a character prays to a god, the narrator often supplies the god's response, indicating compliance or rejection. In book 1, Chryses appeals to Apollo, seeking punishment for the Greeks. At the end of the request, the narrator indicates the god's answer: "Thus he spoke in prayer, and Phoebus Apollo heard him" (1.43). The narrative signal "and Phoebus Apollo heard him" indicates to the audience that the god will work to bring about the substance of the prayer. In this case, Apollo brings a plague upon the Greek camp. The narrator has chosen to prepare the audience for the fulfillment of this prayer by marking the god's positive reaction. (This prediction is also persuasive and accurate, leading the audience to await its fulfillment.)

In contrast, the narrator may choose to omit a prediction, withholding information about the subsequent narrative. An example is found in book 3, when Menelaus prays to Zeus during his duel with Paris. He calls upon the god to punish Paris for violating his trust as a host. In this case, the narrator moves immediately from the words of the prayer to a description of Menelaus hurling his spear: "Thus he spoke, and he hefted and hurled his long-shadowing spear" (cf. 3.349–56). The audience does not learn whether Zeus has heard this prayer, for the narrator refrains from introducing any information. The audience does not know how—or whether—Zeus will respond to Menelaus' appeal. In fact, it is not Zeus but Aphrodite who intervenes on Paris' behalf. Menelaus fails at this juncture to avenge the abduction of his wife. While the audience knows Paris will eventually pay for his actions, it has received no advance indication of Aphrodite's dramatic rescue. Of course, the narrator often omits introducing a prediction, but the absence of the narrator's indication of the divine reaction to this prayer is noteworthy. Such predictions are generally introduced when a mortal prays to a god; the audience thus comes to rely upon receiving such information.[11] When such a prediction is omitted in book 3, the effect is suspense: the audience lacks information regarding what may occur.[12]

Let us now follow the narrator's strategy of alternatives regarding predictions. If the narrator chooses to present a prediction, the prediction itself may be persuasive or not persuasive to the audience. Since our interest is in the audience's expectations, the factor of persuasiveness is crucial: if a prediction is not persuasive, it will not generate an expectation. The persuasiveness of a prediction depends in part upon the source of the prediction. Predictions occur in a variety of narrative contexts, some of which confer plausibility. In book 21, when Lycaon approaches Achilles, the narrator remarks: "On the twelfth day, the gods put [Lycaon] in the hands of Achilles, who would send him to Hades" (21.46–48). In this case, the narrator signals the imminent death of Lycaon. Because this prediction derives from the narrator—on whom the audience relies—it is persuasive to the audience, generating an expectation of Lycaon's demise: the audience awaits the presentation of such a scene. While every prediction promotes a possible outcome, certainly not all predictions are persuasive. In book 1, Achilles calls an assembly and addresses Agamemnon. His first response to their critical situation is a suggestion that the Greeks return home (1.59–61). Surely the audience does not find plausible an early departure of the Greeks—before sacking Troy. In the case of Achilles' suggestion, although a prediction is introduced, it does not generate an expectation. The audience may wait to see what alternative plan the Greeks adopt to avoid abandoning their quest, but this prediction produces no expectation.[13]

A variety of voices present the story of the *Iliad*. The narrator anticipates certain events, the gods make promises, and heroes boast of future victory. The audience relies upon predictions of the narrator to guide its anticipations, for the narrator's anticipations are persuasive. The narrator's indication of Apollo's compliance to Chryses' request or his anticipation of Lycaon's death are examples of predictions that generate expectations, leading the audience to be confident of a particular outcome. If a prediction comes in the narrator's own voice, we may label it an *authoritative prediction*. Such authority is accorded by the conventions of the genre: without hesitation, the audience accepts it as reliable and accurate. The narrator's predictions are authoritative, for part of the implied contract between the narrator and the audience is that the narrator will be trustworthy. The audience relies upon the narrator, with good reason in the majority of cases.[14]

The narrator may also assign predictions to other voices that are persuasive to the audience.[15] Although divine prophecies have a different status from narratorial predictions (and therefore have a different effect upon the audience), such predictions are often authoritative. When Athene promises gifts to Achilles (1.212–14) or when Zeus guarantees to honor Achilles by bringing victory to the Trojans (1.522–30), the audience confidently awaits such outcomes. These guarantees are compelling, because what the gods guarantee has a good chance of coming about. The promises of the gods and comments in the narrator's own voice are the audience's most frequent sources of reliable guidance. Still the narrator's foreshadowing has a different authority from divine prophecy; the effect upon the audience differs because Zeus does not fulfill everything he proposes.[16] In book 8, Zeus threatens to hurl to Tartarus any gods who oppose his prohibition against aiding the Greeks or Trojans. Later, when it becomes apparent that Poseidon and probably Hera have disobeyed him, he responds with nothing more than a second threat (8.5–17, 15.4–219). The narrator, however, is expected to fulfill what he promises. There exists then a hierarchy of predictions. The most persuasive—the most authoritative—predictions are the narrator's. Divine predictions may be regarded with somewhat more caution but in general are also authoritative.

Mortal plans and suggestions as a group do not generate such confident expectations. The words of mortal characters do not normally possess the credibility of the gods' or the narrator's predictions. In a work such as the *Iliad,* which emphasizes the gulf between prescient gods and unknowing mortals, there is a marked difference in the capacity to anticipate the course of future events. At times, the narrator makes utterly clear that a character is speaking out of ignorance. In book 2, after Zeus sends a deceptive dream to Agamemnon, the Greek leader wakes up with hopes of taking Troy. The narrator comments: "[The dream] left Agamemnon there, believing things in his heart that were not to be accomplished" (2.35-36). Predictions in the voice of mortal characters are automatically suspect not only due to their status but because they are often soon shown to be false, they are contradicted by other authoritative predictions, or they contradict the tradition. Agamemnon vows never to return Chryses' daughter (1.29-31), but the immediately succeeding narrative shows him to have spoken rashly: he agrees to return her at 1.116-17, less than 100 lines later. When Hector boasts that he will kill Achilles, the audience knows full well that, in fact, Achilles will be victorious (18.305-9; cf., e.g., 15.68, 17.201-8). Another situation occurs if a character's prediction contradicts the general outline of the traditional story: the audience will view such untraditional possibilities with skepticism. Achilles threatens to return to Phthia (1.169-71): this would violate the epic tradition and in fact is contradicted by the subsequent narrative, in which Thetis advises him merely to withdraw from battle (1.421-22; cf. 1.488-92). Authoritative predictions also make clear to the audience that Achilles will remain in Troy (2.694). Although any prediction raises the possibility of fulfillment, in general, what mortal characters say is not persuasive. The audience is expected to discriminate within such a hierarchy of predictions.[17] While it relies upon certain pronouncements, it may remain skeptical toward others.

In certain contexts, however, the words of mortals do generate expectations. In book 1, Achilles describes the Greek defeat that will follow his withdrawal from battle (1.240-44, 1.338-44). Achilles' words are compelling for two reasons. First, they are introduced by elaborate solemnity. As he makes his first oath, Achilles holds the divinely bestowed scepter (1.233-39); later he calls on the gods to witness (1.338-39). Second, and more importantly, Achilles' words are supported by other authoritative predictions. In this case, divine and narratorial predictions endorse Achilles' picture of Hector driving the Greeks to their ships. When authoritative predictions confirm that a event will take place, reinforcement occurs. Here, Athene's promise that Achilles will receive recompense and Zeus' guarantee of a Trojan victory (1.212-14, 1.508-30) reinforce Achilles' predictions of a Greek defeat. Some mortal predictions are persuasive then, because they form part of a set—or network—of predictions. It is quite common in Homeric epic for the narrator to present repeated, rather than single, predictions with respect to a later event. Because Achilles' predictions concerning the Greek defeat belong to such a network, they fall into the exceptional category of persuasive mortal predictions.[18]

We have now examined two sets of alternatives: the narrator may give or not give a prediction; the prediction may or may not generate an expectation, that is, it may or may not be persuasive. The third set of alternatives concerns accuracy and fulfillment: is the prediction true or false? If the narrator introduces a persuasive prediction, the prediction is either wholly accurate or it is inaccurate in some way. This determination is made, of course, by examining the subsequent narrative and comparing the prediction with its fulfillment or lack of fulfillment. Certain persuasive predictions are accurate in a very straightforward sense. Thetis promises Achilles she will go to Zeus (1.427-29); Zeus predicts the deaths of Sarpedon, Patroclus, and Hector (15.64-68). These predictions are persuasive and accurate; their fulfillment occurs in the subsequent narrative. Yet when Zeus says that Achilles will send Patroclus to battle *after* Hector drives the Greeks to the Myrmidon camp, this divine prediction is persuasive but false (15.61-65).

Of course, predictions vary in precision. Zeus' prophecy of the deaths of Sarpedon, Patroclus, and Hector is the picture of clarity. Alternatively, the narrator more vaguely anticipates Patroclus' death (11.604). In a sense, all predictions are partial or incomplete in some way, for the narrative's fullest presentation of an event naturally comes at the moment of enactment.[19] The network of predictions anticipating Patroclus' confrontation with Hector only sketches in advance the event itself, while the presentation of Patroclus' death in book 16 is fuller and more elaborate than any of the predictions of that event.[20]

We are now in a position to analyze foreshadowing and misdirection in terms of these three sets of alternatives. Foreshadowing occurs when the narrator—in his own voice or perhaps in that of a character—introduces a persuasive prediction that is accurately fulfilled. The narrator (1) chooses to give information, (2) makes the source of the prediction persuasive, and (3) keeps the fulfillment consistent with the prediction. Much fine work on Homeric foreshadowing has shown how the narrator uses an extensive system of narrative preparation to unify this long narrative poem.[21] Although centering the action around one main event—the wrath of Achilles—the narrator anticipates events that occur later in the epic and even beyond its final book. The narrator prepares his audience for these subsequent events by carefully introducing predictions early in the epic and then reinforcing the resultant expectations by giving progressively more detailed predictions as the work proceeds. Foreshadowing economically concentrates the attention of the audience upon particular upcoming events. The audience is prepared far in advance for the Greek defeat, the death of Patroclus, and the return and vengeance of Achilles.

Misdirection, however, occurs when a prediction (1) is given, (2) is persuasive, and (3) is false or misleading in some way. I distinguish three types of misdirection. The first type, false anticipation, describes the situation where the fulfillment of authoritative predictions is delayed. These predictions are misleading because they encourage the expectation that something will happen soon, while the enactment itself is postponed. For example, the audience expects Achilles to meet and kill Hector—a true expectation—but the final meeting is put off until book 22. Although the relevant authoritative predictions are persuasive and true and the audience's expectations are ultimately satisfied, in the short term the expectation for timely fulfillment is disappointed (this is examined in chap. 4). In the second type, thematic misdirection (explored in chap. 6), authoritative predictions turn out to be outright false. Events of great importance to the course of the epic are subject to manipulation by the introduction of false authoritative predictions. Zeus' prediction that Achilles will send Patroclus to battle when Hector reaches Achilles' ships is not true: Achilles acts far in advance. Zeus' prophecy is persuasive but false. A third possibility occurs when the narrator chooses to withhold information where it is normally given, so that the audience lacks guidance toward what will happen. The absence of authoritative predictions creates epic suspense (discussed in chap. 5).

This approach of narrative analysis allows us to ask at any point of the narrative: What does the audience now know? What are its expectations? Does it find a particular prediction persuasive? Oddly, the audience is in a paradoxical position. It possesses knowledge of what will happen based on its familiarity with the tradition and the authoritative predictions introduced within the narrative. At same time, the audience does not precisely know what scenes will be presented or how the narrative will unfold. The interplay then between the audience's familiarity with the general story and its experience of what is actually presented in the *Iliad* is not straightforward. The audience may know the basic story line without having a definite idea of what the narrator will present in this particular narrative. While Homeric foreshadowing furnishes the audience with an outline of the narrative, the narrator manipulates the audience's orientation toward these events by means of false and misleading predictions. At each stage of the narrative, the audience may compare what it knows will happen with various misleading predictions in the *Iliad*. We may distinguish the plot of the *Iliad* from the narrative. The plot is what actually happens in the story of the *Iliad*: that sequence of events—often anticipated—that advances the action, leading ultimately to the burial of Hector. The narrative includes not only the plot but also the presentation of various possibilities that are formulated, vividly explored, and ultimately rejected. While the plot can be simply recapitulated—Achilles' withdrawal, the Greek defeat, the death of Patroclus, Achilles' return—the narrative includes the entire presentation, including, for example, Achilles' suggestion to return to Greece.[22] These alternatives to the plot lead in various directions—sometimes at odds with the tradition itself.

The narrator's strategy, which involves both foreshadowing and misdirection, forces the audience to consider the epic tradition in a new way. A tension between foreshadowing and misdirection results because the narrator encourages the audience to adopt different perspectives. Foreshadowing is conservative: it reliably looks ahead to the later action of the epic. When Zeus or the narrator predicts, for example, the death of Patroclus, the audience is freed from contemplating the alternative. To a great extent, it no longer needs to reflect upon Patroclus not facing Hector, Achilles' last minute rescue of his friend, or the safe return of Achilles and Patroclus to Greece after sacking Troy. Foreshadowing reinforces the tradition or at least eliminates the possibility of an alternative outcome. Foreshadowing—coupled with a knowledge of the tradition—

links the audience's experience with a "divine" perspective, akin to the gods': it is objective, detached, and prescient. Without the introduction of misdirection, the audience would remain at this position.

Misdirection is one way of probing what might have happened, by raising expectations for what does not belong to the plot of the *Iliad* or the traditional story line. Misdirection undercuts the tradition and leads the audience to consider other outcomes to the story. By doing so, the narrator puts the audience into a situation experienced by mortal characters: this situation is characterized by doubt, delay, frustration, and false expectation. Homeric misdirection encourages the audience to adopt this second viewpoint, as it loses its previous self-assurance and is reduced to a "mortal" perspective. In the analysis to follow we must gauge the effects that both foreshadowing and misdirection have on the audience.

The *Iliad* is a narrative that risks being simplified in such an analysis. As we shall see, Zeus is usually reliable, but not always; the narrator does not without exception accurately prepare the audience. Indeed, as the epic comes to a close, the hierarchy of predictions is partially inverted: mortal characters' predictions—used to anticipate events beyond the scope of the *Iliad*—assume the authority of divine proclamation and the narrator's commentary.

Chapter 3

Iliad 1 and Alternatives to the Epic Tradition

This chapter examines unpersuasive false predictions in the first book of the *Iliad*. I isolate such passages, show they are not persuasive, and then discuss their effects upon the audience. These predictions—voiced by mortal characters—are false, that is, they are not fulfilled. Because unpersuasive predictions do not generate expectations, this is not a question of misdirection. These predictions, however, do allow the narrator to propose alternatives—briefly articulated and quickly dismissed—to the plot of the *Iliad* and to the epic tradition. Although the narrator raises possibilities at odds with the overall movement of the epic, the audience recognizes that these possibilities will remain unrealized. In the first book of the epic, the narrator does not contradict the tradition or his own authoritative predictions, but he has adopted a method of storytelling that treats with careful attention what might have happened as well as what happens. The narrator's repeated introduction of such alternatives—here and throughout the epic—supports my contention that he has chosen to articulate such alternatives for his audience's reflection. Even though untraditional episodes do not take place, the narrator stretches the tradition for his audience. As the narrator marks out the limits of the tradition by going beyond those boundaries in this speculative manner, the overall effect is to put the tradition itself under scrutiny at each stage of the story.

Two general considerations should be kept in mind. The first is the problem of assessing the effect of these predictions upon the audience. Although any prediction raises the possibility of fulfillment, the predictions of mortal characters are not usually persuasive to the audience (as suggested in the previous chapter). Still the following analysis argues that the predictions of Chryses, Agamemnon, Achilles, and Nestor are introduced as a means of raising various possibilities that cause the audience to recall its prior assumptions. Even unpersuasive predictions may open up the audience's sensitivity to what might transpire.

The second consideration is related to the first and concerns the relationship between the plot and the narrative.[1] The plot is the relatively simple sequence of events in *Iliad* 1, which culminates in Achilles' request to Zeus for a Greek defeat. It has been argued that the whole of the *Iliad* represents a long series of events linked by a clear chain of cause and effect.[2] Agamemnon's rejection of Chryses' offer of ransom leads to a plague sent by Apollo. In response, Achilles call an assembly where Agamemnon slights his worth; Achilles withdraws from battle in anger, vowing that the Greeks will regret his absence when they fight at their ships. This is the "positive" side of book 1, the path that the plot actually follows. And yet much more is presented in book 1. The plot should be contrasted with the narrative, everything that is introduced. The inevitability of the sequence of events leading to Achilles' withdrawal and the Greek defeat is repeatedly undermined. The narrator offers the audience alternative scenarios to the plot at four critical junctures, and in each case he introduces those alternatives with mortals' predictions. In comparing plot with narrative, we see how many of these possibilities raised in the narrative would—if realized—contradict the audience's knowledge of the tradition or its anticipations generated by the poem itself. By explicating the interaction between narrative and plot (or the tradition), we will be in a position to recover an essential feature of the way the *Iliad* is told. The narrator sets the straightforward action of *Iliad* 1 against a context of potential violations of the expected course of events, indicating that—if not for certain actions—the story might have turned out differently. Let us examine the first book in greater detail, with such considerations in mind.

The first scene in the *Iliad* describes the supplication by Chryses, who offers ransom for his daughter. In appealing for her return, Chryses begins with a wish that the Greeks sack Troy and then sail home successfully:

"'Ἀτρείδαι τε καὶ ἄλλοι ἐυκνήμιδες Ἀχαιοί,
ὑμῖν μὲν θεοὶ δοῖεν Ὀλύμπια δώματ' ἔχοντες
ἐκπέρσαι Πριάμοιο πόλιν, εὖ δ' οἴκαδ' ἱκέσθαι."

"Sons of Atreus and you other strong-greaved Achaeans,

to you may the gods, who have their homes on Olympus, grant
Priam's city to be plundered and a fair homecoming thereafter."
(1.17–19)

Agamemnon rejects this, but the immediate response is approval: the
rest of the Greek army wishes to respect the priest by accepting the
ransom.

Ἔνθ' ἄλλοι μὲν πάντες ἐπευφήμησαν Ἀχαιοὶ
αἰδεῖσθαί θ' ἱερῆα καὶ ἀγλαὰ δέχθαι ἄποινα.

Then all the rest of the Achaeans cried out in favour
that the priest be respected and the shining ransom be taken.
(1.22–23)

Although Agamemnon drives the old man away with threats, the narrator does not move directly from the offer of ransom to its rejection. Instead he interposes an alternative (which is quickly dismissed) by indicating the army's wishes before Agamemnon acts to overrule them. By first presenting a positive reaction by the Greeks, the narrator suggests—for the brief space of two lines—the possibility that Chryses' offer might be accepted. Chryses' approach to the Greek camp presents a choice: the Greeks may either accept or reject the ransom. Although the second option prevails, the narrator has formulated both possibilities. We may schematically outline this scene as follows (the choice taken is underlined):

Event	Possible Responses
Chryses' offer (1.12–21).	1. Acceptance (1.22–23).
	2. <u>Rejection (1.24–33).</u>

Let us consider the effect of this passage upon the audience. Chryses' appeal is a prediction: it is directed to the possible future action of accepting ransom, victory, and homecoming. But his words are not persuasive for three reasons. First, his voice does not have the authority of, for example, the narrator or Zeus. Simply because the priest offers ransom does not mean his appeal will meet with success. Second, his offer is almost immediately rejected. While the audience may consider such a possibility for two lines before Agamemnon makes his refusal, no fully developed expectation is allowed to form during such a limited period. Third, Chryses' words fail to persuade the audience, for acceptance of his offer would contradict the plot as outlined just before the scene, when the audience learns that Apollo would be angry at Agamemnon for dishonoring his priest (1.9–12). The possibility of accepting ransom and the gods' good favor is not persuasive, yet it is articulated for the audience's consideration.

As he rejects the offer of ransom, Agamemnon says the daughter will spend her old age in Argos serving him:

"τὴν δ' ἐγὼ οὐ λύσω· πρίν μιν καὶ γῆρας ἔπεισιν
ἡμετέρῳ ἐνι οἴκῳ, ἐν Ἄργει, τηλόθι πάτρης,
ἱστὸν ἐποιχομένην καὶ ἐμὸν λέχος ἀντιόωσαν."

"The girl I will not give back; sooner will old age come upon her
in my own house, in Argos, far from her own land,
going up and down by the loom and being in my bed as my
    companion."

(1.29–31)

Yet Agamemnon's words are not compelling either. He asserts that he will not release the woman because he wishes to keep her in Mycenae after the war. Again his is not a voice of authority, and in fact he retracts his statement in the next 100 lines (cf. 1.116). In addition, the audience learns in the proem that Agamemnon will quarrel with Achilles—though the substance of that dispute is not anticipated. Neither character's prediction is persuasive to the audience. What then is the effect of allowing Chryses and Agamemnon to express these possibilities?

The words of both Chryses and Agamemnon belong to the category of wishful thinking. Both scenarios look beyond the end of the *Iliad* and contrast sharply with the tales of the Greeks' homecoming as told in the *nostoi* tradition. The *Odyssey* tells of quarrels, storms, and shipwrecks afflicting the heroes in their attempts to get home. Odysseus and Menelaus wander for many years before seeing their homelands; the lesser Ajax dies in a shipwreck; on returning to Mycenae, Agamemnon is murdered by his wife's lover.[3] Chryses is merely expressing his goodwill toward the Greeks in order to secure his daughter's return. Yet he articulates what must have been the Greeks' keenest desire: to sack Troy and to return home safely. No wonder the army approves receiving the ransom! With this brief glimpse, the narrator implicitly contrasts an unrealizable hope of uncomplicated Greek success against the evils that the audience knows await the Greeks after they sack Troy. In recognizing the Greeks' ignorance of what lies ahead, the audience is in a position to appreciate the poignancy of Chryses' words.

Agamemnon will return Chryses' daughter, thus eliminating the hope of her serving him. Yet he surely hopes one day to savor his military victory, perhaps attended by another slave woman: according to the tradition, it is Cassandra. Agamemnon, of course, has no inkling of what lies in store for him on his return home. But the audience knows that Agamemnon's success in Troy is overshadowed by his treacherous death in Mycenae. His wish for care by slave women is immediately recognized as misguided. At one level, describing the daughter's future servitude is a cruel threat to the father. Yet the narrator may even inspire his audience—which knows of Agamemnon's abrupt demise—to pity Agamemnon.[4]

These two examples demonstrate the narrator's impulse to offer alternatives not only to the immediate events of book 1 but to the larger tradition. The audience will appreciate the narrator's adherence to the tradition: he presents predictions that are not compelling and are soon dismissed. All the time, however, he uses mortal characters' predictions to gesture toward alternative stories for the audience's contemplation. In the assembly scene that follows, we find a similar situation. By juxtaposing unpersuasive predictions against the plot, the narrator demonstrates the various possibilities open to him as storyteller.[5]

When Achilles calls an assembly, his first words suggest the desperate situation of the Greeks:

"'Ἀτρεΐδη, νῦν ἄμμε παλιμπλαγχθέντας ὀΐω
ἂψ ἀπονοστήσειν, εἴ κεν θάνατόν γε φύγοιμεν,
εἰ δὴ ὁμοῦ πόλεμός τε δαμᾷ καὶ λοιμὸς Ἀχαιούς.''

"Son of Atreus, I believe now that we, driven back,
shall return home again if we possibly should escape death,
if fighting and plague together are to destroy the Achaeans."
(1.59–61)

This is remarkable. Achilles' first speech in the *Iliad* begins with a suggestion that the Greeks sail home in order to escape the combined evils of war and plague. It is true that he then goes on to propose seeking help from Calchas (perhaps Apollo's anger is due to a fault with a prayer or sacrifice), but again we find a situation—the plague—leading to two possible responses articulated by a character's suggestions.

Event	Possible Responses
The plague (1.44–57).	1. Sail home (1.59–61).
	2. <u>Consult Calchas (1.62–67).</u>

When Calchas explains that Chryses' daughter (Chryseis) must be returned to appease the god, Agamemnon reluctantly agrees. His insistence, however, that he be awarded some other prize triggers the quarrel with Achilles. Agamemnon begins by proposing that the Greek leaders voluntarily make good his loss. Achilles counters with a suggestion that amends will be made after the sack of Troy. Agamemnon is suspicious and threatens to forcibly take another's war-prize. Three possibilities follow Agamemnon's obedience to the seer's advice:

Event	Possible Responses
Agamemnon's loss of Chryseis (1.94–117).	1. Voluntary gift (1.118–20).
	2. Amends after Troy's sack (1.127–29).
	3. Agamemnon to use force (1.137–39).

The actual outcome is deferred until after the assembly breaks up. While Agamemnon continues to threaten force, Achilles tolerates Agamemnon's act of taking Briseis (cf. 1.298–303).[6]

The argument at this point escalates. Achilles questions his own presence at Troy—he has not suffered from the Trojans—and recalls Agamemnon's previous unfair distribution of spoils. Achilles then asserts his intention to sail home to Phthia. When Agamemnon belittles Achilles' value to the Greeks, Achilles contemplates slaying Agamemnon. He is on the point of drawing his sword when Athene appears. Achilles' address to the goddess makes clear his mood:

"τίπτ' αὖτ', αἰγιόχοιο Διὸς τέκος, εἰλήλουθας;
ἦ ἵνα ὕβριν ἴδῃ Ἀγαμέμνονος Ἀτρεΐδαο;
ἀλλ' ἔκ τοι ἐρέω, τὸ δὲ καὶ τελέεσθαι ὀΐω
ἧς ὑπεροπλίῃσι τάχ' ἄν ποτε θυμὸν ὀλέσσῃ."

"Why have you come now once more, o child of Zeus of the
   aegis?
Is it that you may see the outrageousness of the son of Atreus,
   Agamemnon?
Yet I will tell you this then, and I think it shall be accomplished.
By such acts of arrogance he may even lose his own life."
(1.202-5)

Athene, however, persuades him to attack Agamemnon with words alone. The quarrel has provoked several reactions:

Event	Possible Responses
Quarrel (1.101-68).	1. Achilles to return home (1.169-71).
	2. Achilles to slay Agamemnon (1.188-205).
	3. <u>Abuse Agamemnon with words (1.206-47).</u>

Nestor attempts to reconcile the two leaders. He says such internal bickering would please the Trojans. He admits that each leader deserves some degree of respect and proposes a solution: Agamemnon should not usurp Achilles' right to Briseis, while Achilles should recognize Agamemnon's authority since Agamemnon rules more men. This attempt at peacemaking fails.

Event	Possible Responses
Nestor intervenes (1.247-84).	1. Reconciliation by Nestor (esp. 1.274-84).
	2. Achilles withdraws from battle; <u>Agamemnon takes Briseis (1.306-48).</u>

At each of these four critical junctures in the assembly, mortals' predictions suggest the various paths the story could follow. Achilles, Calchas, Agamemnon, and Nestor (and Athene) propose, suggest, or threaten various actions. We find distinct options in response to the plague, Agamemnon's agreement to return the priest's daughter, the dispute between Achilles and Agamemnon, and Nestor's call for restraint. The Greek army earlier wished to accept Chryses' offer of ransom; if Agamemnon had accepted the priest's original offer, Chryses would have no reason to seek help from Apollo.[7] The plague's devastation has now led Achilles to contemplate sailing home. After Calchas' advice, Agamemnon might have submitted to Achilles' proposal of waiting for recompense until after the Greeks' victory. This would certainly interrupt events leading to the quarrel. Achilles is on the point of killing Agamemnon, when Athene intervenes. If she had not, the Greeks would have lost their leader, and the entire expedition would be thrown into doubt. Finally, the two leaders might have heeded Nestor's plea for reconciliation. At each stage of the narrative, the narrator introduces explicit alternatives to the actual outcome.[8] The plot leads to Achilles' withdrawal from battle, but the narrative explores far more than the limited sequence of events reaching such a result.

While never actually violating the tradition in the first book of the *Iliad,* the narrator does offer a distinctive view of the epic tradition. Let us now consider the assembly scene from the audience's perspective. An undisputed feature—perhaps the defining feature—of the Trojan War tradition is the Greek sack of Troy. Although the audience expects the eventual sack of Troy, the narrator suggests various scenarios in book 1 that place this outcome in question. Achilles twice proposes leaving before the city is sacked (1.59-61, 1.169-71). First he says that the whole army should leave. This, of course, would not be persuasive to the audience. If the entire army leaves and the city of Troy survives, this poem would move outside the tradition of Trojan song. Then, in anger, Achilles asserts he will leave with the Myrmidons. The Greeks could be successful without Achilles and his men—they still vastly outnumber the Trojans[9]—but his departure is likely to confound the audience. The succeeding narrative somewhat indirectly indicates that Achilles will not leave. Athene tells him gifts will be his if he restrains himself (1.212-14); Thetis tells him to stay by the ships and refrain from war until she goes to seek Zeus' help (1.421-22); the narrator reminds us Achilles is still at the ships (1.488-92).[10] Besides a premature departure, Achilles also contemplates slaying Agamemnon (1.194–221). This would undoubtedly violate the tradition.[11] Agamemnon is the leader of the expedition seeking the return of his brother's wife. If Agamemnon were to die at the hands of Achilles, the expedition would be jeopardized.[12] Others have dismissed these alternatives as "imaginary" or "merely rhetorical," yet the audience confronts scenarios that contradict its expectations based on familiarity with the tradition.[13] We should attempt to determine the effect this presentation has upon the audience. How seriously will the audience take these possibilities?

The narrator is not attempting to deceive his audience in these episodes. His project is subtler than that. The audience has in mind the inevitable sack of Troy. The narrator begins with a clear prediction of Achilles' anger. When the audience takes into account the tradition and the announcements of the proem, the alternatives presented are not compelling. In fact, the narrator controls the audience's reaction to these possibilities by explicitly anticipating the quarrel ahead of time; in particular, he predicts that Agamemnon's treatment of the priest will lead to conflict with Achilles (1.6–12). The audience expects the quarrel to take place. The narrator merely makes the audience aware of various alternatives as potential detours to the path the plot follows, making it sensitive to a wider range of possibilities.

With such alternatives, the narrator not only challenges the traditional story known to his audience but also juxtaposes these alternatives with his own pronouncements in the proem. Of course, there is presumably overlap between the *Iliad*'s plot and the epic tradition. Although we will never know the exact degree of innovation in the *Iliad,* from the proem we can reconstruct the plot the narrator intends to present. The first-time audience depends on the narrator's hints and predictions to learn what episodes will be presented. The narrator clearly announces Achilles' wrath in the proem: whether this theme is traditional or not, the audience expects to hear of it in this song. When Chryses approaches the Greek camp, the audience assumes that Achilles will soon be angered. But again the narrator formulates alternatives that, at some level, suggest that Achilles' anger is not inevitable. Agamemnon could accept either Chryses' original ransom or Achilles' proposal to receive amends after Troy is sacked; Nestor might have successfully reconciled the two leaders. Any one of these possibilities, although not in violation of the tradition, would—if realized—lead the plot away from the story of destructive anger that the narrator promises to present.[14]

The narrator's strategy of alternatives encourages the audience to view the events at Troy as contingent in an important sense. Although the Alexandrian commentators debated this issue along somewhat different lines, we find a valuable perspective in an argument dating from antiquity and preserved in the scholia. On the third line of the *Iliad,* "[the wrath of Achilles] sent many heroes to Hades," a commentator remarks: νῦν γὰρ δοκεῖ λέγειν ὡς οὐ διὰ τὴν Μοῖραν, ἀλλὰ τὴν μῆνιν Ἀχιλλέως ἀπώλοντο ("[The poet] now appears to say that they perished not because of fate (Moira), but rather due to the wrath of Achilles"). These lines in the proem are interpreted as emphasizing the passion of Achilles over the larger forces of the divine order. Fate did not cause the death of many heroes; it was Achilles' anger at Agamemnon. In response, another commentator on *Iliad* 1.3 cites Hector's remark to Andromache:

"μοῖραν δ' οὔ τινά φημι πεφυγμένον ἔμμεναι ἀνδρῶν."

"I think that no man has escaped his fate [Moira]."

(6.488)

This line is introduced to emphasize the controlling power of destiny and to argue against the interpretation that mortals have any control over events. Presumably this is an Alexandrian controversy (a *problema*):[15] Why did certain heroes die at Troy? Was it fate or Achilles' anger? While the ancient debate follows its own line of inquiry, let us adapt this controversy for our own interpretative purposes. We need not argue that only Achilles' actions or fate alone determines what happens. Each is a significant factor. In the *Iliad,* we find a narrator juxtaposing the possibility of alternative outcomes against the dictates of fate. At some level, Achilles is free to leave Troy and return home; yet he is fated to die at Troy, being "most short-lived" (ὠκυμορώτατος—1.505).

If we move outside the narrative itself to the perspective of the poet, we find a situation corresponding to the debate over the relative importance of Achilles' passions and inflexible fate. In terms of poetic freedom, Homer may in some sense tell any story he likes. And yet he is a traditional poet. The tradition—in some ways, the poet's destiny—places limits upon the outcome of his story.[16] The presentation of alternatives indicates the poet's awareness of this situation. Even as he tells a traditional story, his inclination is to show possibilities that contradict the tradition. He demonstrates that the traditional story is just one of the many stories that might be told. By examining the complex interplay between plot and narrative, we are in a position to consider the audience's receptivity to innovation and Homer's larger aesthetic goals. In the next three chapters, we turn to misdirection, where the narrator introduces persuasive false predictions that force the audience to question more deeply its assumed knowledge with respect to how the narrative will develop. After this survey of misdirection, we may more securely assess the overall effect repeated challenges to the tradition have on the audience.

Chapter 4

Misdirection 1: False Anticipation

This chapter examines false anticipation, at first glance a relatively simple type of misdirection. False anticipation occurs when the narrator introduces true, persuasive predictions, yet the fulfillment of such predictions is unexpectedly postponed. While there are other ways in which the audience's expectations may be manipulated—predictions may be false in different ways—here the narrator delays the enactment of authoritative predictions. The audience's expectation is correct as far as what will happen, but it is misled as to the moment of presentation. In book 11, for example, the narrator suggests that Hector will soon enjoy his victory, but the Trojans' successful drive to the ships is postponed. The audience correctly anticipates Hector's success but is led to expect it to happen well in advance of its actual occurrence.

This chapter explores two other examples of false anticipation in detail: the commencement of battle (books 2-4) and Achilles' meeting with Hector (books 20-22). In the first case, we find the armies facing each other at the beginning of book 3. Although every indication has been given that fighting will start, battle is postponed. Such delayed fulfillment has been recognized by scholars, who refer to it as retardation, expansion, or postponement. Kirk notes that although the armies are brought to the point of engagement, the "constant series of delays is a result of a fundamental compositional technique of books 1-4 and some of their successors."[1] In examining this "fundamental compositional technique," we do not find simple delay. The narrator does more than postpone the start of battle: he prepares the audience for battle only to frustrate that expectation. In fact, three similar sequences are introduced—each of which could lead to the expected outcome—yet the audience has no means of determining which sequence will be interrupted and which will actually lead to the realization of earlier predictions. Each time the narrator suggests that he is about to present the opening battle scene, the audience expects that to be the moment of fulfillment, only to be frustrated twice in its assumption. This analysis reveals the narrator's skill in maintaining the audience's alertness for climactic situations throughout the epic.

False anticipation can occur only when the audience knows the outcome ahead of time. Here we begin to appreciate the complex epistemological position of the audience. Homeric misdirection works only when the audience knows, or thinks it knows, something. Indeed, it knows a great deal, since it is privy to divine conversations and authoritative comments by the narrator. As a general rule, the narrator reliably guides its expectations in terms of what events will take place. But the audience's knowledge is not absolute; the audience is not left confidently to await the presentation of preordained events. The audience is also ignorant, for it does not know how, or when, the events themselves will take place. Its expectations of the start of battle, a Greek defeat, or Hector's death are subject to manipulation. While the audience finds itself in a privileged position—superior to that of mortal characters within the story—it is paradoxically vulnerable to false anticipation. The audience correctly anticipates the start of battle in book 2 and Achilles' meeting with Hector in book 20, yet the narrator manipulates these expectations by disguising the actual moment of fulfillment. Each potential sequence leading to the expected outcome might be interrupted. In each case, the audience knows very well what is coming, yet the narrator has designed his narrative so that the audience cannot know when it is coming.

In building upon the work of Kirk and others to explain the mechanism of false anticipation, I examine the narrative in the *Iliad* in terms of movement toward a well-defined endpoint. The narrator marks this endpoint by authoritative predictions, which are recognized by the audience. The narrator has several options other than following a rapid path to fulfillment. While the audience correctly anticipates a Greek defeat or the death of Patroclus, for example, the narrator may introduce delay in three ways: by retarding, by interrupting, or by reversing the narrative's direction.[2] In each case, fulfillment is put off, but the effects are different. First, the narrator may merely slow or retard the movement toward fulfillment of the expected outcome. For example, when the audience anticipates the start of battle, the catalog of ships ultimately leads there, but in veritable slow motion. The narrator has not misled the audience, but he does delay commencement of battle in exhaustively enumerating the Greek and Trojan forces. Second, the narrator may interrupt movement toward the expected result. In book 20, Achilles seeks Hector but first encounters Aeneas. This moves the plot neither closer to nor further from the final meeting of Hector with Achilles, but the scene with Aeneas postpones the presentation of the climactic scene that is finally presented in book 22. Third—and most interesting—the narrator may reverse the movement, turning the narrative in a totally unanticipated direction.[3] A noteworthy feature of this type of delay is that it actually carries the story away from the *Iliad*'s plot as well as the epic tradition. At the start of book 3, for example, the narrative movement does not merely slow or stop. It actually reverses, moving away from the start of battle as the Greeks and Trojans discuss how to end the war by negotiation. When the narrator actually drives the narrative away from the expected goal, the audience must seriously ponder such alternative outcomes. The prelude to battle in books 2-4 is not merely lengthy; unexpected episodes— which appear to preclude the necessity of battle—intervene when every indication has been given that battle is about to begin. These reversals in narrative movement threaten the integrity of the story. In addition to frustrating the audience's expectations, the episode of the duel between Paris and Menelaus leads to the possibility of a negotiated settlement of the Trojan War, which would be contrary to the epic tradition (I discuss these "untraditional" episodes at length in chap. 5). False anticipation is actually a complicated phenomenon. At one level, it consists of delay, yet the narrator effects that delay by a variety of means including retarding, interrupting, or reversing the movement toward an expected outcome. With these issues in mind, let us examine books 2-4 from the perspective of the audience's expectations.

The Commencement of Battle: Books 2-4

The audience anticipates the start of battle in book 2, yet fighting actually begins at the end of book 4. The audience's expectation is correct, but the narrator leads the audience to expect the commencement of battle far in advance of its presentation. The audience's expectations are determined in part by predictions in book 1 that anticipate a Greek defeat. In the proem, the narrator begins by announcing Achilles' dispute with Agamemnon. We learn that the wrath of Achilles will cause much trouble for the Greeks: many heroes will die after Achilles and Agamemnon quarrel (1.1-7). Later, in the assembly scene, Athene dissuades Achilles from killing Agamemnon by promising eventual compensation for Agamemnon's treatment, presumably at the resolution of this dispute (1.212-14). Specific details of an imminent Greek defeat are then introduced. As he is about to leave the assembly, Achilles swears an oath that without him the Greeks will be unable to stop Hector.

"ἦ ποτ' Ἀχιλλῆος ποθὴ ἵξεται υἷας Ἀχαιῶν
σύμπαντας. τότε δ' οὔ τι δυνήσεαι ἀχνύμενός περ
χραισμεῖν, εὖτ' ἂν πολλοὶ ὑφ' Ἕκτορος ἀνδροφόνοιο
θνήσκοντες πίπτωσι· σὺ δ' ἔνδοθι θυμὸν ἀμύξεις
χωόμενος ὅ τ' ἄριστον Ἀχαιῶν οὐδὲν ἔτεισας."

"Some day longing for Achilles will come to the sons of the
   Achaeans,
all of them. Then, stricken at heart though you be, you will be
   able
to do nothing, when in their numbers before man-slaughtering
   Hector
they drop and die. And then you will eat out the heart within you
in sorrow, that you did no honor to the best of the Achaeans."
(1.240-44)

In a similar announcement to the heralds fetching Briseis, Achilles says that the Greeks will be in danger as they fight by their ships (1.338-44). He then sends Thetis to Zeus, asking for a Trojan victory (1.408-12; cf. 1.505-10). After Zeus grants this request (1.522-30), Hera rightly suspects Zeus' plan to honor Achilles (1.558-59). These predictions function as a group. While each of the predictions in book 1 emphasizes one aspect of the coming defeat, together they offer a detailed picture.[4] The audience anticipates Achilles' absence from battle, a Greek retreat, and battle at the ships, with the death of many Greeks: all this constitutes a Trojan victory. When the Greeks recognize Agamemnon's treatment of Achilles as a mistake, they will honor Achilles with gifts.[5]

The narrator describes this course of events with different voices, mixing his own comments with divine and mortal promises, requests, and suspicions.[6] In announcing the theme of Achilles' wrath in the proem, the narrator's words are persuasive and authoritative. Divine predictions and promises are normally compelling: here, in addition, we find solemn guarantees from Athene and Zeus.⁷ Achilles' vows, however, set the scene (1.240-44, 1.338-44). Although mortal vows, as argued in chapter 2, do not normally possess the credibility of predictions by gods or the narrator, Achilles' description of the Greek defeat is exceptional, because these predictions of a mortal character are persuasive.⁸ In addition to the solemn vows and invocations, Achilles' words are supported by authoritative predictions. In this case, divine and narratorial predictions endorse Achilles' picture of Hector driving the Greeks to their ships. Athene's promise, Zeus' guarantee, and the narrator's remarks reinforce Achilles' predictions of a Greek defeat.

In book 1, the narrator has carefully prepared the audience for a Greek defeat; what actually transpires in books 2-7 is quite different. The Greek defeat itself does not even begin until book 8, but until battle begins, such a rout cannot take place. The narrator introduces three sequences or successions of scenes moving evidently toward battle. Though the audience's expectations that battle is about to begin are raised, that anticipation is frustrated twice. False anticipation occurs in a series: here there are two instances. The first sequence is interrupted when Agamemnon proposes to test the troops' morale. Paris' offer to duel with Menelaus breaks off the second sequence. The third sequence actually leads to battle at 4.446.

The first sequence of scenes apparently leading to war runs from 2.1 to 2.72, at which time the narrative reverses direction. The first scene in book 2, however, conforms nicely to the predictions of book 1. Zeus lies awake, deciding how to bring defeat to the Greeks (2.3-4). After Zeus sends a deceitful dream to Agamemnon, the Greek leader wakes up deciding to do battle. The narrator's comment, however, makes clear that the Greeks will not take Troy on this day:

"Ὣς ἄρα φωνήσας ἀπεβήσετο, τὸν δ' ἔλιπ' αὐτοῦ
τὰ φρονέοντ' ἀνὰ θυμὸν ἅ ῥ' οὐ τελέεσθαι ἔμελλον.
φῆ γὰρ ὅ γ' αἱρήσειν Πριάμου πόλιν ἤματι κείνῳ,
νήπιος, οὐδὲ τὰ ᾔδη ἅ ῥα Ζεὺς μήδετο ἔργα.

So [the dream] spoke and went away, and left Agamemnon
there, believing things in his heart that were not to be
    accomplished.
For he thought that on that very day he would take Priam's city;

fool, who knew nothing of the things Zeus planned to accomplish.
(2.35-38)

In calling Agamemnon a fool (νήπιος), the narrator reminds the audience that Agamemnon's expectations are ill-founded.[9] Defeat, not victory, awaits him, as the predictions from book 1 have clearly indicated. The audience anticipates that battle will begin, which in turn will lead—unknown by Agamemnon—to a Greek defeat. Yet in his council with the Greek leaders, Agamemnon surprisingly proposes to test the army's morale. In telling the troops that Zeus has deceived him, Agamemnon will pretend to have given up; the Greeks should prepare to depart, for they will never take Troy (2.73-141). There has been no expectation of such a test, and this devious experiment goes awry. The Greek army takes Agamemnon at his word and flees toward the ships, although the Greek leaders are supposed to restrain the troops (cf. 2.75). Hera must send Athene to stop this "homecoming contrary to destiny":

Ἔνθα κεν Ἀργείοισιν ὑπέρμορα νόστος ἐτύχθη,
εἰ μὴ Ἀθηναίην Ἥρη πρὸς μῦθον ἔειπεν·

Then a homecoming contrary to destiny would have come to the
    Argives,
if Hera had not spoken a word to Athene.
(2.155-56)

Only through divine intervention is this early departure avoided.[10]

Agamemnon's test is the first scene postponing the commencement of battle: it disappoints the audience's expectation of battle and Greek defeat. This postponement is not simple retardation or a brief resting point; the narrative has actually moved in a new direction. The logic of this episode leads toward a premature departure by the Greeks. As the narrator's explicit comment at 1.155-56 makes clear, the possibility of the Greeks sailing home is averted only at the last minute by the gods. It takes Hera's quick work to reverse this reversal and reorient the narrative once again toward what the audience had been led to expect.[11] It seems odd that Agamemnon would choose to put off in any way the realization of the Greeks' long-awaited victory.[12] After recounting his dream, Agamemnon may well have suggested arming for battle. Instead, Agamemnon's test and the unanticipated reaction of the Greek army interrupts the movement to battle, contrary to the audience's expectation. For 70 lines, the narrator deviates from the anticipated course of events to entertain the possibility of the Greek army giving up in frustration after nine years of inconclusive fighting.

A second sequence of scenes that seem to signal imminent fighting (2.163-3.15) begins with Hera's order to Athene to reassemble the Greek army. The decision to fight is not immediately renewed. First Thersites challenges Agamemnon (2.212-78). Next Odysseus and Nestor recollect the previous oaths of the Greeks, Calchas' interpretation of an earlier omen, and Zeus' favorable auspices (2.279-368). Agamemnon then exhorts his troops, and the army soon gathers for battle.[13] At this point, the narrator highlights the Greeks' urgency. Nestor advises:

"μηκέτι νῦν δήθ' αὖθι λεγώμεθα, μηδ' ἔτι δηρὸν
ἀμβαλλώμεθα ἔργον, ὃ δὴ θεὸς ἐγγυαλίζει.
ἀλλ' ἄγε, κήρυκες μὲν Ἀχαιῶν χαλκοχιτώνων
λαὸν κηρύσσοντες ἀγειρόντων κατὰ νῆας,
ἡμεῖς δ' ἀθρόοι ὧδε κατὰ στρατὸν εὐρὺν Ἀχαιῶν
ἴομεν, ὄφρα κε θᾶσσον ἐγείρομεν ὀξὺν Ἄρηα."

"Let us talk no more of these things, nor for a long time
set aside the action which the god puts into our hands now.
Come then, let the heralds of the bronze-armored Achaeans
make proclamation to the people and assemble them by the vessels,
and let us go, gathered as we are, down the wide host
of the Achaeans, to stir more quickly the fierce war god."
(2.435-40)

The army is now eager to fight; Menelaus is keen on revenge. The narrator uses *swiftly* and *soon* (ὦκα, αἶψα, τάχα) as leitmotivs heightening the expectancy of battle.[14] The catalog of ships, of course, slows the movement to the first scene of fighting, but this is simple retardation: the audience is not misled. At the start of book 3, the armies march toward each other. Similes prefigure imminent slaughter.[15] After Paris' quick advance and retreat, he proposes a duel (3.67-120). The narrator again breaks off the impetus toward the expected fighting. For a second time, the audience has been led to anticipate fighting, only to witness the armies putting down their arms to await a duel that will settle their conflict. This is the second instance of false anticipation. The duel is inconclusive, but again the movement toward battle has been reversed. The narrative has changed paths and leads toward the possibility of a negotiated settlement.

Divine interference eventually returns the story to its expected plot line: when Aphrodite rescues Paris, Agamemnon claims victory according to the terms of the truce; the gods then incite Pandarus to wound Menelaus—breaking the truce—and a final decision to fight is made (4.221-22). The third sequence of preparation for battle (4.221-445) presents Agamemnon's review of his troops, and this time battle begins (at 4.446). The description of men dying at the close of book 4 echoes the announcement at the beginning of book 2, where the audience first anticipated the coming battle (4.543-44 ≈ 2.39-40).[16] While the first two sequences are interrupted, the third sequence leads to battle in accordance with the audience's expectations.

Although we have been exclusively examining predictions, typical sequences also play a role in generating expectations. Arend, Fenik, and Krischer have demonstrated the patterns (and pervasiveness) of conventional scenes in both Homeric epics. If a sequence of certain elements typically leads to an outcome, the conventionality of such a sequence will generate expectations of that outcome. These anticipatory sequences imply the later result. Schadewaldt has isolated the constituents of one such sequence, the prelude to battle. The narrator presents a selection of nine elements before fighting ensues (the order is variable):[17]

The Prelude Sequence

1. Divine incitement to battle.
2. Mortal decision to fight.
3. Sacrifice.
4. Meal.
5. Gathering of the army.
6. Arming (the whole army or an individual).
7. Marching to battle.
8. Review of troops.
9. Exhortation.[18]

While the prelude sequence varies greatly in the *Iliad*,[19] the narrator uses these nine elements to fashion the three sequences in books 2-4, each of which could lead to battle. As an example, the second sequence, following the test of Agamemnon (2.163-3.15), contains a divine incitement, decision to fight, exhortation, sacrifice, meal, gathering of the troops, and review of the troops. This prelude culminates with the armies marching toward each other.[20] Without exception, the prelude sequence elsewhere in the epic leads to battle. The conventional force of this sequence—in conjunction with explicit predictions—prepares the audience for battle in books 2 and 3, yet the narrator postpones the logical outcome. Although arming is briefly mentioned in the second sequence (2.382-84), there is no individual arming scene in either of the first two sequences. It appears to be reserved for Paris in the duel (3.328-38). Although the audience would not miss an individual arming (none is described in the prelude to book 8, e.g.), the narrator seems to have planned for the arming of Paris in book 3 and therefore avoids one in book 2. This analysis of preludes supports the interpretation that the narrator has deliberately manipulated the audience's expectations.

In books 2-4, we have seen that the audience expects a battle that will lead to a Greek defeat. Although battle eventually begins, the fight itself is postponed: the prelude, or rather three preludes, are stretched over 1,700 lines. Elsewhere the start of battle is simply delayed.[21] Early in the epic, however, the narrator introduces three sequences and twice deviates from the expected outcome. The audience's more immediate expectations are disappointed both times.[22] Although the audience knows that battle will begin—its expectation is correct to this extent—it has no way of knowing in advance which of these potential preludes will bring the armies to battle. The two episodes that interrupt the movement to battle carry the story away from the tradition as well as the *Iliad*'s proclaimed plot. At first the Greeks are eager to sail off without sacking the city. Then Paris and Menelaus are prepared to settle their dispute by a duel rather than continuing the siege and battle. The narrator does not merely slow the advance toward war but pushes the narrative in two entirely different directions. Only divine intervention brings the story back to the outcome anticipated by the audience. Either the departure of the Greeks or the duel—if carried out to completion—would violate the traditional story of a Greek victory over Troy.[23]

Achilles and Hector: Books 20-22

False anticipation occurs throughout the *Iliad*. The unanticipated withdrawal of Hector in book 11 was the example from the third day of battle (books 11-18) introduced in chapter 1.[24] I now wish to examine a second series of false anticipations occurring near the end of the epic. After expectations are raised that Achilles and Hector are about to do battle in book 20, this fateful confrontation is repeatedly postponed. The narrator introduces four sequences that appear to be leading to the final encounter, yet each one is interrupted in one way or another. The audience correctly expects Achilles to slay Hector, but it is misled as to the timing of Achilles' vengeance. Following these sequences, the narrator then uses unpersuasive predictions to suggest alternatives to the *Iliad*'s plot. The audience certainly expects Achilles to kill Hector. But we also find the possibility of Hector escaping or being rescued by a god; even the death of Achilles, rather than Hector, is briefly considered. The narrator not only postpones the final confrontation but also suggests (as in books 1-3) alternative paths that his narrative might have followed.

Achilles' confrontation with Hector follows the Greek defeat at the ships. The narrator eventually prepares the audience for Achilles' return and the vanquishing of Hector, but in the first half of the *Iliad,* he never indicates the circumstances of either event or demonstrates the link between them. Zeus' guarantee to honor Achilles—in conjunction with other predictions in book 1—implies that Achilles will not return to battle until after the Greek defeat.[25] The language describing the hero's return, however, is quite vague. In the catalog, the audience learns that he will soon "stand up" (ἀνστήσεσθαι—2.694). After the second day of battle, Zeus says that Hector will not be stopped until Achilles "arises" (ὄρθαι—8.474).[26] Achilles tells Ajax in book 9 that he will return to battle only after Hector reaches his own ships. At that point, Hector "will be stopped" (σχήσεσθαι—9.655; another ambiguous formulation).[27] This is the first time Achilles himself says anything about stopping Hector, yet he does not specify who will stop him.[28] Finally, in book 15, Zeus' unambiguous announcement clearly predicts Achilles as Hector's killer:[29]

"τοῦ δὲ χολωσάμενος κτενεῖ Ἕκτορα δῖος Ἀχιλλεύς."

"In anger for him [Patroclus] brilliant Achilles shall then kill Hector."

(15.68)

At the end of book 18, Achilles looks ahead to battle but must wait for a new set of armor.[30] The audience anticipates a sequence of Achilles arming, doing battle, and confronting Hector. These expectations are correct, but the narrator first interrupts several potential confrontations and introduces various delays.

Although the prelude to battle in book 19 is typical in many ways (a decision to fight, a sacrifice and meal, arming, marching, and a divine council), the delay that postpones Achilles' actual return is treated thematically within the story. Agamemnon's insistence on delivering the gifts he had previously offered and Odysseus' appeal for a meal override Achilles' eagerness for immediate combat.[31] This retardation is surprising, for the Greeks have long been hoping for Achilles' return. Achilles is put in the unaccustomed position of insisting that the Greeks return to battle. He plays the very role that Nestor, Odysseus, and Patroclus played in earlier councils, where they urged him to fight. For 350 lines, Achilles—and the audience—must wait for battle to begin. The scenes of the return of Briseis, Achilles' compensation, and a renunciation of his anger are placed in such a way as to hinder Achilles' swift return to battle. Even before the false anticipation in books 20-22, Achilles' repeated pleas emphasize the delay, while the narrator self-consciously acknowledges this retardation.[32]

When battle begins in book 20, the audience expects Achilles to seek Hector, the killer of his friend Patroclus. Although the narrator has prepared the audience for this fatal duel, several times he interrupts sequences that could lead there. The first sequence begins as Achilles searches for Hector (20.75-78). This brief sequence is broken off, however, when Apollo sends Aeneas to meet Achilles. During this scene, Poseidon announces the fate of Aeneas (he will survive) and by implication Hector's imminent death.[33] A second sequence that could lead to the final encounter with Hector follows Poseidon's rescue of Aeneas. Achilles looks for further combat (20.351-364), while Hector tells the Trojans that they should not fear Achilles and boasts that he will go meet him (20.371-72). Apollo cuts Hector off with a warning against confronting Achilles, and he obediently retreats (20.375-380). A third sequence actually leads to a challenge. After the slaying of Polydorus, Hector approaches Achilles (20.419-37). The duel begins when Hector hurls his spear. Athene, Achilles' ally, returns it harmlessly to his own feet, and Achilles charges:

αὐτὰρ Ἀχιλλεὺς
ἐμμεμαὼς ἐπόρουσε κατακτάμεναι μενεαίνων,
σμερδαλέα ἰάχων.

>   Meanwhile Achilles
> made a furious charge against him, raging to kill him
> with a terrible cry.
>
> (20.441–43)

This sequence fits nicely with the predictions introduced thus far. Achilles has vowed to avenge the death of Patroclus; he now has the opportunity to dispatch Hector. Yet with Achilles on the point of ending Hector's life, Apollo intervenes a third time and rescues Hector (20.443–44).[34] Achilles then goes on to pursue others; he is confident of soon gaining vengeance (20.452–54).

Three times the narrator explicitly anticipates the meeting between Achilles and Hector. The movement to such a climax is repeatedly brought to a standstill with the intervention of Apollo. First the god sends Aeneas, then he dissuades Hector with words, and finally he rescues Hector. From the audience's perspective, any mention of Hector evokes Achilles' goal of vengeance, but the narrator postpones Achilles' vengeance by interrupting these three potential confrontations. The narrator holds the climactic meeting vividly before the audience's attention, keeping its expectations on edge all the while.

The narrator plays once more on the audience's expectations in a fourth sequence. Book 20 ends with Achilles seeking further "glory" (κῦδος—cf. 20.502–3).[35] After he seizes twelve Trojans for sacrifice at Patroclus' burial, Achilles reaches the river Scamander. The narrator says:

> Ἔνθ' υἷι Πριάμοιο συνήντετο Δαρδανίδαο
> ἐκ ποταμοῦ φεύγοντι...
>
> Then [Achilles] encountered the son of Priam, of the line of
>   Dardanus,
> fleeing from the river...
>
> (21.34–35)

Although Achilles has cornered Lycaon, the identity of this son of Priam is not revealed until the middle of the second line (21.35). Only at that point is "Priam's son" designated as Lycaon: ἐκ ποταμοῦ φεύγοντι, Λυκάονι (21.35). The narrator commonly refers to sons of Priam using *son* with the genitive case of *Priam* (υἷος Πριάμοιο) or the patronymic

Priamides (Πριαμίδης). When the possessive genitive is used, the son's name usually occurs before the genitive, or the context makes clear who is referred to (it is Hector 11 of 25 times). An analogous situation holds for employing the patronymic, which designates Hector 26 of 34 times. Except for this instance in book 21, the hero is always specified in the same line as the phrase *son of Priam*.[36] Achilles has boasted that he would pursue other Trojans and then find Hector. At this point in the narrative—after the killing of numerous Trojans and a recollection of Hector's earlier success (cf. 21.4–5)—Achilles meets a "son of Priam." This subtle gesture is effective, because the audience thinks it knows what is finally coming. For the brief space of a verse and a half, it can only assume that Achilles has encountered his chief antagonist, Hector. Again the narrator reactivates the audience's expectations, only to disappoint them once more. False anticipation occurs in each of these four sequences, any of which could have led to the final meeting of Hector and Achilles. The audience's expectations are raised, then disappointed by interruptions and delays of various types.

Following the encounter with Lycaon, a number of episodes briefly suggest alternative plot outcomes other than what the audience expects. These are not instances of false anticipation but are analogous to the alternatives proposed by unpersuasive predictions found in book 1.[37] I wish to sketch out such possibilities in books 21 and 22. In clogging the river with corpses, Achilles provokes the river god Scamander. The audience has been waiting for the death of Hector, yet Achilles is pursued by divine forces and finds his own life at risk. Although Achilles' death would sharply contradict earlier authoritative predictions, Achilles fears an ignominious death in the waves (21.273–83). Poseidon and Athene arrive immediately to reassure him (21.284–98), but the river gods, Scamander with Simoeis, continue to plan Achilles' demise (cf. 21.316–23). The audience should not find the danger to Achilles compelling; still the possibility is expressed not only by Achilles but by the god Scamander.

Before Achilles' fateful meeting with Hector, several alternatives are presented. Hector's option to enter Troy is considered, when Priam and Hecuba ask him to come within the safety of the city walls (22.37–91). In his monologue, Hector briefly contemplates offering Helen back (22.111–21). Later, Zeus contemplates saving Hector:[38]

"ἀλλ' ἄγετε φράζεσθε, θεοί, καὶ μητιάασθε
ἠέ μιν ἐκ θανάτοιο σαώσομεν, ἦέ μιν ἤδη
Πηλεΐδῃ Ἀχιλῆι δαμάσσομεν ἐσθλὸν ἐόντα."

"But come, gods, consider and take counsel
whether to rescue [Hector] from death, or to subdue him,
a valiant man, at the hands of Achilles, son of Peleus."

(22.174-76)

As with Scamander's threat to Achilles, these three alternatives for Hector—retreat into Troy, negotiation, or divine rescue—are briefly articulated and then quickly dismissed. Hector quickly rejects his parents' pleas (22.78, 22.91); he realizes Achilles will not listen to negotiation (22.122-30); and when Athene objects to Zeus' suggestion to save Hector, the god immediately allows Athene to help Achilles accomplish his goal (22.177-247). The effect of these three passages is not misdirection: unpersuasive predictions by mortal (and here divine) characters briefly express alternatives before the narrative moves on as expected. Still these ideas are explicitly proposed in the narrative.[39] Finally Zeus sets out the scales foretelling Hector's doom (22.209-13). The narrator then presents the scene the audience has long awaited: the duel between Achilles and Hector. Earlier authoritative predictions are at last realized when Achilles slays his opponent (22.306-63).

In books 20-22, the narrator has not simply postponed the ultimate encounter of Achilles and Hector. Throughout the narrative, prominence is given to Hector—whatever Achilles is doing.[40] At first Achilles meets Aeneas while seeking Hector; then Hector is convinced by Apollo to withdraw before confronting him; finally the two heroes challenge one another, but Apollo rescues Hector at the last minute. From the perspective of the first-time audience, each sequence could lead to the final duel.[41] As the narrator heightens the intensity by such repetition, this artfully articulated series of dramatic near confrontations finally culminates in the death of Hector. In effect, the narrator has chosen not to present the awaited scene by the ships, in the plain, or at the Scamander. The narrator briefly essays such possibilities before favoring a scene in front of the walls of Troy, so that all the city—save Andromache—watch Hector die.[42]

This analysis reveals the narrator's skill in maintaining throughout the epic the audience's alertness for climactic situations. The audience correctly anticipates the start of battle in book 2 and Achilles' meeting with Hector in book 20, yet the narrator manipulates these expectations by disguising the moment of actual fulfillment. When false anticipation occurs, the audience is reliably guided in its expectations of what events will take place. The audience knows very well what is coming, but the narrator has presented his story in such a way that the audience cannot know when these events will take place. Each potential sequence leading to the expected outcome can be interrupted, as often happens. As we have seen, the narrator may slow the movement to an expected outcome (with the catalog of ships or the preliminaries in book 19); he may interrupt an expected confrontation (by substituting Aeneas for Hector); or he may reverse the expected course of events (in book 2, the Greeks almost leave Troy; in book 3, a duel all but undermines the inevitable Greek victory; and in book 11, Hector is forced to withdraw from battle). False anticipation occurs early in the epic, in the middle books, and on the closing day of battle. On this score alone, Duckworth's remark that "when approximately two-thirds of the narrative have been set forth, the remainder of the action is forecast in detail" appears to be an overly sanguine view of the audience's foreknowledge. This chapter has demonstrated that an apparently simple operation—postponing an expected event—may actually be manipulated in such a way that the audience's expectations are frustrated time and again.

The most striking sort of delay is the untraditional episode, which not only postpones an anticipated event but drives the narrative in a new, unexpected direction. Retardation and interruption may serve to stimulate an audience's curiosity about when battle will in fact begin, but by reversing the course of the narrative, the narrator leads the audience to ask whether battle will begin at all. For over 300 lines, the Greeks and Trojans enter negotiations for a duel to settle their conflict. Let us now turn to the audience's response to such remarkable episodes as this.

Chapter 5

Misdirection 2: Epic Suspense

Epic suspense, the second type of misdirection to be studied, occurs when authoritative predictions are absent—that is, when the audience is not prepared for a particular outcome. To be sure, authoritative predictions often are not introduced; this does not invariably imply suspense. But when an unexpected episode, such as the duel in book 3, is presented and no authoritative predictions guide the audience's expectations, this situation deserves our attention. The duel between Paris and Menelaus postpones the start of battle by reversing the course of the narrative. Rather than moving toward the start of battle and the Greek defeat, the story goes in an unexpected direction. In such a situation, the audience notices the lack of authoritative predictions, because the narrator does not make clear how, or when, he will return to the anticipated course of events. This chapter examines the duel between Paris and Menelaus in book 3 and Hector's journey to Troy in book 6. During the course of the duel and Hector's journey, the audience—familiar with the epic tradition and expecting a Greek defeat—receives no indication that these episodes will eventually lead back to the expected course of events. I wish to examine the effect upon the audience when the narrator reverses the course of the narrative. Before the unanticipated narrative is itself redirected back to the expected course of events, what will the audience make of such episodes?

Epic suspense occurs when the narrative is moving in an unexpected direction. It is a type of misdirection, because the narrator challenges the audience to consider the consequences of untraditional episodes that conflict with its previous expectations. There are other types of suspense in the *Iliad*.[1] As the audience anticipates the meeting of Hector and Achilles in books 20–22, for example, repeated delays and interruptions lead the audience to wonder when Achilles will meet Hector. By knowing the endpoint, the audience experiences a suspense born from the knowledge that sooner or later the two will meet—only the circumstances are left up in the air. Authoritative predictions are lacking elsewhere in the epic. During the funeral games in book 23, for example, there are no authoritative predictions concerning the winner of each contest, but neither the plot of the *Iliad* nor the epic tradition are at risk. The audience never learns who will win each competition until that contest is over,[2] so a certain sort of suspense may be said to be operating, while the audience and the characters within the story wonder who will prove the victor. Yet Antilochus winning the chariot race will not contradict the expectations of the audience or violate the epic tradition itself. The audience is not seriously challenged, for no preconceptions about the outcome of these episodes are operating. The suspense the audience experiences regarding the outcome is fairly mild, because whatever the outcome is it will not effect the overall plot or threaten the epic tradition at large. In this chapter, I would like to reserve the phrase *epic suspense* for the situation in which the audience's preconceptions are challenged. The audience knows the larger pattern of events based on authoritative predictions and familiarity with the tradition, but it encounters a narrative that goes against what it knows. In book 3, the audience knows battle will recommence and the Greeks will lose; it knows that the Trojan War does not end in a negotiated settlement. In book 6, the audience knows a Trojan victory is coming. The Trojans will not be driven within the city walls until Achilles is honored by the Greeks. Yet in both cases, the audience's knowledge is challenged, for no authoritative predictions during these episodes show the way back.

The only predictions that guide the audience during epic suspense are the predictions of mortal characters. In chapter 3, we examined mortal predictions in book 1 that briefly raised alternatives for the audience's consideration and then were quickly dismissed. With epic suspense, such possibilities are not so quickly abandoned. It is as though Achilles were not driven to kill Agamemnon for a mere 20 lines but went off to his tent, made plans, and for 200 or 300 lines plotted an assassination of the Mycenaean king. During that period, suspense would begin to build: the audience would take such a possibility more seriously, even if it ultimately knew such an event could never take place without violating the larger tradition.

Epic suspense as thus defined is remarkable because in most cases the audience is reliably guided. The audience learns of Zeus' promise of victory to the Trojans, and that promise is persuasively upheld elsewhere. In book 2, the narrator's comments indicate that the hopes of Agamemnon are misguided; in the catalog, Achilles' return is anticipated. Early in the epic, the gods—and the audience—foresee the general outline of a Greek defeat and Achilles' eventual return. The narrator's presence is described by Booth:

> Homer scarcely writes a page without some kind of direct clarification of motives, of expectations, and of the relative importance of events... we move through the *Iliad* with Homer constantly at our elbow, controlling rigorously our beliefs, our interests, and our sympathies.[3]

While I would not describe Homer, or the *Iliad*'s narrator, as "writing a page," this description may be applied to the narrator and his implied audience. By overhearing divine councils and the narrator's comments, the audience enjoys what amounts to a "divine" perspective, confidently possessing knowledge of later events.[4] In books 3 and 6, however, the audience finds itself in an unusual position; its privileged position is altered. In similar situations elsewhere, the narrator generously shapes the audience's anticipations, but in these two books, the narrator appears to withhold such information. The only comments by the narrator are negative and tell the audience that something will *not* occur. Although knowing more than the characters within the story itself, the audience comes closer to sharing those characters' perspective. In general the audience is removed from the action of the epic, confident in its position of superior knowledge relative to that of the characters within the story, but in books 3 and 6, the narrator never announces the outcome in advance, thus encouraging the audience to adopt a new perspective: the viewpoint of mortal characters, which is subject to doubt, reversal, and illusion.

Book 3 is remarkable because the duel appears to preclude the necessity of battle when every indication has been that battle is about to start. The duel—if carried out to its conclusion—would violate the predictions already presented in the epic and upset the larger story line of a Greek defeat of Troy. By the time Hector goes to Troy in book 6, the audience has long awaited a Greek defeat; instead the Trojans are losing. The audience may come to question the validity of earlier predictions—on which the audience had relied to guide its anticipations. Books 3 and 6 elicit a strong reaction from the audience. The narrator uses epic suspense to pose alternatives to the tradition and the *Iliad*'s plot at a level beyond the unpersuasive predictions of book 1. We turn now to the duel in book 3, which raises the possibility of a negotiated settlement—a sharp contradiction to earlier predictions and a violation of the traditional story line.

The Duel: Book 3

In book 3, Paris stops battle and proposes a duel with Menelaus to resolve the conflict between the Greeks and Trojans. This episode—if it were carried out without interruption—would entail two consequences. First, one of the two combatants would die; second, the armies would abide by the outcome. Such a result is interrupted by means of divine intervention. Aphrodite saves Paris on the point of death; Athene then incites Pandarus to shoot the unsuspecting Menelaus, thus breaking the truce. During the preparation for the duel, however, the audience hears nothing of the gods' imminent intervention. Only in book 4 is the audience returned to its prior position of being privy to divine councils, when it learns of the decision to let battle continue. In order to compare the audience's position in book 3 with that enjoyed in the first two books, we first examine three types of scenes that appear throughout the epic: prayers, duels, and divine rescues. After establishing the conventional pattern, the divergent features of such scenes in book 3 become apparent.

The narrator's reticence in offering information in book 3 is perhaps best illustrated by the slight modification of the first recurrent type-scene: the prayer. The narrator normally closes a prayer with a comment on the god's response.[5] When Chryses prays to Apollo in book 1, the narrator indicates Apollo's positive answer:

Ὣς ἔφατ' εὐχόμενος, τοῦ δ' ἔκλυε Φοῖβος Ἀπόλλων.

Thus he spoke in prayer, and Phoebus Apollo heard him.
(1.43 = 1.457)

By indicating the prayer's success, the narrator prepares the audience for a later episode. In book 1, the audience expects Apollo to help the priest (cf. 1.8–13). This anticipatory function of the prayer scene is the general rule.⁶ Yet in book 3, the situation is quite different. The narrator refrains from commenting on two of the three prayers in book 3. Just before the lots determining first throw are shaken, the armies ask Zeus to punish the party responsible for the war (3.318–24). As he is about to hurl his spear, Menelaus seeks vengeance for Paris' crime (3.349–55). In neither case does the narrator indicate the god's response.

Ὣς ἄρ' ἔφαν, πάλλεν δὲ μέγας κορυθαίολος Ἕκτωρ...

So they spoke, and tall Hector of the shining helm shook the lots...

(3.324)

Ἦ ῥα, καὶ ἀμπεπαλὼν προΐει δολιχόσκιον ἔγχος...

So he spoke, and balanced the spear far-shadowed, and threw it...

(3.355)

The third prayer receives a qualified comment. While the armies ask that transgressors of the truce suffer, we learn only that οὐδ' ἄρα πώ σφιν ἐπεκραίαινε Κρονίων ("Zeus would not yet fulfill this"—3.302).⁷ Elsewhere in the epic the narrator uses the prayer scene to anticipate later action, but the prayers in book 3 are modified so that no such information is conveyed.

The second type of scene is the duel, of which there are a number in the *Iliad*. Usually, the audience knows the outcome before a duel takes place. The narrator explicitly predicts the results of the three major duels during battle. Zeus foretells Sarpedon's death at the hands of Patroclus 1,100 lines before he dies.⁸ Numerous predictions anticipate Patroclus' death by Hector.⁹ We have already examined the narrative preparation for the meeting between Achilles and Hector and its outcome. In the duel between Hector and Ajax in book 7 (the only other duel outside the battle narrative),¹⁰ the audience gathers a variety of information in advance. Apollo and Athene agree that this duel will end battle for the day (7.29–30); Helenus assures Hector that he is not yet fated to die (7.52–53); the unusual prayer of the Greeks contains the possibility that the duel may end in a draw:

> "εἰ δὲ καὶ Ἕκτορά περ φιλέεις καὶ κήδεαι αὐτοῦ,
> ἴσην ἀμφοτέροισι βίην καὶ κῦδος ὄπασσον."
>
> "If you [Zeus] also love and care for Hector equally [with Ajax], bestow equal power and glory upon both heroes."
>
> (7.204–5)[11]

Although the narrator does not indicate Zeus' response to this prayer, the audience does not expect Hector to die, due to Helenus' promise and other considerations. Ajax' death would contradict the story of his suicide following the contest of arms with Odysseus (assuming this is traditional). The possibility of a draw is signaled in the prayer: by a principle of narrative economy, the weaker appeal should be realized or not mentioned at all. Elsewhere in the *Iliad,* the narrator anticipates the victor of each duel, but the victor of the duel in book 3 is not indicated beforehand, promoting an atmosphere of uncertainty over the outcome.

Regarding divine rescues, there is great variety in the epic. In book 3, as Menelaus drags away Paris, the audience has received no advance notice of any intervention. Aphrodite, who rescues Paris, is not mentioned until her sudden appearance (3.373–82). Yet the narrator often prepares the audience for such intervention. A comparison between Aphrodite's rescue and other divine rescues in the *Iliad* reveals this contrast. The other rescues occur in books 5, 20, and 21. As she counsels Diomedes, Athene foresees the action of Aphrodite to save Aeneas (5.129–32).[12] Apollo encourages Aeneas to face Achilles (20.104–7), and Poseidon makes it clear that Aeneas must survive (20.301–8).[13] In book 21, Apollo remains at Agenor's side, ready to save him (21.544–49). In three of five rescues, the audience is prepared beforehand for the outcome. The only wholly unanticipated rescue—other than Aphrodite's in book 3—occurs in book 20, when Apollo unexpectedly saves Hector.[14] Regarding Aphrodite's sudden appearance in book 3, the audience misses any anticipatory signals. Instead of Aphrodite, Iris, the only divinity previously introduced, brings the news of the duel to Helen (3.121–40). Given Aphrodite's interest in Helen and Paris, we might have expected her at least to have sent Iris. Is this a deliberate ploy to keep Aphrodite off the scene until she appears in the nick of time?[15] In books 1 and 2, the audience enjoys a position of privileged foreknowledge. In book 3, that status is substantially altered. Instead of the almost routine anticipation found with prayers, duels, and rescues introduced elsewhere, predictions are omitted in situations where we normally expect to find them. Rather than linking the audience's perspective with the gods, the narrator brings the audience closer to a fallible, "mortal" perspective on the future.

The only guidance the audience receives are the predictions and hopes of the mortal characters. In examining these, I begin with the various formulations of the terms of the duel, and then compare the characters' expectations with those of the audience. In his initial proposal, Paris lays out the terms of the duel clearly enough:

"ὁππότερος δέ κε νικήσῃ κρείσσων τε γένηται
κτήμαθ' ἑλὼν εὖ πάντα γυναῖκά τε οἴκαδ' ἀγέσθω.
οἱ δ' ἄλλοι φιλότητα καὶ ὅρκια πιστὰ ταμόντες
ναίοιτε Τροίην ἐριβώλακα, τοὶ δὲ νεέσθων
Ἄργος ἐς ἱππόβοτον καὶ Ἀχαιίδα καλλιγύναικα."

"Whoever wins and proves stronger, let him
fairly take the possessions and the woman, and lead her
   homeward.
But may the rest, having cut oaths of faith and friendship,
dwell in Troy where the soil is rich, while those others return home
to horse-pasturing Argos and Achaea, the land of fair women."
(3.71-75)

The winner of the duel will receive Helen and her goods; the two armies are to pledge oaths of friendship. After the duel, the Trojans will stay in Troy, and the Greeks will sail home. In announcing Paris' proposal, Hector uses similar language (3.71-72 = 3.92-93). While Paris and Hector only mention a victor, Menelaus and (later) Agamemnon explicitly foresee death coming to one of the fighters.[16] As he invokes the gods as witnesses, Agamemnon makes a formal proclamation: if Paris kills Menelaus, Paris will keep Helen and her goods, and the Greeks will sail home; if Menelaus kills Paris, Helen and her things are to be returned, and an additional payment should be paid to the Greeks (3.276-87). The various proposed terms contain somewhat different emphases. It is unclear whether death is a necessary outcome; Agamemnon is the first to introduce the idea of a Trojan penalty. It is hardly surprising that none of the characters anticipates Aphrodite's intervention. In the end, although Menelaus proves to be the winner according to the original terms, Helen is not returned, nor does the truce endure.[17]

For 400 lines, the hopes and expectations of mortal characters are all that guide the audience's experience. What do the characters within the story expect the duel to accomplish? The immediate response to Paris' challenge by the Greek army is silence (3.95). Although this is a common response to any challenge (and usually indicates hesitation), here it may well indicate surprise. The Greeks hardly expect Paris, who has been responsible for the war, to offer Menelaus an opportunity for vengeance.[18] Paris' retreat when he first sees Menelaus reinforces the unlikelihood of his proposing a duel (cf. 3.30-37). And yet he offers to fight 30 lines later. In accepting the challenge, Menelaus is suspicious and insists on Priam's presence to ensure that the Trojans abide by their oaths (3.105-10). Following these reactions of surprise and suspicion, both armies are confident that the war has finally come to an end (3.111-12). The audience, of course, must juxtapose such a response with its knowledge of the tradition and its recollection of earlier authoritative predictions.

Priam appears to anticipate the worst for his son. After witnessing the oaths, he turns to leave, saying that he cannot bear to watch his son fight (3.303-13).[19] Although in book 2 Odysseus and Nestor recalled prophecies of the eventual sack of Troy, here the Greeks appear prepared to settle for the return of Helen and the death of Paris. When Menelaus proves the stronger, Aphrodite rescues Paris; Agamemnon accordingly claims victory for his brother (3.456-60). The gods intervene a second time, when Athene incites Pandarus to shoot Menelaus. Although the Greeks and the Trojans had hopes that the war would be over, they now must return to battle.

Naturally the audience follows this scene differently. The audience scarcely expects the duel actually to end the war, as the armies hope, for that would contradict Zeus' promise to Thetis of a Greek defeat and the narrator's prediction of Achilles' return. Nor can this duel result in the death of either contestant if the tradition is to be respected: Paris should survive to kill Achilles with Apollo's help at the walls of Troy, while Menelaus will return home with Helen after Troy is sacked. The audience comes to this episode with knowledge superior to that of the mortal characters, but for several hundred lines, the only indication of what will occur is found in mortal predictions that are based on a view of the future without fixed preconceptions about the future. Until now, the audience shared the divine perspective, and in book 3, the audience still knows more. But it now misses reminders of that knowledge. No authoritative predictions reinforce its previous assumptions. While it has not forgotten earlier authoritative predictions, it is brought closer to the limited viewpoint of mortal characters. In book 4, the audience is returned to its privileged position. When the narrator presents Hera insisting that war continue and Athene being sent to the battlefield, the audience finally sees how the apparent implications of the duel will be overruled. The potential for a negotiated settlement is disrupted by this second divine intervention.

In book 3, the narrator structures the narrative so that the audience experiences a strong degree of suspense. It knows that the duel must be terminated if the story is to continue, yet the narrator gives no indication how that will be accomplished: the duel's outcome remains a mystery. The audience must set its own previous ideas about what is likely to happen against the narrative, which at this point moves in an entirely different direction. The audience has no idea of what will happen to interrupt this digression. In a sense, it expects renewed battle and an ensuing Greek defeat, yet it does not know how the narrator will return the narrative to its former track. It can only wait to see how the narrator takes the armies from the prospect of a truce and negotiated settlement back to battle and a Trojan victory. Throughout book 3 (over 400 lines), the audience must contrast its previously formed expectations with this unsettling episode. In a passage where the narrator has given no indication of the outcome, the means of interrupting the obvious consequences of that sequence come as a surprise.

The duel in book 3 is striking for a number of reasons. It is chronologically out of place. No one expects Menelaus and Paris to wait until the tenth year of the war to try to resolve their differences in such a manner. It has been argued that its placement early in the epic reminds the audience of the original cause of the war.[20] This view has some merit, but I believe this duel is unsettling in a more fundamental way. If successfully brought to a conclusion, the Greeks would sail home, and the Trojans would live on in peace. The consequences of this duel would contradict the traditional story by bringing the Trojan War to an early and peaceful end. Although the audience naturally resists this alternative outcome to the ultimate victory of the Greeks, the narrator gives no indication of how he will derail such a possibility. The duel resolves nothing; it fails to advance the plot. Still the narrator vividly presents this episode before rejecting it in favor of the traditional story. By withholding his usual guidance, the narrator compels the audience to confront with some degree of seriousness the duel as an alternative to the expected (i.e., traditional) course of events.

Such "untraditional" episodes lead away from the tradition and, in this case, the plot as well. We have already seen other examples. In book 1, the narrator depicts Achilles on the point of killing Agamemnon; in book 2, the Greek army rushes to their ships, eager to return home; in book 3, Paris and Menelaus agree to settle their dispute by individual combat. Each of these episodes—if not interrupted—would lead to scenarios contrary to the Greek sack of Troy. In surveying the *Iliad,* we find that the narrator presents numerous episodes that have the potential to undermine the tradition. In book 2, we learn that if Athena had not intervened to interrupt a "homecoming contrary to destiny," the Greeks would have left Troy and traveled home. Throughout the epic, we find the formulation "Then A would have happened, if B had not occurred." Menelaus, Nestor, and Aeneas almost die (5.311-13, 7.104-8, 8.90-91; cf. 20.288-91); Hector nearly burns the Greek fleet (8.217-19); and Troy comes close to being prematurely sacked (16.698-701, 21.544-46; cf. 20.29-30, 21.515-17). Although each of these episodes is interrupted, the narrator is repeatedly pushing the narrative toward untraditional outcomes. The most prominent instance is Achilles' threat to return to Greece (1.169-71, 9.356-63; cf. 9.393-429).[21] The *Iliad*'s narrator is continually exploring ways in which the traditional story line could be upset.[22] The "A if not B" formulation is simply the most explicit acknowledgment that the narrative has moved in such an unexpected direction. These troubling situations have long been noted. The Alexandrian scholars called Athena's intervention in book 2 a "reversal of fortune" (*peripeteia*).[23] In more recent times, these episodes have been characterized as "imaginary possibilities."[24] Schadewaldt, however, holds that the audience should seriously consider these alternatives.[25]

According to tradition, the war ends with the sack of Troy. Although the event itself falls outside the scope of the *Iliad,* Zeus and the narrator predict this outcome.[26] I think it fair to call the ultimate victory of the Greeks the defining feature of songs about Troy. Yet the narrator introduces three alternative ways in which the war could end. In the first scenario, all the Greeks might choose to leave due to failure. Achilles suggests this during the plague (1.59-61), while Agamemnon's test almost leads to such an outcome (2.149-56). Agamemnon fears that if Menelaus dies, the army will give up (4.170-82). After the rout in book 8, Achilles advises the Greeks to return home (9.417–20). The recurrence of the theme of a premature homecoming makes such a possibility appear all the more likely (cf. 9.26–28, 14.74–81). The narrator is continually showing that the traditional story line might have been altered.[27] A second scenario of Trojan victory would be their success in driving the Greeks away. Rather than the Greeks choosing to leave, the Trojans might force the issue. Both Agamemnon and Hector contemplate such a possibility.[28] Given Zeus' promise to Thetis for a Trojan victory, the audience, too, must wonder at the extent of the Trojans' success: at what point will they be stopped?[29] A negotiated settlement is the third untraditional scenario. We first hear of a treaty during Agamemnon's speech to his troops (2.123–24). At that time neither he nor the audience considers this likely. Yet 1,000 lines later, the two armies are, indeed, making oaths and swearing to abide by the outcome of the duel (3.264–324). Antenor later urges the Trojans to comply with such terms (7.350–53).[30]

On numerous occasions, the narrator raises the prospect of the war ending in a manner contrary to the tradition. The narrator never actually violates the traditional story line, as far as we can tell. By the end of the *Iliad,* Hector is dead, Achilles looks grimly ahead to his own death, and Priam and Andromache anticipate all too accurately the sack of the city and its aftermath.[31] The *Iliad* remains a traditional poem to this extent: the outcome of the war is not ultimately changed. But the narrator makes clear at each stage of the narrative that—were it not for a particular action, decision, or intervention—the story of the Trojan War would have been fundamentally altered.

In book 3, the narrator allows the duel to follow an unconstrained path, without reminding the audience that this episode will not actually end the war. The audience is confronted by an episode that appears to have a logic of its own, as this alternative outcome is explored. The narrator has temporarily suspended the tradition itself; from the narrator's perspective, previous authoritative predictions are ignored, and of course the audience is dependent to a great extent upon sharing that perspective. When authoritative predictions are absent, the audience responds differently to the narrative. Throughout the course of book 3, the audience is immersed in the duel between Paris and Menelaus, which contradicts Zeus' promise to Thetis and the expected outcome of the war. In a way, the narrator invites the audience to forget what it already knows and encourages it to believe, at least for the duration of this scene, that the war may be resolved in this manner.[32] The persuasiveness of such untraditional scenes largely depends on the narrator's skills as an effective dramatist. I will return to the cumulative effect of such challenges to the tradition in chapter 7. For now, let us say that in book 3 the audience surely knows the narrator will return to telling the tale of the wrath of Achilles and the sack of Troy. Still at some level it must reconsider its preconceptions about what can, or will, be told in an epic tale set in Troy.

In chapter 4, I quoted Kirk's remark that delays in the early books were part of the narrator's fundamental compositional technique. We are now in a position to refine that description. First, not only in the early books but throughout the epic, the narrator introduces episodes that postpone the announced plot of a Greek defeat followed by Achilles' return. This is an integral feature of the *Iliad*'s narrative. Second, the narrator does more than introduce delays; he interrupts the plot with untraditional episodes leading away from the anticipated plot. The expansive catalog of ships might be said to delay the start of battle; the duel in book 3, however, does not simply slow or halt the story's movement toward battle, since the narrator actually "switches tracks." The narrative begins to travel in an entirely different direction, a direction opposed to what has been foretold. In a sense, even Achilles' plan to kill Agamemnon in book 1 suspends the plot. In narrative terms, however, it lasts only 20 lines. The plan or idea is barely expressed before it is rejected. The "homecoming contrary to destiny" in book 2 is somewhat longer. The duel in book 3 lasts for several hundred lines. With this longer stretch of an unexpected episode, the audience is forced to consider an alternate ending to the *Iliad*.

Let us not take book 3 in isolation. We have studied two related aspects of the audience's experience during the first four books: false anticipation and epic suspense. When the narrator informs the audience that battle will begin yet postpones the fulfillment of that expectation, we find the audience's expectations manipulated in one way. The narrative resists realizing previous authoritative signals. By contrast, epic suspense follows from a lack of information. The audience is uncertain how the narrator will return to the story he has promised. With epic suspense, the narrative leads away from the tradition, in contradiction to the audience's expectations.[33]

Book 3 itself contains many typical elements: a challenge, the casting of lots, an arming scene, prayers, and a duel. In terms of compositional elements, we may consider book 3 quite conventional. Yet this duel is one of many examples in the *Iliad* that demonstrates the narrator's skill in adapting typical scenes from the tradition to the larger dramatic movement of the epic. This episode is introduced in such a way as to interrupt the start of battle and to call into question the necessity of battle at all. This is not an unwarranted intrusion; the narrator has deliberately interrupted his narrative to offer an alternative path away from the epic tradition.[34]

Hector's Journey to Troy: Book 6

In book 3, the narrative follows an unexpected path. Suspense occurs as the audience—without guidance from authoritative predictions—waits for a return to the expected story line. Once battle begins in book 4, the plot of the *Iliad* is again "suspended," when Diomedes leads the Greeks to success contrary to Zeus' promise and to the audience's expectations. In book 6, the narrator raises the possibility of bringing about the anticipated Greek defeat, when Hector goes to Troy with a request for a prayer. Perhaps with the gods' help, the Trojans will begin to find success. The narrator does not initiate a Greek defeat, as the audience might assume, but rather offers a new perspective on Hector and the Trojans. The narrator exploits the lack of Trojan success as a means of returning Hector to his family in the besieged city.[35] In concentrated fashion, the narrator shows Hector the warrior as son, brother, husband, and father.[36] Although the audience anticipates his meeting with Hecuba, his mother, there is no indication that he will meet Paris until 6.280 and Andromache and Asyanax until 6.365—several hundred lines into the episode. The narrator disguises his design, revealing the sequence of Hector's encounters only one stage at a time.[37] As in book 3, the narrator presents this episode without any authoritative predictions: his comments are only negative. While the audience has its own expectations based on earlier comments, the anticipations voiced in book 6 are exclusively those of mortal characters. The audience, not knowing in advance whom Hector will meet or what the consequences of his trip will be, is again led to share the mortal perspective. Rather than a Greek defeat, battle on this day soon ends with a duel, but first the narrator offers the Trojan perspective of the war. Our focus then is the audience's expectation about the consequences of Hector's journey to Troy.

When battle begins in book 4, the audience expects Zeus to bring defeat to the Greeks. Except for a few Trojan assaults, however, the

Greeks are quite successful in battle, as Diomedes takes center stage.[38] In book 6, another "A if not B" formulation indicates the danger to Troy:

ἔνθα κεν αὖτε Τρῶες ἀρηιφίλων ὑπ᾽ Ἀχαιῶν
Ἴλιον εἰσανέβησαν ἀναλκείῃσι δαμέντες
εἰ μὴ ἄρ᾽ Αἰνείᾳ τε καὶ Ἕκτορι εἶπε παραστὰς
Πριαμίδης Ἕλενος, οἰωνοπόλων ὄχ᾽ ἄριστος.

And then once more the Trojans would have climbed back
within Ilium's wall, subdued by terror before the warlike Achaeans,
if Priam's son, Helenus, best by far of the augurs,
had not stood beside Aeneas and Hector and spoken a word to them.

(6.73–76)

Far from enjoying the success Achilles had requested, the Trojans—if not for Helenus' plan—would have been unable to continue fighting outside the city walls. After advising Aeneas and Hector to exhort the troops, Helenus asks Hector to return to Troy and request that a prayer be made to Athene.

"καί οἱ ὑποσχέσθαι δυοκαίδεκα βοῦς ἐνὶ νηῷ
ἤνις ἠκέστας ἱερευσέμεν, αἴ κ᾽ ἐλεήσῃ
ἄστυ τε καὶ Τρώων ἀλόχους καὶ νήπια τέκνα,
ὥς κεν Τυδέος υἱὸν ἀπόσχῃ Ἰλίου ἱρῆς,
ἄγριον αἰχμητήν, κρατερὸν μήστωρα φόβοιο,
ὃν δὴ ἐγὼ κάρτιστον Ἀχαιῶν φημι γενέσθαι."

"Let [Hecuba] promise to dedicate within the shrine twelve heifers,
yearlings, never broken, if only [Athene] will have pity
on the town of Troy, and the Trojans wives, and their innocent children.
So she might hold back from sacred Ilium the son of Tydeus [Diomedes],
that wild spear-fighter, the strong one who drives men to thoughts of terror,
who I think now has become the strongest of all the Achaeans."

(6.93–98)

According to Helenus, the Trojans' goal is to keep Diomedes from Troy. Hector, however, tells the army that he will confer with the elder counselors and wives in Troy and see to it that prayers are made and hecatombs are promised (6.111-15). Since antiquity, critics have noticed that Hector's version of his trip, as presented to the Trojan army, differs from what Helenus has proposed. Although Helenus only mentions the need to see Hecuba and the priestesses to stop Diomedes (6.86-88), Hector tells the troops that he will speak to the "senators" of Troy (γέρουσιν βουλευτῇσι—6.113-14). Hector also mentions prayers and hecatombs but omits any reference to Diomedes specifically.[39] On reaching his parents' house, Hector conveys Helenus' precise request: ask Athene to keep Diomedes from Troy (6.90-97 ≈ 6.271-78). He follows his brother's instructions. Yet Hector's itinerary is not clear in advance, since two possibilities have been presented, both including prayer and sacrifice. Because the two versions conflict, it is unclear to the audience which Trojans Hector will visit. In fact, although Hector does follow the advice of Helenus in seeing his mother, he goes on to do much more that has not yet been anticipated.

After Hector delivers Helenus' request, Hecuba urges a respite. Hector refuses, saying he must find Paris (6.280-85). The preceding narrative has not anticipated this second stage of the journey: neither Helenus nor Hector mentioned Paris. Hector's trip to Troy was first proposed almost 200 lines earlier (6.86-101), yet Paris is not mentioned until 6.280. The audience anticipated a meeting with Hecuba or perhaps the council of elders. Paris returned to Troy in book 3, when Aphrodite rescued him, yet no mention of him is made with respect to Hector's trip. The narrator now reveals the next stage in Hector's encounters, and the audience awaits a scene with Paris.[40]

While Hector is on his way to Paris, Hecuba gathers the priestesses at Athene's temple. After placing the *peplos* on the knees of Athene's statue, Theano, the priestess, prays:

"πότνι' Ἀθηναίη, ῥυσίπτολι, δῖα θεάων,
ἆξον δὴ ἔγχος Διομήδεος, ἠδὲ καὶ αὐτὸν
πρηνέα δὸς πεσέειν Σκαιῶν προπάροιθε πυλάων,
ὄφρα τοι αὐτίκα νῦν δυοκαίδεκα βοῦς ἐνὶ νηῷ
ἤνις ἠκέστας ἱερεύσομεν, αἴ κ' ἐλεήσῃς
ἄστυ τε καὶ Τρώων ἀλόχους καὶ νήπια τέκνα."
Ὣς ἔφατ' εὐχομένη, ἀνένευε δὲ Παλλὰς Ἀθήνη.

> "O lady, Athene, our city's defender, shining among goddesses:
> break the spear of Diomedes, and grant that this man be hurled on his face
> before the Scaean gates, so we may instantly dedicate within your shrine
> twelve heifers, yearlings, never broken, if only you will have pity
> on the town of Troy, and the Trojan wives, and their innocent children."
> Thus she spoke in prayer, but Pallas Athene turned her head from her in rejection.
>
> (6.305-11)

The prayer in Troy does not jibe with Helenus' instructions from the battlefield: Theano has altered the substance of the prayer. Both Helenus and Hector were explicit that the request to Athene should be: "Keep [ἀπόσχῃ] Diomedes from Troy" (6.97-98, 6.277-78). Yet Theano asks for his death in battle: "Grant that this man be hurled on his face before the Scaean gates."[41] Before following Hector further, let us examine the audience's response to the ostensible purpose of Hector's journey.

The audience has been awaiting the Greek defeat ever since battle began, yet Diomedes and the Greeks have brought the Trojans to desperate straits. Helenus' plan appears to offer a solution. If Athene stops Diomedes—or merely withdraws her active support—perhaps the Trojans can begin their drive to the Greek ships.[42] The "A if not B" formulation introduces Helenus' plan. This often is the narrator's signal that events are about to shift in a new direction (cf., e.g., 2.155-56). Hector repeats Helenus' request to Hecuba, and the prospect of Athene's aid or at least acquiescence reinforces the expectation that the narrator will now present the long awaited Trojan victory. Theano's prayer upsets this expectation. By seeking Diomedes' death, she asks what Athene will never grant: the goddess is a champion of the Greeks and will certainly not allow the death of Diomedes, her recent favorite. Although the narrator often uses prayers to anticipate later scenes, Athene's response is an outright denial—the only such rejection in either Homeric epic. The audience learns only that Diomedes will not die. The ostensible goal of Hector's journey is unsuccessful: the gods will not help the Trojans. In fact, the narrator has not yet revealed the dramatic climax in the story of Hector's journey.

After finding Paris at home, Hector rebukes his brother, who then agrees to return to battle (6.313-42). Helen asks him to stay, but Hector says he hopes to see his wife and son, for he is unsure whether he will return again from battle (6.363-68). The pattern here reflects the previous encounter. Refusing Hecuba's offer to drink, Hector says he must go after Paris. Paris had not been mentioned at all in book 6.[43] When visiting Helen and Paris, Hector again refuses to stay. The audience now learns that he is going to visit his wife and son—again not previously mentioned. In any scene in which Hector returns to Troy, it is possible that he may meet his wife, but for this particular journey, the audience has no reason to expect a visit to either Paris or Andromache. The narrator introduces no authoritative predictions, leaving the audience to rely on the characters' predictions for guidance. The first indication of Hector's intention to see his wife and son (or of the narrator's intention to present such a scene) occurs over 270 lines after Helenus tells Hector to go to Troy.

Again expectations are jarred: Andromache and Astyanax are not at home. They have gone to the wall out of concern for the Trojans (6.386-89). Hector prepares to return to battle:

εὖτε πύλας ἵκανε διερχόμενος μέγα ἄστυ
Σκαιάς, τῇ ἄρ' ἔμελλε διεξίμεναι πεδίονδε,
ἔνθ' ἄλοχος πολύδωρος ἐναντίη ἦλθε θέουσα
Ἀνδρομάχη, θυγάτηρ μεγαλήτορος Ἠετίωνος.

So on his way through the great city he had come to the gates,
the Scaean gates, where he was about to go out into the plain,
there his own richly-dowered wife came running to meet him,
Andromache, the daughter of high-hearted Eetion.
(6.392-95)

Hector, just on the point of returning to battle, meets Andromache by the walls.[44] When he first indicated his intention to see his wife and son, the audience anticipated their meeting. Once this new expectation had been raised, however, Hector was unsuccessful in finding them at home. As Hector reaches the gates, the ancient commentators note the audience's concern: "[The poet] says this so that the audience becomes more anguished."[45] Andromache finds him at the last moment.

The conversation of husband and wife looks to the future—without comment by the narrator. At first a dismal picture is imagined. Hector's death will make Andromache a widow; their child will be an orphan. Hector acknowledges that one day Troy will fall and vividly imagines Andromache in slavery. The atmosphere is uniformly bleak: death seems preferable to the fate awaiting them.[46] Then Hector reaches for his son, and the child's cry at the sight of his daunting helmet inspires laughter (6.466-71). Hector's mood changes:

ἐκ δὲ γέλασσε πατήρ τε φίλος καὶ πότνια μήτηρ·
αὐτίκ' ἀπὸ κρατὸς κόρυθ' εἵλετο φαίδιμος Ἕκτωρ,
καὶ τὴν μὲν κατέθηκεν ἐπὶ χθονὶ παμφανόωσαν·
αὐτὰρ ὅ γ' ὃν φίλον υἱὸν ἐπεὶ κύσε πῆλέ τε χερσίν...

Then his beloved father laughed out, and his honored mother,
and at once glorious Hector lifted the helmet from his head
and laid it, all shining, upon the ground.
Then taking up his dear son he tossed him about in his arms, and
  kissed him...

(6.471-74)

Hector goes on to make an optimistic prayer to Zeus on behalf of Astyanax: may his son prove to be a greater warrior than he is (6.476-81). Turning to Andromache, Hector proclaims that "no man goes to Hades before his appointed time."[47] He then leaves his wife and child and meets up with Paris. Again Hector's words are optimistic.

"ἀλλ' ἴομεν. τὰ δ' ὄπισθεν ἀρεσσόμεθ', αἴ κέ ποθι Ζεὺς
δώῃ ἐπουρανίοισι θεοῖς αἰειγενέτῃσι
κρητῆρα στήσασθαι ἐλεύθερον ἐν μεγάροισιν,
ἐκ Τροίης ἐλάσαντας ἐυκνήμιδας Ἀχαιούς."

"Let us go now; some day hereafter we will make amends
if Zeus with the immortal gods in the sky ever grants it,
by setting up in our houses the wine-bowl of liberty
after we have driven the strong-greaved Achaeans out of Troy."

(6.526-29)

Hector hopes that, with the help of Zeus, the Trojans may drive back the Greeks. Hector and Paris then pass through the Scaean Gates and return to battle. The simile of the galloping horse, which precedes their meeting, exhibits Paris' high spirits as well (6.503-14), and this shared optimism is infectious. At the beginning of book 7, the Trojans rally. The return of Hector and Paris to their fellow warriors is compared to a fair wind coming to waiting sailors (7.1-7).

Athene's reaction to the Trojan rally in book 7 leads the audience to expect her intervention on behalf of the Greeks (7.17-22). This is precisely what Apollo asks:

"τίπτε σὺ δὴ αὖ μεμαυῖα, Διὸς θύγατερ μεγάλοιο,
ἦλθες ἀπ' Οὐλύμποιο, μέγας δέ σε θυμὸς ἀνῆκεν;
ἦ ἵνα δὴ Δαναοῖσι μάχης ἑτεραλκέα νίκην
δῷς; ἐπεὶ οὔ τι Τρῶας ἀπολλυμένους ἐλεαίρεις."

"What can be your desire this time, o daughter of great Zeus,
that you came down from Olympus at the urging of your mighty
    spirit?
To give the Danaans victory in the battle, turning it back?
Since you have no pity at all for the Trojans who are dying."
(7.24-27)

At the first glimmer of Trojan success—which finally would realize the audience's expectations—Athene again intervenes on behalf of the Greeks. Yet here, when Apollo suggests that they bring the day's battle to an end with a duel, she agrees (7.29-36). Athene accepts in spirit Helenus' original proposal, which initially caused Hector to return to Troy. This divine negotiation effectively terminates Diomedes' preeminence without forcing Athene to oppose her ally. The duel between Hector and Ajax in book 7, not a prayer to Athene, achieves the Trojans' original wish.[48] The Greek defeat comes on the next day of battle, presented in book 8.

Hector's journey to Troy should be examined from the audience's perspective. In the short term, Hector's journey appears to offer a means of advancing the plot as expected. If Diomedes is stopped, Hector may have the opportunity to drive the Greeks to their ships. Perhaps Hector is not the best choice for a messenger, but he delivers the request in any case. Athene, however, rejects Theano's (stronger) petition for Diomedes' death. The Greeks led by Diomedes are stopped only in book 7, when Athene agrees to the duel proposed by Apollo. The episode of Hector's journey serves the larger design of the epic, but not as the audience may have assumed: it does not initiate a Greek defeat but offers a new perspective on Hector. No compelling predictions guide the audience. Though its previous expectations certainly lie in the background, the audience must consider this journey a spontaneous venture.

Hector's meeting with his family is the more immediate function of the trip. A second consequence is the articulation of a more distant picture, since the narrator also presents the war from the Trojans' perspective. The fate of Troy is treated not by narrator or providential deity but from within the drama as Hector and Andromache ponder their fate. In their eyes, the future first appears to include military defeat, the sack of Troy, the death of Hector, the slavery of Andromache, and Astyanax' future as an orphan. This undoubtedly reinforces the audience's view of the war's traditional outcome.[49] The narrator, however, never explicitly confirms these forebodings and indeed presents an alternative vision. As Hector picks up his child, he becomes sanguine: he prays that perhaps Astyanax will grow up to be a great warrior. The substance of this prayer is not corrected by the narrator. The narrator omits the gods' reaction to this prayer and does not later correct the wishful thinking that Hector and Paris may one day drive the Greeks away from Troy.[50] The earlier fear of disaster is balanced by Hector's newfound optimism. At first Hector anticipates the inevitable Greek victory—an expectation shared by the audience. Then he hopes for Trojan success. Without intruding comments of his own, the narrator allows the audience to consider these contradictory pictures. Each has some validity, for Hector's optimism coincides with Zeus' promise of a Trojan victory. Because the worries and hopes of Hector and the Trojans have been presented without authoritative comment during this episode, the audience must assess both views without the aid of the narrator's commentary.[51]

In books 3 and 6, the narrator poses alternatives to the tradition and the *Iliad*'s plot that produce epic suspense. Epic suspense most obviously links the audience with characters because the only predictions introduced into the narrative are those of mortal characters. While the audience is still in a superior position to mortal characters, that position of privilege is based on authoritative predictions outlining the plot and on familiarity with the tradition. Both the inevitability of a traditional conclusion and the reliability of authoritative predictions have, as we have seen in this chapter, been called into question. The duel raises the possibility of a negotiated settlement, which contrasts sharply with the traditional outcome of the war. Then Hector's journey seems to provide a means of producing Trojan success; instead, a divinely sanctioned duel brings battle to a halt. The effect is remarkable. The audience is normally removed from the action of the epic, confident in its position of superior knowledge relative to that of the characters within the story, yet in books 3 and 6, the narrator allows mortal characters to contemplate the future. The audience is led to adopt this new perspective, the viewpoint of mortal characters, which is subject to doubt, illusion, and reversal. In a sense, all misdirection has the effect of reducing the audience to this fallible position. In chapter 7, I further develop the shared experience of miscalculation—both the audience's and that of the characters.

Chapter 6

Misdirection 3: Thematic Misdirection

This chapter examines thematic misdirection, which is brought about by false authoritative predictions. In contrast to false anticipation, where the presentation of an expected event is merely postponed, with thematic misdirection authoritative predictions anticipate events that do not take place. The substance of the prediction—not merely the apparent time of fulfillment—is false or exceedingly misleading. The themes of a Trojan victory and burial for a fallen hero are subject to thematic misdirection.[1] These both play a central role in the narrative, developing throughout the epic. Regarding the threat of Trojan victory, authoritative predictions support the false picture of the Greek fleet in flames before the Myrmidons' intervention. The predictions by Zeus and Achilles concerning the extent of this victory imply destruction of most of the Greek fleet before Hector is stopped. This puts into doubt an eventual Greek homecoming, even if the Greeks eventually rally to sack Troy. Once again, misdirection challenges the audience's assumption that the traditional story line will be respected. The second theme of burial—or its denial—reaches a climax when Achilles threatens to throw Hector's body to scavenging birds and dogs. Although he does ransom Hector's body in book 24, until then it appears that Achilles will mutilate Hector's corpse. This is evidently supported by the narrator's comments. Zeus' predictions are not invariably reliable, and Achilles often belies his predictions by his own action—or inaction. Yet regarding the Trojan victory and the burial of Hector, an apparently consistent network of predictions points the audience in the wrong direction, and the narrator refrains from correcting such false persuasive predictions.

The Trojan Victory and Its Limits

Our first instance of thematic misdirection concerns the predictions anticipating the Trojan victory. As we shall see, the audience is misled regarding its extent. Let us begin by surveying the sequence of events on the four days of battle and the audience's expectations. In book 1, Zeus promises to honor Achilles' request for a Greek defeat. When battle begins in book 4, the Trojans do not immediately drive back the Greeks. The Trojan victory is left in abeyance during the first day of battle. On the second day of battle (book 8), Zeus prohibits divine interference, and the Trojans take the upper hand. On the third day, as we have seen, Zeus promises Hector a victory until sundown. Hector breaks through the Greek wall, burns the ship of Protesilaus, kills Patroclus, and wins the armor of Achilles. On the final day of fighting, Achilles drives the Trojans back to their city and slays Hector before the walls of Troy. The audience receives much accurate information about this sequence of events. As we saw in chapter 4, the audience not only foresees the Trojan victory but knows that beyond it lies Achilles' return to battle and eventually the sack of Troy. The narrator makes it very clear that the Greek setback will be temporary.

The limits of Trojan success are spoken of in several ways. Zeus originally assures Thetis that the Greeks will suffer defeat until the Greeks honor Achilles (1.508-30). In book 8, Zeus announces that Hector will not be stopped until Achilles acts (8.470-77). The god's promise in book 11 is for a single day: at sunset Hector presumably will lose Zeus' support (11.191-94 ≈ 11.206-9). This network of predictions leads the audience to expect that Achilles will stop Hector at the end of the day. Although Hector ignores the qualification of Zeus' promise, Polydamas foresees the aftermath of the Trojan assault. Both Agamemnon and Nestor ask the gods that the Greeks not be utterly destroyed, and their wishes are acknowledged.[2] The audience is misled, however, regarding how much damage Hector will do before the Greeks drive him back. Although Achilles' return at sunset marks the end of Hector's day of glory, the audience never learns precisely what Hector will accomplish before then. Because some authoritative predictions about Hector's success are vaguely worded while others are factually incorrect, the narrator encourages the expectation that Hector will do considerable damage to the Greek fleet before any aid comes from the Myrmidons. The audience is led to anticipate mistakenly the burning of much of the Greek fleet, as Zeus' predictions—which normally are quite reliable—reinforce the hopes and fears of mortal characters. The entire network of predictions is misleading, for the narrator never qualifies or corrects such false predictions.

The predictions of mortal characters partially constitute a set of predictions anticipating the threat to the Greek camp. Previously in the *Iliad*, the Greek camp—situated at the ships—was not in danger. Hera says that, as long as Achilles was fighting, the Trojans never ventured far from the city (5.788-91).[3] Yet without his services, Achilles predicts that Agamemnon will not keep the Greeks "safe by their ships" (1.338-44). After the Greek wall is built, the ships become the focus of Trojan boast and Greek concern. Hector vows to cross the wall and burn the ships (8.178-83). Although diverted on the second day of battle, that night he presents a strategy.[4] The Trojans will set watch fires to prevent the Greeks from escaping at night; in the morning, the Trojans will battle the Greeks at their ships (8.526-41). Corresponding to the Trojan threat is the anxiety of the Greeks. In the embassy to Achilles, Odysseus appeals for help in saving the ships (9.230-46). Phoenix' opening and closing words emphasize his fear for the fleet threatened with fire (9.434-38, 9.601-2). Agamemnon's first question to the returning ambassadors concerns the danger to the ships (9.673-75). The Trojan threat against the ships recurs as a leitmotiv throughout the third day of battle.[5] Schadewaldt calls *the ships* a catchword for the coming disaster.[6]

Why does the narrator choose to emphasize the ships? What makes them so important? There are two answers: one in purely military terms, the other with respect to the tradition. In purely strategic terms, the ships define an area of control and safety for the Greeks. Defending the ships means protecting men and supplies in the camp. But in addition the ships function as vessels of transport.[7] The catalog of ships in book 2 reminds the audience that this expedition began as a naval operation. The narrator surveys the Greek forces by naming the number of ships and the leaders of each contingent (2.493-760). Elsewhere the ships are described in ominous terms. They have brought war to Troy, as Idomeneus grimly tells Deiphobus:[8]

"νῦν δ' ἐνθάδε νῆες ἔνεικαν
σοί τε κακὸν καὶ πατρὶ καὶ ἄλλοισι Τρώεσσιν."

"And now the ships have brought evil to this place
for you and your father and the rest of the Trojans."

(13.453-54)

Conversely, these ships furnish the means for accomplishing the journey from Troy back to Greece. After sacking Troy, according to the tradition, the Greeks will sail home in triumph.⁹ This latter capacity of the ships is endangered by Zeus' promise of Trojan victory. For the Greeks to accomplish a homecoming after the war, the ships must survive the war intact. The narrator highlights the danger to the ships, because any threat to the ships jeopardizes the Greeks' *nostos*. Odysseus puts it most bluntly:

"ταῦτ' αἰνῶς δείδοικα κατὰ φρένα, μή οἱ ἀπειλὰς
ἐκτελέσωσι θεοί, ἡμῖν δὲ δὴ αἴσιμον εἴη
φθίσθαι ἐνὶ Τροίῃ ἑκὰς Ἄργεος ἱπποβότοιο."

"All this I fear terribly in my heart, lest the gods
accomplish all these threats, and lest for us it be destiny
to die here in Troy, far away from horse-pasturing Argos."
(9.244-46)

While Odysseus is painting the worst possible picture, the fear that the ships' destruction will leave the Greeks to die far from their homeland is shared by Idomeneus and Agamemnon (13.225-27, 14.69-70; cf. 15.504-5, 15.699-700). The idea of dying away from home also bears on Achilles' rationale for leaving (9.412-13; cf. 9.434, 9.622).¹⁰

A coherent network of predictions—either authoritative or without authoritative correction—suggests that the ships will not be successfully defended. Although the audience is assured that the Greeks will eventually rally, it appears that this reversal will come too late. The audience's expectation that the Greeks will return home (in accordance with the tradition) is undermined by predictions that Achilles will not act until Hector has destroyed much of the fleet. Of course if the Greeks lose only their ships, can protect the lives of the men in the army, and can later sack Troy, it would be possible to build more ships. The fleet's destruction, however, implies the loss of much of their military force. As the narrator highlights the importance of defending the ships, the audience seizes upon predictions regarding the extent of the damage Hector will inflict before he is driven back. Let us consider the most emphatic announcements.

In book 9, Odysseus, Phoenix, and Ajax each attempt to persuade Achilles to return to help the Greeks in battle. Achilles' final word to the ambassadors is that he will not return to battle until the Greek ships are in flames and the Trojans reach his ships.

"οὐ γὰρ πρὶν πολέμοιο μεδήσομαι αἱματόεντος,
πρίν γ' υἱὸν Πριάμοιο δαΐφρονος, Ἕκτορα δῖον,
Μυρμιδόνων ἐπί τε κλισίας καὶ νῆας ἱκέσθαι
κτείνοντ' Ἀργείους, κατά τε σμῦξαι πυρὶ νῆας.
ἀμφὶ δέ τοι τῇ ἐμῇ κλισίῃ καὶ νηῒ μελαίνῃ
Ἕκτορα καὶ μεμαῶτα μάχης σχήσεσθαι ὀΐω."

"For I will not think of bloody war again,
until the son of wise Priam, godlike Hector,
reaches the huts and ships of the Myrmidons
slaughtering the Argives, and the [other] ships are consumed with fire.
But around my hut and my black ship
I think Hector will be stopped for all his desire for battle."

(9.650–55)

The Myrmidons' ships are at the extreme end of the Greek camp (8.222–26 = 11.5–9).[11] Achilles' threat implies that Hector will destroy most of the fleet before reaching Achilles' camp to force his return. In fact, Achilles changes his mind in book 16, when Patroclus' appeal succeeds. As Achilles tells his friend:

"ἀλλὰ τὰ μὲν προτετύχθαι ἐάσομεν· οὐδ' ἄρα πως ἦν
ἀσπερχὲς κεχολῶσθαι ἐνὶ φρεσίν· ἤτοι ἔφην γε
οὐ πρὶν μηνιθμὸν καταπαυσέμεν, ἀλλ' ὁπότ' ἂν δὴ
νῆας ἐμὰς ἀφίκηται ἀϋτή τε πτόλεμός τε."

"Still we will let all this be a thing of the past; and it was not
in my heart to be angry forever; and yet I have said
I would not give over my anger until that time came
when the fighting with all its clamour reached my own ships."

(16.60–63)

Achilles had planned to wait for Hector's arrival at his own camp, yet Patroclus' appeal is effective. Long before Hector reaches Achilles' ships, Achilles sends Patroclus and the Myrmidons to stop the Trojans. Hector throws fire on only one ship in book 16—that of Protesilaus. It is remarkable, however, that in books 8–15 authoritative predictions reinforce, rather than correct, Achilles' vow that no aid will come until Hector reaches his own ships: this leads the audience to expect the Greek fleet to suffer more damage than it actually does in book 16.

This misleading network of predictions consists of threats and worries by the Trojans and Greeks respectively, Achilles' final response to the ambassadors, and authoritative predictions by Zeus and the narrator. While the predictions of mortal characters are often suspect, the audience relies upon Zeus and the narrator for trustworthy guidance. First let us consider Zeus' prophecies. Regarding the limit of Hector's victory, Zeus predicts that Hector will not be stopped until Achilles "rises" (ὄρθαι) as they fight over the dead Patroclus "in the most terrible straits" (στείνει ἐν αἰνοτάτῳ) by the ships (8.475-76). This is false. Patroclus does not lie by the Greek ships after he is killed. He is killed on the battlefield, where the struggle over his corpse takes place.[12] This inaccurate prediction implies that Hector will be at the ships when Achilles finally returns to battle, while the Greeks continue to defend their camp. This is Zeus' first significant false prediction.

Awakening after Hera's seduction in book 15, Zeus is determined to fulfill his promise to Thetis by championing Hector's efforts. He announces that Hector will drive the Greeks to their ships; after killing Sarpedon, Patroclus will be killed by Hector; then Achilles will kill Hector, and Troy eventually will be sacked (15.53-77). Zeus' prophecy is accurate in many respects. Except for the sack of Troy, all this takes place in the next eight books. But Zeus' statement regarding Patroclus' appearance is false:

"αὐτὰρ Ἀχαιοὺς
αὖτις ἀποστρέψῃσιν ἀνάλκιδα φύζαν ἐνόρσας,
φεύγοντες δ' ἐν νηυσὶ πολυκλήϊσι πέσωσι
Πηλεΐδεω Ἀχιλῆος· ὁ δ' ἀνστήσει ὃν ἑταῖρον
Πάτροκλον."

"But let [Hector] drive strengthless panic into the Achaeans, and turn them back once more;
let [the Greeks] be driven in flight and tumble back onto the benched ships
of Achilles, Peleus' son. And he shall rouse up Patroclus his companion."

(15.61-65)[13]

Given the sequence of this prophecy, Zeus appears to be saying that the

Greeks will fall back to the ships of Achilles, and that only then will Achilles send Patroclus to battle. If the Greeks rally at this point, their homecoming would be seriously at risk, for if Hector reaches the extreme end of the Greek camp, the rest of the fleet would presumably be destroyed.[14] Zeus' predictions in books 8 and 15 apparently support Achilles' predictions that no one will help the Greeks until Hector reaches the ships of the Myrmidons.

In general, the narrator's comments are very reliable and helpful in anticipating events. Yet with respect to the limits of Hector's victory and the safety of the Greek fleet, he never corrects Achilles' proclamation or the anticipations of the Greeks and Trojans, as he frequently does elsewhere (cf., e.g., 18.310-13). Not only does he let Zeus' false predictions stand, but his own misleading (if not false) comment in book 15 again reinforces the network as a whole:

Ἕκτορι γάρ οἱ θυμὸς ἐβούλετο κῦδος ὀρέξαι
Πριαμίδῃ, ἵνα νηυσὶ κορωνίσι θεσπιδαὲς πῦρ
ἐμβάλοι ἀκάματον, Θέτιδος δ' ἐξαίσιον ἀρὴν
πᾶσαν ἐπικρήνειε· τὸ γὰρ μένε μητίετα Ζεύς,
νηὸς καιομένης σέλας ὀφθαλμοῖσιν ἰδέσθαι.

Zeus' desire was to give glory to the son of Priam,
Hector, that he might throw inhuman weariless
fire on the curved ships, and so make completely accomplished
the prayer of Thetis. Therefore Zeus of the counsels awaited
the sight before his eyes of the flare of a burning ship.
(15.596-600)

The narrator mentions Hector's glory, the burning of the ships, and Thetis' wish. Nowhere in the narrator's comment is there any indication that Achilles is about to change his mind to save the fleet. Until Achilles reverses himself in book 16, the audience must entertain the possibility of a fleet in flames—and a homecoming at risk.[15]

Various theories have tried to account for the discrepancies between the predictions in books 8-15 and the events of book 16. These entail examining Achilles' character, altering the text, or minimizing the importance of the discrepancies. First let us consider Achilles' character. From the audience's perspective, Achilles has previously made rash predictions and threats in the epic. His vow to return home during the quarrel with

80 / *Homeric Misdirection*

Agamemnon was not realized (1.169-71). He changes his mind several times in response to the embassy. First he vows to leave in the morning; then he says he will wait until morning to decide; and finally he reverses himself and says he will wait for Hector at his ships (cf. 9.356-63, 9.618-19, 9.650-55). How much faith can the audience have in a hero who has previously acted contrary to his word? Still the audience's response to Achilles' announcements is normally guided by other predictions that reinforce or correct his expressed intentions. Certainly many of his unfulfilled threats are not persuasive to the audience. Early in the epic, the audience knows that Achilles is not going home, for authoritative predictions make it clear that Achilles is speaking rashly. In book 1, Thetis tells Achilles to remain in anger by his ships (1.421-22; cf. 1.212-14); Achilles' return to battle is then mentioned in the catalog (2.694, 2.859-61, 2.873-75). Although Odysseus reports his threat to leave at the Greek council (9.677-92), Achilles is still watching the battle in book 11, and of course Zeus has foretold his return (8.473-77). When the audience hears Achilles' threats, it generally knows whether or not they will be realized, due to authoritative predictions that offer a truer picture of the future.[16] As demonstrated above, however, Achilles' threat regarding Hector's attack is not corrected; rather, authoritative predictions reinforce his vow that he will wait until the Myrmidon camp is threatened. Certainly Achilles' temperament is mercurial, but in the case of stopping Hector, his anticipations are corroborated by other persuasive predictions.

A second approach, advocated by both ancient and modern scholars, is to achieve consistency between prediction and outcome by removing the offending lines of Zeus' prophecies. Zeus' description of Patroclus "lying by the ships" (8.475-76) was athetized in antiquity on the grounds that it was false.[17] Aristarchus and Aristophanes athetized Zeus' entire second prophecy (15.56-77); Zenodotus deleted most of it (15.64-77). Two reasons were explicitly advanced for removing these lines: the first is repetition. The ancient critics often objected to repetition in the *Iliad*: in Zeus' prophecy in book 15, Patroclus' death is unnecessarily reiterated (according to this argument) and the sack of Troy has already been referred to.[18] Although it is true that the narrator often avoids repetition, this is not a fixed rule of Homeric narrative.[19] Passages containing summary and recapitulation are found elsewhere in the *Iliad* and do more than just summarize.[20] New information is almost always introduced, raising new and more detailed expectations. Zeus' prophecy in book 15 contains the first explicit prediction that Hector will kill Patroclus and that Achilles will kill Hector. And each time Hector is in the midst of success, the audience is reminded that his victory will be short-lived, and that his death and the sack of Troy impend.[21] Zeus' prophecy just precedes Hector's attack upon the Greek ships: his day of glory is reaching its climax. Yet here the audience learns of his death at the hands of Achilles, as the narrator shifts its expectations to these later events involving Hector. Such "summaries" as Zeus' prophecy either represent a regular type of interpolation or are a regular stylistic feature of Homeric narrative.[22]

The second reason for removing these lines is their falsity, or inaccuracy.[23] The Greeks do not retreat to Achilles' ships; Achilles sends Patroclus to battle when Hector is still fighting at the ship of Protesilaus. How can we explain Zeus getting it wrong? Chapters 4 and 5 have demonstrated how the narrator has manipulated the audience's expectations in a variety of ways. Fulfillment is postponed, and untraditional episodes challenge the traditional story line. Regarding the extent of Hector's victory, we have misdirection of another sort: the entire network of predictions—formed by Zeus' prophecies, Achilles' threat, and other mortals' predictions—generates the consistent (but false) expectation that Hector will drive the Greeks to Achilles' ships at the extreme end of the Greek camp. The Greek fleet will suffer great damage, as Hector gains the opportunity to burn the abandoned fleet. Only then will Achilles send Patroclus to battle. The audience may see Zeus' prophecy as adding more detail to what was said in earlier predictions: Achilles will send Patroclus (he will not go himself), but not until the Greeks flee to the Myrmidon camp. While a scholarly desire for consistency advocates removal, this study argues for retaining the lines with their full import: in books 8 and 15, the narrator uses Zeus' remarks to mislead his audience.

A hypothesis formulated by Schadewaldt offers a third explanation of Zeus' false predictions: the "principle of inexactitude."[24] Schadewaldt argues that the narrator has little regard for precise details; the audience is concerned only with the general movement and would not notice slight discrepancies. Since Homer is an oral poet, his original audience heard the *Iliad* performed. If the performance took days or perhaps weeks, surely no one would remember such details. Is it legitimate then to ground an argument for misdirection upon such close attention to the actual verbal formulation? Admittedly, my analysis has given great emphasis to the precise phrasing found in the narrative. Achilles will "rise" when

Patroclus lies "in the most terrible straits" by the ships. Achilles will send Patroclus "when the Greeks fall back to Achilles' camp." If the audience notes these false leads, it will have trouble reconciling Hector's attack on the ships with the larger tradition of the Greeks sailing home. While I have emphasized the telling effect of false predictions, Schadewaldt prefers to diminish the importance of such discrepancies.

I think the principle of inexactitude helps to explain certain inconcinnities. Athene, for example, intervenes in book 1 to prevent Achilles' murder of Agamemnon, yet Thetis tells Achilles that the gods are away in Ethiopia (1.423-27). There are two middays on the third day of battle (11.84-91, 16.777-80).[25] Regarding these cases, I think, Schadewaldt is correct: the audience is not bothered by the contradiction in either case, for it is of a trivial nature. Concerning the Trojan victory, however, I maintain that the narrator is choosing his words carefully and expects his audience to pay attention. The traditional story tells of a Greek sack of Troy. The narrator of the *Iliad* has chosen to present a Greek defeat, all the while making the audience aware that a reversal is coming. This major theme has been developed with great care. The audience has become sensitive to the limits of Trojan success, suspecting that the Greeks will rally before the fleet is lost. A central issue for the Greeks— and the audience—is the timing of Achilles' return. Any relevant predictions will be carefully attended to. When predictions raise the possibility that the Greek fleet will be destroyed—calling into question the Greek homecoming—this will surely attract the audience's attention. I think the principle of inexactitude does not apply in the case of the Trojan victory.

The audience may not always fix its attention on the finer details. Yet in the proem, the narrator evokes a picture of great destruction as the result of Achilles' intransigence. Later, more detailed predictions reinforce this scenario. While the audience may not retain all the details in connection with Hector's attack, the narrator has manipulated the audience's expectations regarding the limits of Trojan success. The narrator could easily have corrected Achilles' rash threat, yet he does not. Zeus' false predictions and the narrator's vague comments increase, rather than reduce, the audience's worry that Hector will accomplish his threats against the Greek fleet. (On the effects of the Meleager story, see the Appendix.) When Zeus confers a temporary invincibility upon Hector and when the narrator emphasizes the danger to the fleet and then does nothing to reassure the audience about the Greek defense, the audience is left to wonder once again if part of the traditional story line may be abandoned.

The Fate of Hector's Corpse

We now turn to the case of Hector's burial, a second important example of thematic misdirection. When Achilles finally returns to battle and avenges the death of Patroclus by killing Hector, the central focus of the epic turns to the fate of Hector's corpse. Achilles' threats to mutilate the body of Hector are nowhere contradicted, and in fact, comments by the narrator appear to confirm this plan of vengeance. In book 24, Achilles ransoms Hector's body to Priam, but the audience is given little indication ahead of time that he will do so; instead the audience is led to expect that Achilles will continue his savage treatment of Hector's corpse. While the tradition itself is not seriously challenged, the audience is misled regarding the plot of the final portion of the epic.

An articulated sequence of the death and burial of fallen heroes provides a basic structure to the final third of the *Iliad*. The sequence of deaths builds to a climax: in book 16, Patroclus kills Sarpedon but then is killed by Hector; finally, in book 22, Achilles slays Hector. The consequences are evident: while Zeus loses his son Sarpedon, Hector's slaying of Patroclus brings Achilles himself back to battle; the loss of Hector spells imminent destruction for Troy. The narrator normally prepares the audience far in advance for a hero's death. Care for the heroes' corpses is not as decisive for the outcome of the Trojan War, yet it too is given great emphasis in the narrative. The burial of Sarpedon occurs soon after his death in book 16, as the gods Death and Sleep escort him to his home in Lycia. The poem as a whole culminates in two burials. The celebration of Patroclus' funeral games comes in book 23; and the entire epic closes with Hector's burial in Troy. Predictions of burial, however, are not introduced as readily as those for the deaths of heroes. The theme of mutilating a corpse—or denial of burial—is developed throughout the epic and reaches a climax with Achilles' threats against Hector. The work of Bassett, Segal, and Griffin has made clear the centrality of this issue to the narrative.[26] Without reiterating the insightful analysis of these critics, I would like to sketch out briefly how the treatment of fallen heroes evolves in the *Iliad*.

On the first day of battle (books 2–7), there are few instances of threat or concern about the fate of a hero's corpse; no acts of mutilation take place.²⁷ To the contrary, great respect and care is given to the dead. Before his duel with Ajax in book 7, Hector announces the terms concerning the vanquished warrior: if Hector is slain, his killer may strip his arms but must return the body for the pyre; if Hector kills his opponent, he will dedicate the spoils to Apollo but will return his opponent's body to the Greeks for burial (7.76-91). Although the duel—interrupted by darkness—is called a draw, burial would have been assured to the potential loser. That night, both Nestor and Priam propose a truce so that both armies may bury the dead from the first day of battle. War ceases for a day; only after the funeral rites of burning pyres, gathering bones, and setting up markers does battle recommence (cf. 7.324-436).²⁸ Early in the epic—outside the proem—there is no expectation of the savagery to follow.

On the second day of battle (book 8), only a single threat of mutilation is made,²⁹ yet that night the atmosphere is wholly altered. The agreement concerning burial is not renewed. The plain is evidently littered with dead warriors, for the Trojans and the Greeks must each find a space clear of bodies to set up camp or council.³⁰ On their night mission, Diomedes and Odysseus make their way through the slaughter of that day's fighting:

βάν ῥ᾽ ἴμεν ὥς τε λέοντε δύω διὰ νύκτα μέλαιναν,
ἂμ φόνον, ἂν νέκυας, διά τ᾽ ἔντεα καὶ μέλαν αἷμα.

They went on their way like two lions into the black night
through the carnage, the corpses, the war gear, and dark blood.
(10.297-98)

When these Greek spies confront Dolon, the first decapitation of the epic takes place (10.454-57). The third day of battle begins not only with the threat and worry of mutilation but with two acts of mutilation presented (11.146-47, 11.261).³¹ Zeus worries about the fate of Sarpedon's corpse. After Hector slays Patroclus, the Trojan attack on the ships is utterly forgotten as the armies fight an extended battle over the body of Patroclus. The threat of mutilation recurs as a leitmotiv in books 16-18.

The final day of battle includes several acts of mutilation (including a beheading) by Achilles.³² The theme of mutilation thus recurs and intensifies in the *Iliad,* with special prominence after the deaths of Sarpedon and Patroclus and surrounding Achilles' meeting with Hector.[33] Segal calls book 22 the climax of the theme of the mutilation of the corpse. Hecuba worries that Hector's corpse will be fed to the dogs (22.86-89). Hector twice attempts to negotiate with Achilles for burial— once when they first meet, and again after he is mortally wounded. Both times he is unsuccessful (22.250-72, 22.338-60). Weeping at the sight of her dead husband being dragged around the city, Andromache assumes he will never be buried (22.508-14). The heroes and their families evidently place great value upon burial; in narrative terms, this issue is also of central importance to the course of the epic, as the audience becomes sensitive to this shift toward savagery.[34] First there are relatively civilized dealings between the armies, but in the final third of the epic, we find desperate responses to the threat of ignominious violation.

Let us now consider the audience's expectations regarding such episodes. I begin by contrasting the anticipation of a hero's death with the absence of narrative preparation regarding burial. The narrator uses his own comments and those of the gods (primarily Zeus) to prepare the audience for the deaths of Sarpedon, Patroclus, and Hector.[35] Zeus is the first to predict Sarpedon's death—1,200 lines before it occurs. Zeus, Hera, and the narrator reiterate the inevitable outcome of Sarpedon's duel with Patroclus, just before it takes place.[36] Zeus also foresees Patroclus' death—first mentioned eight books and over 5,000 lines before he dies. In books 15 and 16, numerous authoritative predictions remind the audience that Patroclus will die at the hands of Hector.[37] Zeus predicts Hector's death seven books (again almost 5,000 lines) before he dies. Divine and narratorial comments keep this outcome before the audience's attention, while the Trojans, the dying Patroclus, and Achilles all foresee it.[38] For each hero's death, we find extensive preparation far in advance of the event and continuing up to its presentation. The audience is reliably prepared for the killing of each major hero.

In contrast to the foreshadowing of death in battle is the narrative situation regarding burial. Although the threat and act of mutilation gain in ferocity, there is a remarkable silence preceding the burial of these heroes. The exception is Sarpedon, whose burial is planned before he dies. When Zeus agonizes over Sarpedon's imminent death, Hera suggests that he should have Sarpedon's body conveyed to Lycia for burial rites performed by the family (16.450-57). When Patroclus attempts to mutilate the corpse and Glaucus urges Hector to prevent it, the audience realizes that Sarpedon's body is not in danger of mutilation:

Zeus has already planned Sarpedon's funeral.[39] Yet the case of Sarpedon is unique. After Patroclus dies, an extended battle takes place over the corpse. Hector continues to threaten mutilation, yet the first clear indication that Patroclus' body will be saved occurs almost 1,000 lines after his death—just before Achilles' appearance at the trench. Hector dies in book 22, but Achilles agrees to his burial over 1,000 lines later.[40] All three heroes are threatened with mutilation, but burial is assured ahead of time only for Sarpedon. The narrator does not introduce authoritative predictions concerning the fate of the bodies of Patroclus or Hector until long after their deaths.[41]

The audience anticipates the death of each hero but is left in suspense regarding burial for Patroclus and Hector. Let us now examine the predictions that anticipate mutilation rather than burial. To what extent is the audience persuaded that Hector or Achilles will actually carry out their threats? Hector tells the dying Patroclus that his body will be fed to the birds (16.836). In the ensuing battle over the corpse, Hector's intention is obvious:

Ἕκτωρ μὲν Πάτροκλον ἐπεὶ κλυτὰ τεύχε' ἀπηύρα,
ἕλχ', ἵν' ἀπ' ὤμοιιν κεφαλὴν τάμοι ὀξέι χαλκῷ,
τὸν δὲ νέκυν Τρῳῆσιν ἐρυσσάμενος κυσὶ δοίη.

But Hector, when he had stripped from Patroclus the glorious armour,
dragged at him, meaning to cut his head from his shoulders with the sharp bronze,
to haul off the body and give it to the dogs of Troy.
(17.125-27)

Zeus grants Hector victory until sundown. Hector has broken through the wall, burned a ship, killed Patroclus, and won Achilles' armor. He now seeks the further "triumph" of insulting Patroclus' body. Despite his hope that Patroclus will not be given to the dogs (cf. 17.268-73),[42] Zeus does not intervene as he did for Sarpedon. The burden of defending Patroclus' body falls to the Greeks, as Menelaus realizes that even Achilles cannot help without his armor (17.711-14). When they fail to save Patroclus (18.151-68), only Iris' swift message to Achilles secures burial for Patroclus' body:

καί νύ κεν εἴρυσσέν τε καὶ ἄσπετον ἤρατο κῦδος,
εἰ μὴ Πηλείωνι ποδήνεμος ὠκέα Ἶρις
ἄγγελος ἦλθε θέουσ' ἀπ' Ὀλύμπου θωρήσσεσθαι,
κρύβδα Διὸς ἄλλων τε θεῶν· πρὸ γὰρ ἧκέ μιν Ἥρη.

And now [Hector] would have dragged [the corpse] away and won
   glory forever
had not swift wind-footed Iris come running from Olympus
with a message for Peleus' son to arm. She came secretly
from Zeus and the other gods, since it was Hera who sent her.
(18.165-68)[43]

With Achilles' supernatural appearance at the trench, the Greeks succeed in rescuing the body of Patroclus (18.203-33). Until this scene, however, the audience has witnessed only the concern of the Greeks and the threats of the Trojans. Without divine intervention and Achilles' last minute appearance, the likely outcome appears to be that Hector would have indeed carried out his threats. No authoritative predictions actually anticipate Patroclus' mutilation, but the audience is never assured in advance that Patroclus will gain burial until the actual rescue: until then, the fate of Patroclus' corpse is left open.

Hector makes his threats against Patroclus' body on the battlefield, but Achilles' threats against Hector are of a different sort. Achilles plans his vengeance in a more calculated manner—before his return to battle—and he gains the opportunity to fulfill his threat, when Hector's body is brought to the Greek camp. Achilles makes numerous threats of mutilation in books 18-24. Against the corpse of Lycaon, only Achilles' words are presented (21.122-25), but in the next scene, the narrator presents him feeding Asteropaeus to fish and eels (21.200-204). Achilles plans to decapitate twelve Trojans (this is carried out at Patroclus' funeral), and he repeatedly threatens to feed Hector's body to the birds and dogs.[44] In order to assess the audience's expectations as to whether Achilles will actually deny Hector burial, let us consider two aspects of Achilles' character, both of which evolve over the course of the epic: his treatment of the enemy, and his ability to anticipate the future.

When Achilles returns to battle in book 20, he has changed in terms of how he treats the Trojans. Although he has not yet been shown fighting, the audience learns of his earlier deeds in several retrospective scenes. Andromache recalls the sack of Thebe, when her father, Eetion, was killed by Achilles. At that time, Achilles honored him with burial and ransomed Andromache's mother (6.414-28). We learn that Antiphus and Lycaon had previously been ransomed by Achilles (11.104-6, 21.40-43; cf. 24.751-53). These flashbacks paint a uniform picture of Achilles: he was willing to ransom rather than kill the enemy—even in the heat of battle. He evidently respected the dead: there is no mention of savagery.[45] When Achilles learns of Patroclus' death, he undergoes a transformation. Contemplating vengeance, he plans not only to kill Hector, but delays the burial of Patroclus so that he may "carry Hector's head." Part of his reprisal entails the sacrifice of twelve Trojans. Such are his intentions before entering battle (18.334-37).

On his single day of combat, Achilles fights in a rage. He corners the Trojans at the river and chooses twelve for human sacrifice (21.26-32). In his encounter with Lycaon, he eloquently rejects any possibility of ransom, kills him, and vaunts over his corpse. He describes vividly how fish will eat Lycaon's flesh; Lycaon's mother will never mourn her son (21.122-25). In his next encounter, he leaves Asteropaeus' body by the side of the river:

τὸν δὲ κατ' αὐτόθι λεῖπεν, ἐπεὶ φίλον ἦτορ ἀπηύρα,
κείμενον ἐν ψαμάθοισι, δίαινε δέ μιν μέλαν ὕδωρ.
τὸν μὲν ἄρ' ἐγχέλυές τε καὶ ἰχθύες ἀμφεπένοντο,
δημὸν ἐρεπτόμενοι ἐπινεφρίδιον κείροντες.

[Achilles] left him there, when he had snatched his spirit away from him,
sprawled in the sands and drenched in the dark water.
And about [Asteropaeus] the eels and fish were busy
tearing him and nibbling the fat that lay by his kidneys.

(21.201-4)

This is the only scene in the *Iliad* where the narrator presents animals feeding upon a slain warrior's body.[46] Schadewaldt notes that Achilles' actions here show us what he is capable of: he is the only hero to carry out a stated threat of mutilation.[47] In book 22, Achilles refuses to consider an agreement to return Hector's body for burial. He repeats his threat to feed Hector to birds and dogs (22.335-36) and denies a dying request. No ransom will be enough, not even Hector's weight in gold:

"οὐδ' ὥς σέ γε πότνια μήτηρ
ἐνθεμένη λεχέεσσι γοήσεται, ὅν τέκεν αὐτή,
ἀλλὰ κύνες τε καὶ οἰωνοὶ κατὰ πάντα δάσονται."

"Not even shall the lady your mother,
who herself bore you, lay you on the death-bed and mourn you:
no, the dogs and the birds will have you all for their feasting."
(22.352–54)

Achilles then pierces Hector's ankles and drags him around the city.[48]

Ignoring the more gruesome aspects of Achilles' threats, I now consider their persuasiveness. One might suppose that Achilles' plans of mutilation were conceived in anger, and that, although some were carried out in the heat of battle, he would not continue such acts after he returned to camp.[49] This is plausible given his earlier behavior toward the enemy. Yet after battle, he still wishes to feed Hector to the dogs, and his promise to sacrifice the twelve youths is carried out. Although Aphrodite and Apollo offer temporary protection, the fate of Hector's corpse is undecided when the funeral games begin in book 23.[50] At the beginning of book 24, Achilles still habitually drags Hector's body (24.15–18). At this point the gods intervene more forcefully. Zeus sends Thetis with an order for Achilles; the hero then agrees to ransom Hector (24.139–40).[51] The predictions of mortal characters are usually not persuasive to the audience. Yet as we have seen, the narrator often corrects or reinforces such predictions. In the case of Hector's burial, however, he introduces no authoritative predictions contradicting Achilles' threats against Hector; Hector's burial is never mentioned in Zeus' prophecies.[52] Achilles' threats of human sacrifice and mutilation are partially accomplished in books 21–23. The audience may be cautious about accepting Achilles' pronouncements as reliable, but until Thetis' final conference with her son in book 24, Achilles appears eager and capable of fulfilling his threats.

Achilles undergoes another change: he is able to foresee the future. After he learns of Patroclus' death, Achilles comes to see his own fate without illusion. Earlier he acted contrary to his vows—threatening to leave Troy, vowing no assistance until the Greek fleet was in flames. Now, with the loss of his friend, Achilles immediately realizes he will never return to Greece and resolutely accepts his fate to die soon after Hector.[53] Indeed, Achilles is unique among the heroes in the *Iliad,* because he foresees his own death well before it occurs. Unlike his outbursts in the early books, which led to inaction, Achilles' vision—including his plans of vengeance—is now unclouded. Achilles succeeds in killing Hector. After he leaves battle, his ire does not subside. Achilles sacrifices twelve youths on his friend's pyre and promises the ghost of Patroclus that he will feed Hector to the dogs (23.179-83).[54] His manner may be frightening, but his foresight is clear. After battle, the only intention Achilles fails to realize is his threat to feed Hector to the dogs and birds.

The opening to the entire epic sets a tone that is consistent with Achilles' threats. In the proem, the narrator anticipates the wrath of Achilles and its consequences. Not only will trouble come to the Greeks, but the bodies of heroes will be eaten by birds and dogs:[55]

Μῆνιν ἄειδε, θεά, Πηληιάδεω Ἀχιλῆος
οὐλομένην, ἣ μυρί' Ἀχαιοῖς ἄλγε' ἔθηκε,
πολλὰς δ' ἰφθίμους ψυχὰς Ἄιδι προίαψεν
ἡρώων, αὐτοὺς δὲ ἑλώρια τεῦχε κύνεσσιν
οἰωνοῖσί τε δαῖτα, Διὸς δ' ἐτελείετο βουλή.

Sing, goddess, the wrath of Peleus' son Achilles
and its devastation, which put pains thousandfold upon the
    Achaeans;
it hurled the strong souls of heroes in their multitudes
    to the house of Hades,
but gave their bodies to be the delicate feasting
of dogs and birds; so the will of Zeus was accomplished.

(1.1-5)

According to Griffin, the wrath of Achilles is "accursed" (οὐλομένην) because "its result was that mighty heroes became food for scavenging dogs and birds."[56] In spite of the many threats concerning mutilation by birds and dogs, such a scene is never presented in the *Iliad*. This is the only instance in which an authoritative suggestion that a specific scene will be presented is never followed up. Every other event anticipated in the proem is presented in the *Iliad*.[57] This is the narrator's usual practice.[58] The proem misleads the audience to this extent: in other invocations, the events anticipated are always presented in the narrative. The announcement here signals a theme that will be developed throughout the epic; the audience may well expect a scene in which dogs and birds feed upon a corpse. While no authoritative predictions anticipate an actual scene of Hector's body fed to scavengers, Achilles' threats—in the absence of correction by the narrator—acquire compelling power. In a sense, tacit acceptance by the narrator raises Achilles' threats to the status of authoritative predictions.

I am stressing a single passage found at the epic's beginning as support for the threats of Achilles. Would the audience retain this suggestion throughout the entire epic? I believe it would because the narrator introduces this theme and continues to make it central to the epic.[59] From the start, the audience is made aware of the possibly savage consequences of Achilles' anger. Of all the verses in a poem, the proem would be most carefully attended. While hearing Achilles' plans and witnessing his other actions, the audience receives no assurance of funeral rites for Hector. Achilles appears as capable of feeding Hector to the dogs out of battle, as he is of leaving Asteropaeus for fish to feed on in the heat of battle. My conclusion is that the audience is led to expect such a scene of mutilation.

Against this, many have seen Hector's burial as a fitting conclusion to the *Iliad*. Segal calls it "a natural close to a poem dwelling upon the mutilation of the corpse."[60] Yet a work of literature that treats the theme of caring for the dead need not end with burial. However satisfying this final scene may appear in retrospect, the question still remains of the first-time audience's expectations. The narrator provokes the audience's attention, yet until book 24, there is no clear indication that Hector's body will receive burial. All other ransoms in the epic are denied; Achilles' decision to ransom Hector is unique. Achilles himself suggests that Agamemnon and the other Greeks will not view it with favor (24.650-55).

Other endings to this narrative are possible. Macleod says that Hector's dying prediction of Achilles' death in book 22 could indicate the narrator's intention to depict Achilles' own fateful attack on Troy. J.A.K. Thomson speculated that in the "original" story Achilles cuts off the head of Hector.[61] A comparison with Roman literature supports this point. The epic modeled most closely upon the *Iliad* and *Odyssey*, Vergil's *Aeneid*, closes on a jarring note of violence. The madness (*furor*) that pervades the epic is not softened at the end but consumes Aeneas in the final chilling scene (*Aeneid* 12.940-52).[62] The *Iliad* could have had another ending. Although Achilles achieves a reconciliation with the Greeks in book 23, he may not yield on the burial of his friend's slayer.[63] In fact, he continues to violate Hector's corpse after he makes his peace with the Greeks. For the sake of argument, we might consider another narrative, in which Asteropaeus is fed to fish and eels in battle but the mutilation of Hector's corpse by dogs and birds is reserved for a later scene by the ships. Griffin suggests that the fate of Asteropaeus—mutilated in the river by scavengers of the watery element—may be seen as a member in a sequence. The final climactic scene would be Hector's mutilation by land scavengers after battle.[64]

In this chapter, I have argued that the narrator introduces persuasive predictions that turn out to be false. Zeus is generally reliable, yet his predictions mislead the audience regarding the extent of Hector's success at the ships. Achilles' predictions are not always persuasive, yet I have argued that the audience has good reason to expect the foul mutilation of Hector's corpse—chief among the factors is the narrator's silence regarding the fulfillment of such threats. I oppose the view that the audience knows in advance the action of this epic in some detail. While some events are unambiguously predicted, other events of considerable importance are left to the audience's imagination. Thematic misdirection goes further than deceptive timing or suspense: the audience is encouraged to believe that the Greek fleet will be in flames when the Myrmidons return to battle and that Achilles will mutilate—not ransom—Hector's body.

Achilles' anger is the key to the *Iliad*'s plot. It manifests itself in various ways that the audience may not always anticipate. These two examples of thematic misdirection bear divergent relations to the epic tradition. The Trojan victory must be only temporary if the prediction of Achilles' return and Troy's sack are to be realized. If the plot and tradition are to be respected, the Greek army and ships must be saved. Yet the predictions concerning Hector's attack on the ships appear to put the homecoming of the Greeks in jeopardy. An audience that expects the Greeks to return home must confront this disturbing set of predictions. The sequence of death and burial, however, appears in a different light. It is likely that the death of particular heroes was part of the tradition: Antilochus, Achilles, and Ajax die at Troy; Agamemnon on his return to Mycenae; Odysseus and Menelaus live long enough to enjoy the spoils of victory, such as they are. In the *Iliad*, death in battle is usually foreshadowed, and such predictions not only stimulate the audience's anticipation but may tally with the tradition. In the case of burial (or conversely mutilation), we can only speculate about the tradition, but the narrator may well have enjoyed more freedom.[65] In any case, a hero's burial is not anticipated with the same clarity as his death. The narrator presents a suspenseful fight over the corpse of Patroclus and arouses the audience's concern that Achilles will accomplish his threats. Even the *Iliad*'s proem appears to signal that something other than respect for the Trojan dead will bring this poem to an end.

Chapter 7

The *Iliad* and the Audience: Mortal Miscalculation

This chapter addresses the significance of misdirection for the audience. My first objective is to consider the effects misdirection has on the audience—in particular, how a continual disappointment of expectations leads the audience to adopt a different perspective. While foreshadowing links the audience to the omniscient gods, misdirection links the experience of the audience to that of characters within the story. To speak of misdirection in the *Iliad* is potentially ambiguous. So far I have confined its application to the narrator's techniques of raising false expectations on the part of the implied audience. Yet throughout the story itself, the heroes—and sometimes the gods—are unable to foresee where events will lead. Agamemnon, Achilles, Hector, and even Zeus are subject to illusion and miscalculation. These two phenomena—a narrator misleading his audience and heroic characters suffering from delusion—are not utterly distinct. In the story of the *Iliad,* the experience of the audience is treated thematically; or conversely, the deception and miscalculation within the epic is reflected in the audience's experience in hearing the tale. The theme of mortal miscalculation develops throughout the story of the *Iliad,* linking the audience hearing this narrative to characters within the story. My second objective is to speculate on how misdirection will affect audiences other than the implied one. How will a historical listening audience be affected by misdirection? What response will the modern reader and rereader have? After focusing narrowly on the narrator and the implied audience, it is worth considering the meaning of misdirection for actual auditors and readers.

In the preceding analysis, the *Iliad*'s narrative has been examined from the audience's perspective in terms of its knowledge and expectations. Rather than using the inconsistencies, abrupt shifts, and untraditional episodes to distinguish singer A's portion of the epic from that of singer B's or alternatively dismissing the inconcinnities as insignificant, I have offered a radically different interpretation. I think the false predictions and unexpected turns of the narrative are introduced to produce a deliberate, intentional effect upon the audience. The narrator introduces false and misleading predictions as part of a strategy to mislead the audience. A unified epic, composed by a single author, need not be utterly free of inconsistency and contradiction if those misrepresentations produce a deliberately intended effect. Chapters 4–6 have been devoted to a demonstration of how several relatively simple techniques—delay, withholding information, and introducing false authoritative predictions—put the audience in the uncomfortable position of not knowing how the story will unfold.

This examination begins with the audience's affinity with the mortal characters' perspective on the future. This is not the only—or the most obvious—point of view available to the audience. The narrator offers his own viewpoint; the gods offer another; mortal characters, a third. The contrast between these three perspectives proves illuminating. The audience relies upon the narrator and in some sense shares his perspective.[1] The *Iliad* is his narrative; as he presents this story he often comments on it. The narrator can encourage the audience to adopt other viewpoints, however, by introducing predictions in the voice of gods and mortal characters. The audience's expectations will never wholly coincide with such internal points of view, because the audience is a spectator outside the narrative action, while the gods and heroes are fictional creations residing within the story. Still, foreshadowing and misdirection bring the audience very close to such perspectives.

At the beginning of the epic, knowledge resides with the gods, and the audience shares such a perspective. Divine providence, no less than immortality, separates the gods from unwitting mortals.[2] Although the gods foresee how events will turn out, the participants in battle do not share such prescience. The Greeks and Trojans repeatedly confront crises without a sense of what is happening or what is likely to follow. We need not seek far for examples of mortal ignorance and delusion. Early in the epic, the Greeks must consult Calchas regarding the causes of the plague. In book 2, Agamemnon trusts the deceptive dream from Zeus and plans a deceptive trial of his troops' morale. The armies expect the duel in book 3 to end the war. With a false promise of glory, Athene deceives Pandarus into breaking the truce. In each case, individual characters or entire armies act out of ignorance. The epistemological gap between the gods and the warriors at Troy is succinctly described by Griffin: "The plan of Zeus is a mystery to Agamemnon, Hector, and even Achilles."[3]

The narrator often highlights human illusion and miscalculation by setting the ignorance of certain characters against a context of knowledgeable spectators. Apollo alone hears Chryses' prayer; Agamemnon and the Greeks know nothing of the priest's request. As he draws his sword to kill Agamemnon before the assembly of Greeks, Achilles alone witnesses the sudden appearance of Athene; his meeting with Thetis takes place on a lonely stretch of beach far from the Greek camp. When Hera voices her suspicions of Zeus' promise to Thetis, the Olympian gods look ahead to a Greek defeat. In book 8, Zeus issues his prohibition of divine interference. Each of these events occurs at the divine level, unknown to any mortal—except, in part, to Chryses and Achilles. The privileged audience is linked to the gods since it is privy to private conversations and secret meetings, "overhearing" Chryses' prayer, Achilles' request to Thetis, and Thetis' approach to Zeus. With access to the narrator's comments and to divine guarantees, which sketch out the course of the Greek defeat in advance, the audience is in a position to know, for example, that Zeus' dream in book 2 is deceptive and that Agamemnon's hopes are unfounded. Such foreshadowing offers the audience a "divine" perspective upon the events at Troy.[4]

The mortal characters' perspective is like—and unlike—that of the audience. While the audience at times adopts a providential viewpoint, the narrator often brings the audience's expectations into coincidence with those of characters within the epic. In book 3, the audience and the armies both expect battle to begin: the duel is as much a surprise to the audience as to the Greeks and Trojans. In book 6, Hector's expectation of success agrees with the audience's anticipation of a Trojan victory following Zeus' promise to Thetis; simultaneously, the prospect of the city sacked and Andromache in slavery conforms to the audience's knowledge of the tradition. In book 19, the audience anticipates Achilles' return to battle and confrontation with Hector. Frustration at delays by breakfast, gift giving, and oaths are the common experience of Achilles and the audience. In each of these situations, the audience's expectations—some mistaken, some accurate—are brought into agreement with those of mortal characters.[5]

Because the narrator offers both divine and mortal perspectives, the audience alternates between detachment and involvement. But the audience is linked to the mortal characters in another manner that evolves over the course of the epic. I have made much of the miscalculation of mortal characters. Through much of the narrative, mortal characters base their actions on mistaken assumptions. This situation, however, does not remain static. The heroes gradually discover more about what had previously seemed incomprehensible. By the close of the *Iliad,* the gods' exclusive capacity to foresee the future has diminished in importance, while the mortal characters come to anticipate with prophetic certainty the events that will soon overtake them. In book 24, Priam is guided by Hermes to Achilles' camp; Andromache foresees the destruction of Troy and its aftermath; Achilles has shed his previous illusions about altering his destiny. Although mortal characters begin in ignorance and serve as a foil to the gods' virtual omniscience, this dichotomy collapses by the end of the poem. The narrator presents a dynamic situation in which heroes and heroines eventually come to realize and acknowledge their fate.

This shift from ignorance to recognition is best illustrated with the examples of Hector and Achilles. Martin Mueller has shown how the careers of Hector and Achilles follow a pendulumlike swing from knowledge, to delusion, back to an ultimate recognition of previous folly and subsequent fate. As we shall see, the audience follows a similar development.

Hector undergoes a change in the course of the epic: he swings from reasonable expectation to wildly unrealistic hope, back to sure knowledge. Early in the epic, Hector appears to accept the likely outcome of the war. In his first speech to Andromache, he foresees his own death, the sack of Troy, and Andromache's days in slavery (6.447–65). Mueller argues that after Hector goes outside the walls he becomes subject to delusion. Though enjoying Zeus' favor on the second and third days of battle, he makes unrealistic boasts and strategic mistakes that lead to a Trojan rout and his own death.[6] On the night before his greatest success, Hector predicts that he will subdue Diomedes and wishes for divine honor and immortality:

"αὔριον ἣν ἀρετὴν διαείσεται, εἴ κ' ἐμὸν ἔγχος
μείνῃ ἐπερχόμενον· ἀλλ' ἐν πρώτοισιν, ὀίω,
κείσεται οὐτηθείς, πολέες δ' ἀμφ' αὐτὸν ἑταῖροι,

ἠελίου ἀνιόντος ἐς αὔριον· εἰ γὰρ ἐγὼν ὣς
εἴην ἀθάνατος καὶ ἀγήρως ἤματα πάντα,
τιοίμην δ' ὡς τίετ' Ἀθηναίη καὶ Ἀπόλλων,
ὡς νῦν ἡμέρη ἥδε κακὸν φέρει Ἀργείοισιν."

"Tomorrow [Diomedes] will learn his own strength, if he can stand up to
my spear's advance; but sooner than this I think, in the foremost
he will go down under the stroke, and many companions about him
as the sun goes up into tomorrow. Oh, if I only
could be as this in all my days, immortal and ageless
and be held in honor as Athene and Apollo are honored
as surely as this oncoming day brings evil to the Argives."
(8.535-41)

In fact, Diomedes wounds Hector on the following day. Still Hector revives, crosses the Greek wall, kills Patroclus, and wins Achilles' armor. Zeus' comments in book 17 express the tension between Hector's momentary invincibility and his imminent destruction:

"ἆ δείλ', οὐδέ τί τοι θάνατος καταθύμιός ἐστιν,
ὅς δή τοι σχεδὸν εἶσι· σὺ δ' ἄμβροτα τεύχεα δύνεις
ἀνδρὸς ἀριστῆος, τόν τε τρομέουσι καὶ ἄλλοι·
τοῦ δὴ ἑταῖρον ἔπεφνες ἐνηέα τε κρατερόν τε,
τεύχεα δ' οὐ κατὰ κόσμον ἀπὸ κρατός τε καὶ ὤμων
εἵλευ· ἀτάρ τοι νῦν γε μέγα κράτος ἐγγυαλίξω,
τῶν ποινὴν ὅ τοι οὔ τι μάχης ἒκ νοστήσαντι
δέξεται Ἀνδρομάχη κλυτὰ τεύχεα Πηλείωνος."

"Ah, poor wretch! There is no thought of death in your mind now,
and yet death stands close beside you as you put on the immortal armour
of a surpassing man. There are others who tremble before him.
Now you have killed this man's dear friend, who was strong and gentle, and
taken the armor from his shoulders and head, as you should not have done.

Still for the present I will invest you with great strength
to make up for it that you will not come home out of the fighting, nor
Andromache take from your hands the glorious arms of Achilles."
(17.201-8)

After two days of success, Hector ignores the cautionary words of Polydamas, the Trojan seer, boasting that he will seek out Achilles (18.305-9).

In book 22, according to Mueller, comes the moment of Hector's disillusionment.[7] Pondering before the walls whether to enter the city or face Achilles, Hector acknowledges that the Trojan rout has resulted from his ill-considered plans. He briefly contemplates offering Helen back, but realizes this will never appease Achilles (22.99-131). Although Athene (disguised as Deiphobus) tricks Hector into facing Achilles, Hector soon recognizes this final deception. Before his encounter with Achilles, Hector realizes he is going to his death:

"ὦ πόποι, ἦ μάλα δή με θεοὶ θάνατόνδε κάλεσσαν·
Δηίφοβον γὰρ ἔγωγ' ἐφάμην ἥρωα παρεῖναι·
ἀλλ' ὁ μὲν ἐν τείχει, ἐμὲ δ' ἐξαπάτησεν Ἀθήνη.
νῦν δὲ δὴ ἐγγύθι μοι θάνατος κακός, οὐδ' ἔτ' ἄνευθεν,
οὐδ' ἀλέη· ἦ γάρ ῥα πάλαι τό γε φίλτερον ἦεν
Ζηνί τε καὶ Διὸς υἷι ἑκηβόλῳ, οἵ με πάρος γε
πρόφρονες εἰρύατο· νῦν αὖτέ με μοῖρα κιχάνει.
μὴ μὰν ἀσπουδί γε καὶ ἀκλειῶς ἀπολοίμην,
ἀλλὰ μέγα ῥέξας τι καὶ ἐσσομένοισι πυθέσθαι."

"No use! Here at last the gods have summoned me deathward.
I thought Deiphobus the hero was here close beside me
but now evil death is close to me, and no longer far away;
there is no way out. So it must long since have been pleasing this way
to Zeus and Zeus' son who strikes from afar, though before this
they defended me gladly. But now my death is upon me.
Let me at least not die inglorious without a struggle,
but do some big thing first, that men to come shall know of it."
(22.297-305)

Hector dies fully conscious of his past mistakes. His dying words accurately prophesy Achilles' own end.

Achilles' perceptions oscillate as well. His centrality to the entire work derives not so much from the sympathy he elicits as from his epistemological complexity. Achilles begins with an awareness that he is destined to die young. His initial complaint to Thetis acknowledges that he is "short-lived" (μινυνθάδιος—1.352). Indeed, Thetis grounds her request to Zeus upon this premise. If Achilles is "destined for a most untimely death" (ὠκυμορώτατος), he should not be dishonored by Agamemnon as well (1.505-10; cf. 1.416). Yet as the epic progresses, this very destiny is precisely what Achilles calls into question. In book 9, he not only rejects Agamemnon's offer of gifts but tells Odysseus of two choices facing him: a short, glorious life or a long, obscure, quiet one. He says he will choose the latter by returning home and leaving the war to others (9.410-16; cf. 9.393-400). At this point in the narrative, Achilles appears to have forgotten what he previously admitted. He entertains an alternative to his fate of a brief, heroic existence. When he grants Patroclus' request for armor in book 16, his dreams continue: he hopes that only he and Patroclus will survive to take the city of Troy (16.97-100).

Like Hector, Achilles is subject to unrealistic illusions: he badly misjudges the consequences of his request for a Greek defeat and of allowing Patroclus to wear his armor. In fact, his prayer to Zeus for Patroclus' return from battle is denied; neither Achilles nor Patroclus survive to see the sack of Troy.[8] After the death of Patroclus, Achilles comes to accept his own fate: he meets Hector knowing that his death will soon follow.[9] The Olympian gods play no role in foretelling the death of Achilles at the Scaean Gates.[10] The audience hears of his death not from Zeus or the narrator but from Achilles, who confronts what he has known all along. The *Iliad* ends not with Achilles' death but rather with his clear vision of what awaits him. Mueller describes his knowledge in the final books as having "the finality and authority that other heroes acquire only in their dying words."[11] In describing the pattern of Achilles and Hector, we find that each hero begins with realistic expectations but comes to deny what he had previously accepted. At the end, each realizes the mistakes of the past and accepts what he had admitted at the beginning.

At a different level, the implied audience undergoes a similar development. While hearing a story is in many ways incongruous with fighting a battle, we might compare the pattern of Hector and Achilles with the audience's experience in hearing the *Iliad*'s narrative. Just as heroes ponder the outcome of battle, the audience has expectations about the story. The movement from realistic expectation, to doubt, back to final recognition applies to the audience no less than to Achilles or Hector. The audience comes to the performance of the *Iliad* familiar with the epic tradition and begins in a position of knowledge superior to those within the story. Yet in the course of the epic, the narrator repeatedly frustrates the audience's expectations. He introduces snags and impediments that make a straightforward hearing of the poem impossible. Although the audience knows that the Greeks will suffer defeat and that Achilles will slay Hector, it is led to anticipate these events before they actually occur. The audience has begun with some degree of assurance that only particular events can occur if the tradition is to be respected. The narrator challenges that assumption by introducing untraditional episodes, such as the duel in book 3, which has the potential to bring the war to a premature end. The duel is presented in such a way as to encourage the audience to suspend its knowledge of the tradition. Even Zeus' and the narrator's own comments (regarding Hector's threat to burn the ships and Achilles' vow to violate Hector's corpse) point the audience in the wrong direction. The audience's trust in authoritative predictions—its trust in the narrator as a reliable guide—is undermined. Time and again, the audience's expectations are upset in a variety of ways.

At the start, the audience has confidence in its ability to foresee the course of the narrative. As the epic unfolds, that confidence is challenged; the narrator attacks any possible complacency in the audience. By the end of the epic, however, the audience regains an unambiguous picture of what events will ultimately transpire. As the narrator respects the tradition in the final scenes of the epic, the audience returns to what it knew all along. In book 24, after ransoming Hector's corpse, Achilles guarantees an eleven-day truce at Priam's request: nine days to collect wood and mourn Hector, a tenth for burial, and the eleventh to make a burial mound. War will recommence on the twelfth day (24.660–70). This plan is put into effect. When Hector's mound is set up on the eleventh day, the epic closes (24.778–803). The audience knows with utter certainty what follows: further war in the immediate future will lead to Achilles' death at the hands of Paris, then Troy will be sacked. The narrator has returned the audience to its former position of prescience;

the tradition is once again honored, and the coming events are clearly foreseen. Just as Achilles and Hector call what they knew into question, the audience, too, is forced into a similar situation. The audience begins at a distance from the heroes, but in parallel development with these heroes, it experiences uncertainty and subsequent recognition of what will soon occur.[12] Achilles and Hector—and the audience—are returned to an acceptance of what they originally knew in the final portion of the epic. Closure is achieved for the audience, for the narrator offers a clear vision of events beyond the end of the *Iliad*. Achilles achieves a personal—and ultimate—sense of closure, realizing that his actions have led him to his own death, which is now foreseen without illusions.[13]

The *Iliad* is an epic of miscalculation on two levels. The audience's experience is treated as an issue within the story itself, for misdirection of the audience reflects the deception and surprise experienced by characters within the narrative. Achilles offers a paradigm for the audience's shifting capacity to predict what will happen. Just as Achilles ends the epic without illusions, so the audience is returned to the comfort of its own assumptions about the outcome of the Trojan War. Mortal miscalculation operates at the level of both story and hearing the story. The audience knowing the traditional story of the Trojan War may wonder what new can be said. Without misdirection, the audience might look unquestioningly to the distant past, never asking how these events might be recounted. It would share only vicariously in the miscalculation and ultimate realization of the heroes at Troy.[14] Hector and Achilles may see clearly at the end, but it is only after tragic mistakes that they come to appreciate their own circumstances. The audience might experience empathy for such unfortunate delusion but would keep at one remove, like the gods. Foreshadowing—coupled with a knowledge of the tradition—offers the audience a confident, detached perspective. The audience would remain at this lofty height, if not for misdirection.

Homeric misdirection encourages the audience to adopt a second, fallible viewpoint. As false predictions upset its expectations, the audience loses its previous self-assurance and is brought closer to a mortal perspective. It is no simple task for a narrator to put the audience into a position analogous to the heroes for whom the outcome is unclear. Yet the narrator plants doubt in his audience and encourages the audience to adopt a less confident position by challenging its assumptions with false predictions and untraditional episodes. Misdirection puts the audience into a situation experienced by mortal characters, a situation characterized by confusion and unrealized expectation.[15] In the course of the epic, the audience wonders no less than the Greeks and Trojans about Achilles' return, the defense of the fleet, and burial of the dead. By forcing the audience to adopt a fresh perspective, the narrator leads the audience closer to the uncertainty experienced by the heroes at Troy. A bond of human fallibility cuts across the boundary that normally separates audience and character. Homeric misdirection more tightly binds the audience with the heroes' experience of miscalculation.

I have stressed the universality of human fallibility. We find support for this view in the narrator's sparing use of seers and oracles.[16] Although Polydamas is Hector's key advisor during battle, Calchas and Helenus have relatively minor roles; Cassandra is not prophetic in the least. Indeed, the art of prophecy is not always an aid; note the case of Ennomus:

Μυσῶν δὲ Χρόμις ἦρχε καὶ Ἔννομος οἰωνιστής·
ἀλλ' οὐκ οἰωνοῖσιν ἐρύσατο κῆρα μέλαιναν,
ἀλλ' ἐδάμη ὑπὸ χερσὶ ποδώκεος Αἰακίδαο
ἐν ποταμῷ, ὅθι περ Τρῶας κεράιζε καὶ ἄλλους.

Chromis, with Ennomus the augur, was lord of the Mysians;
yet his reading of birds could not keep off dark destruction,
but he went down under the hands of swift-running Aeacides
in the river, as he slew other Trojans beside him.

(2.858-61)

For a true seer, the future is clear: he has no doubts. Yet it is precisely such doubt—such skepticism—that the narrator has tried to plant in his audience. By reducing the role of prophecy, the narrator again brings the heroes' situation in the *Iliad* into closer agreement with the audience's position.[17] We might also think of Nestor, who is highly praised as an advisor. Yet even he is repeatedly unsuccessful in his plans for the future. Not only does he fail to reconcile Agamemnon and Achilles in book 1, but most of his ideas are unsuccessful: the embassy to Achilles is rejected, the wall does not protect the Greek fleet, and Patroclus dies after putting on Achilles' armor. Even his advice to Antilochus before the chariot race in book 23 fails to achieve its intended purpose. Nestor's lack of success reemphasizes not only the contingency of events but the limits of human counsel.[18]

Although the human sphere is continually contrasted to the divine, even the gods do not possess prophetic certainty. As Hera's seduction of Zeus in book 14 makes clear, divine knowledge has its limitations. Agamemnon's story of Zeus and Delusion ("Ατη) makes explicit the common experience of gods and mortals (19.86-138).[19] The narrator's status is problematic as well. He invokes the Muses when preparing to present the catalog of ships (2.484-93). Yet this invocation makes clear that mortals know only "glory" (κλέος)—perhaps better translated as "unconfirmed report."[20] I think it is no accident that, less than 100 lines later, the narrator cites the example of Thamyris, a poet who equaled himself to the gods and paid dearly for it.[21] In the end, the audience finds that all perspectives—human or divine, looking to the heroic past with the narrator or to the future with the seer—are fallible.

The preceding analysis has considered an implied audience that comes to the epic with only a knowledge of the tradition. This implied audience has no previous exposure to the *Iliad* itself and will be affected by misdirection in an immediate way. Untraditional episodes will surprise; false predictions will mislead. Yet this is a sophisticated audience whose expectations are not wholly naive, for it knows that in the end the Greeks will sack Troy. This knowledge is expected. The tradition, however, is not an inflexible monolith; at least the narrator does not treat it that way. The audience is led to question its preconceptions about what happened at Troy or—at another level—about which stories can or should be sung. In one sense, it knows that the Greeks will win; in another, that knowledge is put into doubt. Misdirection forces the audience to question the validity of the tradition, as the narrator introduces predictions and events that appear to lead outside the tradition or that contradict what has been foreshadowed elsewhere in the epic.

Let us now turn to the effects misdirection has on an actual audience. In the discussion thus far, I have narrowly focused upon the expectations and response of an implied audience, reconstructed from the text. I wish to speculate upon how historical, nonidealized auditors and readers might experience the *Iliad*. Distinctions must be made between ancient and modern audiences, as well as between listening and reading audiences. The effects of misdirection will differ depending on whether we consider the audience for whom the poet originally composed or a modern reading audience.

We might imagine Homer himself performing for an eighth-century B.C. listening audience.[22] For an ancient, aural audience, we still assume a familiarity with the epic tradition, although the knowledge of actual auditors will vary from a superficial acquaintance to a developed expertise. An essential feature of a singer performing the *Iliad* before an actual audience is the ephemeral nature of the audience's experience. The song is composed in an improvised fashion, and the experience is, in strict terms, nonrepeatable. Each performance will vary depending on day-to-day factors. The effect misdirection would have on such an audience will be similar in a number of ways to that of the implied audience examined at length in this study. Events anticipated by authoritative predictions would be unexpectedly postponed; untraditional episodes would challenge the auditors' expectations about what can or should occur. The audience would find even such a traditional story as the Trojan War beyond its power to control or predict.[23] The common bond of fallibility might emotionally link this audience to the characters. I suspect that the previous discussion of an implied audience brings us much insight into how Homer's own audience may have reacted: with surprise, confusion, and, in the end, recognition. It is possible as well, however, that Homer may have performed the *Iliad*—or something very much like it—on several occasions. If many of his performances were similar (whatever the variation in detail), certain auditors may have come to recognize his impulse to pursue untraditional episodes and surprising turns in plot. A devoted fan following the singer from performance to performance could attain a more sophisticated appreciation of the techniques of misdirection than would have been possible from a single performance. The transcriber of the *Iliad* as we have it, indeed, may have been such a "Homerhead."[24] For all the spontaneity residing in an actual improvised performance, it might have been possible for an auditor who followed the singer to gain an appreciation of misdirection greater than that of a first-time historical audience.

What would that appreciation consist of? This leads us to consider readers and rereaders, who benefit from an intimate knowledge of the narrative. From Hellenistic times until today, scholars and others have studied the *Iliad* as a work of written literature, scrutinizing every line. Yet misdirection has a meaning for readers like us. A full recognition of the common experience of false expectation by characters and audience is best appreciated, I think, by an audience who has heard the *Iliad* performed several times or has read and reread the work. An audience—knowing not only the tradition but the *Iliad* itself—will have a more sophisticated response to misdirection. Its effects will not be lost completely but will operate at a more subtle level. Although surprise itself may be lessened, prior exposure to the *Iliad* may bring a finer appreciation of Homer's methods of raising and manipulating expectations. In describing the joys of rereading, Nabokov argues that a single exposure to a great work of art does not bring true artistic appreciation.[25] For the *Iliad*, only the rereading audience (or a devoted follower of Homer) is in a position to observe the narrator's techniques for manipulating the audience. By rereading, this audience notices that there were misleading predictions even in the proem. Misdirection is recognized as it happens, not only in retrospect. The dictum that Western literature begins with Homer inevitably leads to viewing the *Iliad* as an essentially fixed text whose readers have no doubt how the story will end. The idealized reactions of the implied audience instruct us in our experience of the *Iliad*, because by reading and rereading we risk losing the excitement and atmosphere of unpredictable contingency this narrative offers. Of course, the *Iliad* as a written text repays the rereader, just as it offers something remarkable to the first-time audience.

The narrator has manipulated the expectations of these audiences in somewhat different ways. The implied audience knows the story; it assumes it can foresee what will happen in the tale but is forced to question that knowledge. Although the past may seem reassuring and safe, misdirection confounds such an idea. An audience's knowledge of the tradition does not eliminate the possibility of being surprised. By challenging the complacency of this audience, the narrator eliminates the luxury of calm providence. The rereading audience realizes that its presumption of complete knowledge is misguided. Repeated exposure to this tale can only deepen an awareness of the human propensity for tragic self-deception and error.

To speak of human fallibility and ultimate recognition inevitably evokes another Greek creation: tragedy. The idea that epic has anticipated tragedy in structure and technique has been discussed since before the time of Aristotle.[26] Achilles' return to foresight at the end of the *Iliad* offers a paradigm for tragic "recognition" (ἀναγνώρισις). In the following chapter, I will speak more extensively of the *Iliad*'s influence on later literature. While our attention is still fixed on the audience, however, the *Iliad* prefigures another fifth-century idea: the Socratic insistence on mortal ignorance. Socrates argues that wisdom at the human level consists of recognizing one's own ignorance. Compared to the gods, a mortal sees very dimly. Socrates' mission from Apollo is to demonstrate this point by challenging the assumptions of his fellow citizens. It is very easy to assume knowledge; on examination, such arrogance is often exposed. I find a shared sensibility between Homeric misdirection and the Socratic quest: Socrates would very much appreciate the narrator's methods for leading his audience to question its own assumptions.

Marg has called the *Iliad* an epic about dying and death. Griffin says the focus is heroic life and death.[27] The issue of miscalculation is also found in this epic, operating in a dynamic manner. We find both the characters and the audience confronting the issue of an uncertain future and, in retrospect, acknowledging their own misjudgments. The narrator strengthens the audience's experience by contrasting mortal ignorance with the relative providence of the gods in his story. Mortal limitation becomes an object of contemplation for the audience. Misdirection leads the audience to share a "mortal" outlook, as the narrator unifies the movement within the epic with the experience of hearing—or reading—it, by posing a problem common to both audience and characters: How can one distinguish false hope from reliable expectation?

Chapter 8

Homer and the Tradition

This final chapter considers misdirection in the *Iliad* from the point of view of the actual poet, whom we know as Homer. The historical poet's relationship to the epic tradition is a tantalizing issue. In what ways does he differ from his predecessors in composing epic song? Where does his contribution lie: in the invention of character, in manipulation of formula and typical scene, in the ability to sing a monumental epic on a scale never before produced? Misdirection should be approached from the poet's point of view, in part for the light it sheds upon these questions.

I have examined misdirection in a limited fashion, considering the techniques of misdirection (as the narrator introduces delays, untraditional episodes, and false predictions) and the effects of misdirection (the audience's response, consisting of surprise, questioning, and later, recognition). An investigation of misdirection should be grounded in such an analysis of the text. In chapter 7, I moved on to speculate about the responses of actual audiences. I turn now to the poet—the composer of the *Iliad*—who has created the manipulative narrator. It is worth considering why Homer might have chosen to mislead his audience in this way. What possible motivations may the actual singer have had for misleading his audience? In part, the poet's motivations are short term and practical, subject to the dynamics of the actual oral performance. From this standpoint, we imagine the singer seeking to sustain a livelihood by his craft. Misdirection is one of the means he employs to ensure a captivated audience who rewards him and will return to hear him sing on later occasions. At a deeper level, misdirection implies the poet's relationship to the epic tradition preceding him. While ultimately he remained a traditional poet, Homer's exploration of untraditional episodes and his challenging of the audience's assumptions may also be understood as a response—an assertion of his own independence—toward the epic tradition in which he worked.

The circumstances of the actual oral performance may have encouraged Homer to introduce misdirection with immediate, tangible goals in mind. Historical evidence, literary evidence (treated with caution), and comparative material of more recent date helps us to recreate the circumstances of the performance and the poet's position in society.[1] A picture emerges of either a traveling entertainer or possibly a singer associated with an aristocratic court. Homer could well have performed before audiences in various locales throughout Greece in the late eighth century B.C. The occasion for song would have been a market day, a festival, a competition at funeral games, or perhaps a nightly offering of song at a private gathering. In *The Singer of Tales*, Lord describes how a wild celebration, potential patrons, or a restless audience might affect a performance. The singer's goal would be to engage his audience, thus gaining rewards of a tangible sort. Although Odysseus is not a professional singer, his tale of his own adventures in the *Odyssey* has an effect upon his audience that may well describe a response prized by any singer:

Ὣς ἔφατ', οἱ δ' ἄρα πάντες ἀκὴν ἐγένοντο σιωπῇ,
κηληθμῷ δ' ἔσχοντο κατὰ μέγαρα σκιόεντα.

So [Odysseus] spoke. But they were all silent,
held by the spell of his words through the shadowy halls.
                                        (*Od.* 11.333–34 = *Od.* 13.1–2)

Just as Arete promises additional gifts to Odysseus in the epic situation (*Od.* 11.339–41), the historical singer might profit immediately from the material rewards of food, wine, and valuables, if his song pleased his audience. In the *Odyssey*, the circumstances are unusual (Odysseus needs to secure passage home), but normally the poet's second practical concern would be to receive an invitation to sing again. One tactic would be to promise a different song the next evening. Lord tells us that the best of the Slavic singers from the 1930s would have thirty songs, one for each night of the observance of Ramazan. In the *Odyssey*, Demodocus sings of the affair between Aphrodite and Ares and later tells of the Trojan Horse—each time in response to requests. An alternative to a varied repertoire would be to sing a long continuous song, something that could last several days or even weeks.² The impetus to produce a monumental epic may lie in such pragmatic concerns. By spinning a single tale over many evenings, the poet would obtain a livelihood for that period. The traveling bard might gain a temporary home.

The poet would sing of the gods, battles, the sacking of cities, and travel adventures. The songs would be traditional: by definition, the audience had a basic familiarity with these subjects. Among the various techniques employed to maintain the audience's interest are foreshadowing and misdirection, which—if properly introduced—would help guarantee an interested audience for several reasons. In the *Iliad,* Homer employs foreshadowing as a means of preparing the audience for later episodes. The audience anticipates the Greek defeat, the return of Achilles, and the deaths of Patroclus and Hector. If the poet sings 500, 1,000, or even 2,000 lines at one sitting, his implicit promise to present later scenes will stimulate the audience's desire to discover how he chooses to render these announced episodes. The heart of such drama lies in the audience's anticipation: Homeric foreshadowing leaves the audience wanting to hear more. Although foreshadowing has long been recognized as a Homeric device, I maintain that it may have developed as a practical consequence from the circumstances surrounding an extended performance. The comparative evidence suggests that epics of 15,000 lines or more have been composed without the aid of writing: there is no reason to believe Homer—literate or not—was the first to invent the technique of foreshadowing. As longer songs were sung, the use of foreshadowing may well have become standard practice, in which the immediate goal would be an invitation to return to sing further. Such "features of coming attractions" might have evolved into a convention.³ If foreshadowing became a conventional feature of epic song, it would be subject to manipulation like any other traditional feature, which brings us to a second strategy open to the poet.

Misdirection offers an alternative means of enticing an audience to return for another performance. In chapter 2, I argued that misdirection is dependent upon a regularly used system of foreshadowing. Only if authoritative predictions persuade, can false predictions actually raise false expectations. Once foreshadowing became a standard feature, a poet could seize his audience's attention not only by anticipating a Greek defeat or Odysseus' revenge upon the suitors but by manipulating the audience's expectations. As we have seen, Homer does not tell the *Iliad* in a straightforward manner. The narrative includes delays, untraditional episodes, and authoritative predictions that contradict the plot or the tradition itself. Hearing Achilles' final threat in book 9, the audience may wonder: Will Achilles wait to act until the fleet is in flames? How far will Hector get? Will the homecoming of the Greeks be lost? It is in Homer's interest to leave loose ends. By deliberately keeping certain predictions vague, misleading, and sometimes outright false, Homer provokes his audience and keeps it wondering how the singer will reconcile his tale with the tradition at large.

In the *Odyssey,* Phemius sings to the suitors of the return of Greek heroes from Troy. When Penelope objects, Telemachus defends the poet:

"τὴν γὰρ ἀοιδὴν μᾶλλον ἐπικλείουσ' ἄνθρωποι,
ἥ τις ἀκουόντεσσι νεωτάτη ἀμφιπέληται."

"Men especially applaud the song
which is brand new to the audience."

(*Od.* 1.351–52)

For Phemius' audience, the homecoming of the Greeks is a relatively recent event. Naturally a certain tension arises when Homer introduces a notion of "the latest song" into his own epic about a distant heroic past.[4] Nevertheless, the essential truth here applies to any performer and perhaps most of all to a singer of traditional tales. To a great extent, the poet is constrained by the traditional story line, which has been described as a monolith exerting a tyrannical hold over the poet's freedom.[5] Homer uses misdirection to impart a vivid freshness to a very old story. By presenting alternatives to the tradition and thus challenging the audience's complacency, Homer achieves something remarkable in such a traditional enterprise: he is able to offer a new angle upon the tale of the Trojan War. The preceding analysis must remain in the realm of speculation, but I believe it plausible to see the use of foreshadowing and misdirection in terms of the poet's practical goal of securing a livelihood.

On a loftier plane, misdirection may be understood as an artistic response to the epic tradition. Homer faces a problem—how to explore and question the tradition within which he is working. Given the abiding strength of the traditional story line, how can he adapt this material to his own ends? Misdirection allows Homer to articulate a response to the tradition itself by introducing compelling scenes that clash against that tradition. The Greek army prepares to return home; the duel between Paris and Menelaus might bring the war to a negotiated settlement. From the audience's viewpoint, these episodes are unexpected because they are untraditional. By asserting his independence from the standard story of the Trojan War, the poet expresses an attitude toward the process of storytelling. Of course, Homer raises such possibilities only to reject them. As far as we can tell, he does not violate the tradition in the *Iliad*. It is noteworthy that the poet raises the possibility of untraditional events at all. Homer pulls back each time, but he does so in an extremely self-conscious manner, showing how the traditional story might have been changed. Homer disrupts the natural flow at the last minute, but by sketching out how such a scenario would proceed, he makes it obvious that he could have continued. As the troops rush to their ships in book 2, the poet could simply have shown Athene descending to restrain the Greeks. Instead, Homer goes out of his way to point out that this would have brought about a "homecoming contrary to destiny" (2.155). By this explicit statement, Homer emphasizes how close he has come to altering the standard myth.[6] His style is provocative due to the repeated introduction of alternative paths away from the tradition. Homer explores the myth of the Trojan War by transgressing it in this rhetorical manner.

The introduction of alternatives to the tradition operates at other levels in the epic. Three times Zeus contemplates alternatives to "destiny." In book 4, he considers concluding the war by granting victory to Menelaus, yet this would violate the inevitable (i.e., traditional) Greek victory and Zeus' promise to Thetis of a Greek defeat. "Do it," Hera tells him, "but the other gods will not approve" (cf. 4.13-29). After predicting the death of Sarpedon, Zeus wonders whether he should save his son (16.433-38). Later, Hector's death is anticipated, yet Zeus expresses his wish to save this warrior. This time he yields to Athene (22.174-81). In each case, Zeus pulls back, but it appears that he could have followed his impulse.[7] The objections of Hera and Athene emphasize the resulting confusion or disapproval of other gods, not the dictates of fate. Like the poet, Zeus is willing to contemplate events following a different path, even if he finally acquiesces to what he had previously accepted.

In the last chapter, I argued that Achilles' questioning of his own fate provided a paradigm for the audience's experience of doubting the well-known tradition. Let us return to the choice of Achilles—this time from the poet's vantage. Achilles' contemplation of two fates may also represent a poetic dilemma. While singing, Homer must continually decide between alternative outcomes to each episode.[8] Will Paris or Menelaus be victorious? Will Hector be driven back by Patroclus or Achilles? By explicitly expressing such alternatives for the audience's consideration, Homer distances himself from a predictable telling of the plot of the *Iliad*. Viewing misdirection from one perspective, we find that the audience must attend to reversals and unexpected developments throughout; from another perspective, Homer displays his freedom to move in accordance with or contrary to the plot and the tradition. As Achilles acknowledges his fate by the close of the epic, so Homer acknowledges the tradition as preeminent in some sense. This does little, however, to diminish his challenges.[9] In his recent book *The Language of Heroes*, Martin argues that the speech of heroes is agonistic: heroic discourse is competitive, they speak to win. Martin extends this paradigm to Homer's own activity as bard: the singer is also a competitor. This competitive aspect could be directed toward other singers in a contest, but in a broader sense, the epic tradition to which Homer responds may more concretely be understood as his predecessors. Homer reacts to the story of the Trojan War as it has been sung for many years by driving his song outside its usual course. He not only effectively distinguishes himself from the other poets of the day but locates himself in the tradition that has preceded him.[10]

In his book *Homer and the Heroic Tradition,* Whitman compares Homer to Mozart: both artists worked within a tradition, yet each went far beyond what anyone had previously accomplished, bringing the potential of the tradition to a climax.[11] The analogy with music is valuable—Homer was, after all, a singer—but I think a more fruitful comparison would be with a jazz musician. Both adopt traditional material, and indeed similarities also lie in training and performance.[12] Let us begin with training. The prospective jazz performer learns by listening to and imitating those who have established themselves. Such training consists of the apprentice patterning his own music after that of the masters. This regimen includes a rigorous practice of scales and arpeggios. As Lord tells us, an oral poet also starts out by listening to an older singer and copying his oral song. He accustoms himself to the rhythm and the various constituents of epic song: formulae, type-scenes, similes, and the mixing of speech and narrative. This training constitutes the early phases of an artist's career.[13] In a performance before a critical audience, each jazz rendition derives from work accomplished in practice sessions. Still the performance itself is extemporaneous: as recordings show, no single piece is reduplicated down to the finer flourishes, making each interpretation unique. Similarly, the oral poet may reproduce the same overall story, using the same plot constructed from formulae and type-scenes. Still each song is unlike any other. The idea of a fixed text—a verbatim replica—is outside the grasp of an illiterate oral singer. Each performance—both jazz and oral song—results from prepared patterns that are re-created in a spontaneous composition.

The analogy between the *Iliad* and jazz extends beyond similarities of training and performance. Consider the artist's attitude toward the familiar pattern underlying each performance: in both cases, it is a traditional song. The jazz musician takes a classic tune from Cole Porter or Rogers and Hammerstein, for example. The tune is known to the audience, yet the performance is unpredictable in many ways. Although the melody and chord progressions provide a starting point, the player soon leaves the standard melody and develops it—often until it is barely recognizable. In the process of improvisation, the theme is varied and transposed. When John Coltrane plays "My Favorite Things," he begins with a recognizable rendition but challenges his audience with strange and outrageous digressions and deviations. At times, the audience must wonder, "Is this still 'My Favorite Things'? How will he get us back to the line of melody we know?" The audience experiences a mixture of delight and anxiety: delight in the wonderful and imaginative departures from the song as it has been previously played, and yet anxiety that the song may have been utterly abandoned, lost forever.[14] In this respect, Homeric misdirection comes quite close to the impulse behind the improvisational features of jazz. Homer begins with a well-known song. He then complicates it by introducing false starts and reversals. At times, Homer seems to be singing a new song, quite distinct from the standard epic song of the Trojan War, as he moves away from expected outcomes. Pointed in contradictory directions, the audience may enjoy such novel episodes yet question Homer's ability to bring the song back in line with the tradition. In jazz we speak of exposition, exploration, and recapitulation. The *Iliad* reveals a similar pattern of foreshadowing (reinforcing the tradition), misdirection, and ultimately a return to the tradition.

The poet and the musician remain traditional artists in a very fundamental sense. Both Coltrane and Homer remain true to the classic "melody" in the end. Yet each establishes an independence by demonstrating the freedom to spurn the expected and the traditional time and again throughout the performance. Skill lies not merely in rendering a well-known song but in stretching such standard fare, disappointing expectations, and making a relatively simple song complex. The tradition provides a point of reference; the innovation upon that material expresses a distinctive, individual voice. When the performer leads the audience from his digressions back to the standard song, the audience experiences a heady rush of relief to be back on familiar territory and appreciation for his daring and skill. Neither the jazz musician nor the oral poet has an interest in inventing a new melody or outcome of the song, but each invents the processes by which the theme itself is inverted, abandoned, and ultimately revived. Part of Homer's contribution lies in his mastery of controlling the technique of misdirection as a means of exploring the potential alternatives lying dormant in the epic tradition.

Finally, a few words might be said on the topic of the influence of Homeric misdirection in the *Iliad*. I only briefly sketch out several lines of possible derivation that have been explored by others. At the level of technique in the *Odyssey*, Hellwig and Fenik have both demonstrated that expected episodes are repeatedly delayed. The classic example is the postponement of Odysseus revealing himself—first to the Phaeacians, later to Telemachus, the suitors, Penelope, and his father. With regard to books 5–13 of the *Odyssey*, Rose suggests that the preparation for Odysseus' encounter with the Phaeacians (as authoritatively anticipated by Zeus and Hermes) offers a deceptively optimistic picture in sharp contrast to the actual reception, which is not wholly hospitable, and to Odysseus' departure, which is promised but delayed. Regarding the validity of the traditional outcome, Olson suggests that the repeated references to Agamemnon's disastrous return call into question the ultimate fate of Odysseus. I do not think influence is the right word when comparing the *Iliad* and *Odyssey*; nevertheless, the phenomenon of misdirection occurs in the *Odyssey* as well.[15]

The impulse to question the traditional myth and to explore alternatives flourishes in the fifth century, when the stories of the Trojan War, in particular, were put under intense scrutiny. In his introduction and in book 2 of his *Histories*, Herodotus explores various accounts of the cause of the Trojan War and tests the merits of each possibility. The historian also articulates alternative possibilities within his narrative: each time Croesus, Darius, or Xerxes is about to act, a warning speech articulates a course of action opposed to what is followed. Herodotus thus demonstrates that events might have taken another path. Homer may have influenced (consciously or not) the historian's decision to introduce alternatives within speeches.¹⁶ Further exploration of mythical variation is found, of course, in the Athenian tragedies. Sometimes a tragedy appears to be headed for a new outcome only to be returned to its traditional resolution by intervention (Sophocles' *Philoctetes*, e.g.); at times, the "transgression" is played out in full (Euripides' *Iphigeneia Among the Taurians*). In examining divine prologues, Erbse has shown how deceptive announcements might mislead and challenge the Athenian audience.¹⁷ Vergil's *Aeneid,* which consciously reflects Homeric epic in numerous respects, deserves mention. James O'Hara has recently shown the ways in which optimistic prophecy misleads characters within the epic—a phenomenon that, at some level, reflects the experience of the audience.¹⁸ When the audience of epic, tragedy, or history finds itself in a position of knowledge superior to that of the characters, the author always has the option of manipulating its confident expectations.

In the case of Homeric misdirection, direct influence upon subsequent works is likely but very difficult to prove. In a sense, the *Iliad* provides a blueprint for innovation upon traditional material, yet with any traditional subject, a poet or artist is drawn to explore what has been accepted and handed down. These subsequent poets and historians need not have been using Homer as an immediate model. Any extended work may be unified by far-ranging predictions; any artist may manipulate his audience to some extent. Although we find aspects of misdirection in later Greek and Roman literature, the difficulty lies in distinguishing between direct influence and two artists merely sharing common motives: engaging the audience, exploring alternatives to the myth, and putting a distinctive stamp upon one's own telling.

In this study, I have examined how Homer manipulates his audience and at the same time comments upon the tradition. Homer's success in challenging his audience ultimately depends upon his skill in telling a story. In particular, he must have the ability to convince the audience. The Alexandrian scholars commented on certain passages as possessing "a persuasive quality" (τὸ πιθανόν).¹⁹ When Achilles is about to kill Agamemnon, the audience must find this threat compelling and believable. During the duel between Paris and Menelaus, Homer must promote this wholly unexpected episode as conceivable. By sheer dramatic skill, he provokes the audience into questioning its own assumptions about what is likely to occur. Homeric misdirection may be viewed from various perspectives. In terms of the audience's expectations, we find a careful mixture of accurate foreshadowing and deceptive anticipation. On the poet's side, we find an impulse for engaging the audience (with immediate practical consequences) and a means of expressing an aesthetic response to a tradition that has the danger of becoming ossified. By introducing false predictions and untraditional episodes, Homer has demonstrated his genius in reviving an old and well-known song with an ingredient of uncertainty.

Appendix:
The Myth of Meleager and Homeric Misdirection

The story of Meleager, as told by Phoenix in book 9, appears to have been adapted so that it approximates the situation of Achilles in book 9.[1] In addition, it is used to anticipate the later action in the *Iliad*. Although such anticipation is not as direct as that of predictions, still—in conjunction with predictions—paradigms play a supporting role. Paradigms are fundamentally future oriented: speakers most often introduce them to persuade a person or god to do something. For example, in book 24, Achilles tells Priam the myth of Niobe in order to persuade the Trojan king to eat. Niobe loses her twelve children, yet she overcomes her grief and eats; Priam has lost Hector, but Achilles tells him that he should follow the example of Niobe and eat (24.601-19). The emphasis upon this detail—eating in spite of grief—helps Achilles to persuade Priam. In chapter 6, I examined the way in which the narrator manipulated the audience's expectations regarding Achilles' return to battle. That analysis focused upon predictions, those explicit statements about possible future events. Yet there are other methods of generating both true and false expectations. In chapter 4, the prelude to battle, a typical sequence, was seen as one way of causing the audience to anticipate the conventional outcome of battle. A third means of generating expectations is the use of paradigms. I would briefly like to consider how the story of Meleager may in part anticipate later action and in part mislead the audience.

In book 9, after Achilles has rejected Agamemnon's offer of gifts (conveyed by Odysseus), Phoenix pleads with Achilles. The story of Meleager is part of his attempt to persuade Achilles to return to battle.

119

Most versions of the story of Meleager present, or at least allude to, the following episodes: after Meleager's birth, the three Fates tell his mother, Althaea, that as soon as the log in the fire turns to ash Meleager will die. Althaea pours water on the log, takes it out of the hearth, and puts it in a chest for safekeeping. When Meleager grows up, he kills the Calydonian boar. A quarrel results, and Meleager kills one (or two) of his uncles, Althaea's brothers. In anger, his mother takes the log out of the chest and puts it on the fire. Meleager dies (cf. Bacchylides 5.94–154; Ovid *Met.* 8.270–525). Much of this story is suppressed or ignored in the *Iliad*. Although Meleager does kill the boar, the emphasis is on his anger and withdrawal, the siege of Calydon, and Meleager's eventual return to battle. The story of Meleager is told in such a way that one is led to think of Achilles' situation in book 9. Note the many parallels:

Myth of Meleager	Epic Situation
1. Calydonians and Curetes are at war (9.519–32).	Greeks vs. Trojans.
2. When Meleager fights, the Calydonians are successful (9.550–52).	Achilles helps the Greeks.
3. Meleager is angry with his mother; he withdraws from battle (9.553–60).[2]	Achilles is angry with Agamemnon and withdraws.
4. City of Calydon is threatened.	Greeks ships are threatened.
5. An offer of gifts is made (9.574–87).	Embassy is sent by Agamemnon.

Presumably, certain features of this story are emphasized to make it correspond more closely to Achilles' situation. There is no mention of the magical log, and the killing of Meleager's uncles is only briefly alluded to. But the episodes of his anger and withdrawal (not mentioned elsewhere) are prominent in Phoenix' version.

The story itself is puzzling in several respects. Phoenix introduces the myth with the words: "Thus we hear of the deeds of great men in the old days also, when the swelling anger descended upon them. The heroes would take gifts; they would listen, and be persuaded" (9.524–26). This appears to indicate that Phoenix will tell of a hero who represses his anger and accepts an offer of gifts. We might expect Meleager to yield to the plea of the Calydonians, accept their offer, and return to save the city. Thus Phoenix would say, "So, Achilles, should you accept this offer and return to help the Greeks." Instead, Phoenix says that Meleager refuses the offer and waits until the city is in flames, and that—when he does act—it is too late for him to benefit. As it turns out, Phoenix tells a cautionary tale by offering a negative exemplum: he describes a hero whose actions should not be emulated.[3]

Not only is the myth adapted to the narrative situation in book 9, but the story of Meleager also anticipates the later narrative. The story of Meleager is cautionary or negative because the narrator wishes to use the myth to prefigure Achilles' actions. Just as Meleager refuses to return, so Achilles will also refuse. Meleager waits until his own house is threatened; Achilles says he will wait until his own ships are threatened. In an indirect manner, this myth anticipates the battle at the ships. The story of Meleager accurately anticipates Achilles' actions in several ways:

Myth of Meleager	Epic Situation
6. Meleager refuses the offer (9.585–87).	Achilles refuses the offer.
7. The city is in flames; his bedchamber is bombarded (9.588–89).	One ship is set on fire.
8. Cleopatra approaches Meleager (9.590–94).	Patroclus approaches Achilles.
9. Meleager arms and saves the city (9.595–98).	Achilles sends Patroclus to save the ships.
10. No gifts are given (9.598–99).	Achilles receives gifts from Agamemnon.

First let us look at items 6 and 8. Just as Meleager refuses, so Achilles refuses the offer of Agamemnon. Meleager is persuaded by his wife Cleopatra to return and saves the city of Calydon; similarly, Patroclus successfully persuades Achilles to allow the Myrmidons to return to battle in order to save the Greeks.[4] To this extent, the story of Meleager helps to anticipate later action in the *Iliad*. The fit between the myth and the later narrative, however, is not precise. We do not find an exact one-to-one correspondence with respect to items 7, 9, and 10. Meleager waits until the city is in flames and his own bedchamber is attacked. Achilles, however, acts (by sending Patroclus) after only a single ship is burning. When Achilles relents, he does not return to battle; rather he sends Patroclus. That is, Meleager's return does not prefigure Achilles' own return. And Meleager receives no gifts for his actions; when he finally does act, it is too late to receive compensation. In book 19, however, Achilles receives all the gifts Agamemnon has offered him, in spite of his refusal to fight.

In order to further interpret the myth, let us look at predictions from the rest of the epic. The audience learns a great deal elsewhere that aids its evaluation as to which predictions accurately prefigure the later action and how the story of Meleager may function. We might begin with Patroclus' role. The fact that Achilles sends Patroclus as his surrogate in book 16 is anticipated elsewhere. In book 11, Nestor suggests this idea: Achilles might lend Patroclus his armor and send him in his place (11.790-803). In book 15, Zeus predicts that Achilles will send Patroclus into battle (15.64-65). These two predictions anticipate the events of book 16 and correct any possible expectation that Achilles himself will return. These predictions override the suggestion found in the Meleager story that Achilles himself will return. On the question of gifts, Meleager receives no gifts, but Achilles in a strict sense does, although his loss of Patroclus greatly outweighs the rewards from Agamemnon. However, in book 1, Athene promises Achilles that he will receive compensation for Agamemnon's insult (1.212-14). Zeus vows to Thetis that Achilles will be honored (1.508-30). These divine guarantees are emphatically given. Due to such authoritative predictions found in the epic, the audience would anticipate the lack of agreement on these points between the paradigm and the epic narrative.

I now turn to the circumstances when the angry hero acts (item 7 above). Within the myth, the city of Calydon is in flames. Women and children are being led away to slavery. Meleager's own bedchamber is threatened. Cleopatra approaches her husband; only at this point does Meleager decide to return. The possibility that Achilles will wait until the ships are burning is prefigued by Meleager's prolonged delay until the last possible moment. The city is in flames when Meleager acts, and Achilles says in essence that he will act in the same way: after the Greek ships are burning, he will deal with Hector. This is never contradicted by other predictions.[5] In the story of the *Iliad,* Achilles tells the ambassadors that he will wait until the Greek fleet is in flames and his own camp is threatened (9.650-55). It turns out that he sends Patroclus after only a single ship is burning: he does not wait for Hector to reach his ships. Yet Achilles' threat in book 9 is not contradicted by other authoritative predictions; instead it is reinforced by Zeus' predictions in books 8 and 15 (as discussed in chap. 6). Zeus' two prophecies support the idea that the Greek fleet will be substantially destroyed before the Myrmidons return. He says that Hector will be stopped only when Achilles stirs to action (8.473-77), and he later tells Hera that the Greeks will fall back to the ships of Achilles; at that time Achilles will send Patroclus to help the Greeks (15.61-65). Zeus' prophecies are accurate in many respects, but not with regard to the return of the Myrmidons. The Greek army does not retreat to the ships of Achilles. Only a single ship is set on fire before Achilles acts. Yet Zeus' prophecies—and the story of Meleager—reinforce the audience's expectation that Hector will reach Achilles' camp.

Homer uses the myth of Meleager in conjunction with Achilles' threat and the prophecies of Zeus to encourage the false expectation that Hector will substantially damage the Greek fleet before the Myrmidons return. He misleads his audience concerning the Myrmidons' return. Would the audience take this threat seriously? Do they actually expect the Greek fleet to be burned? If Hector destroys the ships of the Greeks, the basic outline of the traditional story is upset. Yet before Achilles acts in book 16, the audience is forced to consider whether the ships will in fact be saved. As the epic unfolds, the narrator raises various questions that are not answered until later in the epic. In book 1, Zeus promises to honor Achilles by bringing defeat to the Greeks, yet this does not come about until book 8. The audience must await the fulfillment of this expectation. At the time when the story of Meleager is told in book 9, the question is, "When will Achilles return, and how much damage will Hector do before he is stopped?" All indications here and later—not only Hector's threats and the Greeks' worries but the myth of Meleager, Achilles' threat, and Zeus' prophecies—lead to the expectation that only Achilles' ships will be spared. The myth of Meleager helps to reinforce the audience's expectation that the Greek fleet may be in flames before Achilles responds. As with predictions, the paradigm in part anticipates later events, in part its effect is to mislead the audience as to when Achilles— or at least the Myrmidons—will return to battle.

The relationship between myth and epic is complex. In order to interpret the myth of Meleager, we must bear in mind the rest of the epic.

As we have seen, there is no monolithic version of a myth. The stories are flexible; here the story of Meleager is adapted to the epic situation. The myth also anticipates later events, or at least it raises expectations about what might happen. It anticipates Patroclus' success in persuading Achilles, but it also helps to misdirect the audience concerning the point at which Achilles (or Patroclus) will lead the Myrmidons back to battle.

Notes

Chapter 1

1. Hector recalls Zeus' guarantee several times (11.288-89, 12.233-36, 15.490-93, 15.719-25), although not always with the qualification that his success will end at sunset (cf. 18.293-95).
2. Note the striking description of Hector at 11.356: ἀμφὶ δὲ ὄσσε κελαινὴ νὺξ ἐκάλυψε ("black night covered his eyes"). Three similar expressions where either "dark night" or "darkness" covers the victim's eyes recur in the *Iliad*.

--| ἀμφὶ δὲ ὄσσε κελαινὴ νὺξ ἐκάλυψε	(3 times)
τὸν δὲ κατ' ὀφθαλμῶν ἐρεβεννὴ νὺξ ἐκάλυψεν	(3 times)
--|--|-τὸν δὲ σκότος ὄσσε κάλυψε(ν)	(11 times)

In 14 of the 17 cases, these expressions indicate that the hero is about to die (4.461, 4.503, 4.526, 5.659, 6.11, 13.575, 13.580, 14.438-39 [slight variation], 14.519, 16.316, 16.325, 20.393, 20.471, 21.181). In book 11, Hector is only stunned by Diomedes, yet this marked expression jars the audience. Not only does Hector withdraw, but the poet uses an expression that implies Hector's death—at the very moment when success appears to be in his grasp (cf. the other exceptions: Aeneas at 5.309-10 and Andromache at 22.466-67). The ancient commentators' response was to call the authenticity of these lines into question; see Sch. A 11.356: οὐ γέγονε γὰρ σφοδρὰ πληγὴ ... πῶς οὖν ἐσκοτώθη ("For the blow was not severe ... How then did he swoon?"). See Leaf 1900-1902, s.v. 11.356 and Fenik 1968, 93. A similar expression, τῷ δ' αὖθι τέλος θανάτοιο κάλυψεν, describes death itself (5.553; cf. 16.502, 16.855, 22.361).

3. Zeus shows concern for Hector early in this book (11.163-64, 11.181-210) and much later (12.173-74, 12.254-55, 12.290-93, 12.436-38), but immediately following Agememnon's withdrawal—Zeus' explicit signal—Hector is rebuffed and vanishes from view. Schadewaldt (1938, 10-14) notes that after Hector's initial success we hear virtually nothing of Hector's expected *aristeia* until book 12. Paris, who has not been mentioned, leads the Trojans on their assault (11.369-400) and Zeus—rather than Hector—drives Ajax back (11.543-94). The poet

briefly presents Hector at 11.497–507; on Hector's position away from the thick of battle, see Fenik 1968, 106–10.

4. Zeus' promise in book 11 is ultimately fulfilled: in books 15–17, Hector drives the Greeks to their ships, burns the ship of Protesilaus, kills Patroclus, and wins Achilles' armor. See discussion by Schadewaldt (1938, 9–17), who later remarks that, while the poet anticipates the larger design, he does not indicate the precise course of the narrative (54–55). Lord (1960, 92) also concludes that, though the singer always has the end of a sequence in mind, there is always an opportunity for digression.

5. On *athetesis,* see van der Valk 1964, 2:370–476; Pfeiffer 1968, 111–14, 175 n. 6, 230–31, 240. From the time of Wolf (1795), a great deal of ingenuity has been expended on the enterprise of analysis. Leaf 1900–1902 and Wilamowitz 1918 are two good examples of the analysts' reading of the *Iliad;* for an overview, see Clarke 1981 chap. 4. Lord (1960, 94–98) discusses narrative inconsistency on the part of the oral poet. See also Combellack 1965; Gunn 1971; and Goold 1977. Fenik (1968, 69–70, 72, 94, 103) has shown that the associative force of related scenes sometimes outweighs our standards of consistency. An oral theorist would have difficulty, however, arguing that Homer is concerned only with Hector's advance in book 11, for the episode is internally inconsistent: Hector's withdrawal contradicts Zeus' promise.

6. According to Todorov ([1971] 1977, 60), the oral poet never lies; he is fully reliable. Scully (1986, 148) calls the narrator's vision "synoptic and authoritative." Cf. Booth 1961, 3–6; and Scholes and Kellogg 1966, 51–52.

7. Dolezel (1980, 10–12) introduces the concept of the "authentication authority" of a narrator, who is properly "authorized" to present the narrative. Such authority is given by the conventions of the genre. He later considers the possibility that this authority may be destroyed by inconsistency or an "ironic attitude" toward that authority (20–23).

8. See Whitman 1958, esp. 257–60.

9. See Pedrick 1982; Thornton 1984.

10. Schadewaldt (1938, 41, 148) notes another instance: 11.54–55 recall 1.3–4, apparently a signal that what Zeus promised Thetis in book 1 is about to be fulfilled.

11. Chap. 6 fully analyzes the predictions of heroes' deaths.

12. Duckworth 1933, 116; cf. 100–103, 114–15.

13. The fullest accounts of Homeric foreshadowing are Kraut 1863, Wieniewski 1924, and Duckworth 1933, all of which endorse this view. Such an interpretation dates to the early eighteenth century at least. Dacier (1714, 91–94) distinguishes between two types of surprise in connection with Homer: one type of surprise is caused by an unannounced event—wholly without preparation—and a second type, where the event is announced ahead of time yet the precise manner of its fulfillment is left open. She finds only the latter type of surprise in the *Iliad.* For more recent discussion, see Thornton 1984, 67–72; de Jong 1987, 81–90. On *prolepsis* in general, see Genette [1972] 1980, 67–79.

14. Aristotle (*Poetics* 1453B22–26) remarks that poets are not free to change the basic facts: τοὺς μὲν οὖν παρειλημμένους μύθους λύειν οὐκ ἔστιν ("It Is

not possible to alter the traditional plots"). In his correspondence with Goethe, Schiller ([1797] 1905, letter 394, 26 Dec. 1797) speaks of "a calm freedom" (*eine ruhige Freiheit*) enjoyed by the poet, who knows already from the start how the story will end. Schiller also remarks that epic does not work through the type of suspense associated with drama.

15. Schadewaldt 1938, 55. The recent remarks by Tompkins (1986, 211–14) coincide very much with this interpretation.

16. On this point, see Wyatt 1989, 237–40, 251–52. Even these false starts in some sense threaten the integrity of the story (see chap. 4).

17. Nagy (1979, 5) describes the archaic poem as a "formal reflection of the poetry upon its own importance." I do not, however, agree with his assumption that everything in the *Iliad* is traditional.

18. Iser 1974; Genette [1972] 1980; Winkler 1985. As remarked in her introduction, de Jong (1987, xi) explicitly avoids what I propose to do, i.e., examining the "linear structure, the way in which scenes follow upon one another, together forming a unified whole."

19. On the ancient commentators' appreciation of foreshadowing, see Duckworth 1931 and N.J. Richardson 1980.

20. The designation of the addressee of the story ranges from Aristarchus' "auditor" (ἀκροατής) to the "implied reader" of Iser (1974, xii): "This term [the implied reader] incorporates both the restructuring of the potential meaning by the text, and the reader's actualization of this potential through the reading process." Scully (1986, 139–40) contemplates the transhistorical audience, "whose experience in listening or reading could be the same, at least formally, regardless of his time or place." Following Genette, de Jong (1987, 53–60) analyzes the "primary narratee." See also Winkler 1985, 14.

Chapter 2

1. The marks of orality include formulaic language, typical scenes following a set pattern, and mnemonic patterns used to structure the large-scale organization of the epic. The writer or transcriber of the *Iliad* and the date of its transcription are areas of intense controversy that I do not address.

2. While we would learn a great deal from an attempt to re-create the ancient circumstances of such a performance, it would be founded on much speculation and would inevitably fail to capture the flexibility and spontaneity that are essential to the oral epic song.

3. Booth (1961, 156) contrasts the author who knows "how everything turns out in the end" with even the most knowing narrator.

4. Even when the narrator addresses the audience, this is not the actual audience: see Block 1982, 7; de Jong 1987, 29–33.

5. This implied audience is seldom directly addressed by the narrator. For this particular phenomenon in Homer (and Vergil), see Block 1982.

6. A third characteristic is that the implied audience is an oral audience, as the command to the Muse indicates: ἄειδε ("sing"—1.1). My analysis, however, would be little altered if I considered an implied first-time reader, provided this

reader knows the traditional background and reads the book through, never rereading or skipping ahead. The reader must be subject to a continuous presentation. For Winkler (1985, 14), the ideal first-time reader of the *Golden Ass* does not know that the novel concludes with an Isiac redemption. An audience with repeated exposure to the *Iliad* would have a somewhat different experience from that of a first-time audience (see chap. 7). On the expectations of the "primary narratee," see de Jong 1987, 62–64, 93–95.

7. On such allusions, see Gentili 1988, 7–8. The hatred of Hera and Athene for Troy is clear (4.30–67, 20.313–17), yet the reason for it is only alluded to (24.27–30; cf. *Od.* 4.259–89). The allusion to Calchas' past predictions is admittedly perplexing. There is no mention here or later of the sacrifice of Iphigenia (1.106–8; cf. also 2.303–30); Agamemnon later offers any of his three daughters to Achilles (9.144–48 ≈ 9.286–90). Is the narrator assuming that the audience knows of Iphigenia's sacrifice (i.e., are they expected to supply it themselves), or is he deliberately suppressing it—perhaps to make Achilles' human sacrifice in book 23 seem all the more exceptional? It is difficult to determine. See Kullman 1960, 198–99. One scholium (T 1.106; cf. sch. A 1.108-9) asserts that Homer does not know the story of her sacrifice: only the more recent poets (οἱ νεώτεροι) tell of her sacrifice. Comparable allusion is found in the *Odyssey:* e.g., the brief nod to the contest of arms between Odysseus and Ajax (*Od.* 11.543–65; cf. *Od.* 3.109). See Reinhardt 1960, 16–36; Griffin 1980, 66.

8. There is little consensus beyond this as to which episodes or which minor characters were traditional (yet even such characters as Calchas and Nestor are carefully introduced for the audience early on [1.68–72, 1.247–52]), but no one disputes that the traditional background exists. Aristotle notes that the audience of tragedy often was not familiar with the traditional stories (*Poetics* 1451B19–26); see Else 1967, 318–19. Recently, scholars have discussed the possibility of Homer inventing characters (Erbse 1983), Achilles' mortality (Kullmann 1985, 16–17), and even the centrality of the Trojans (Sale 1987). On the invention of mythological paradigms, see Willcock 1964, 1977; Braswell 1971; and Lang 1983. For the overall differences between the *Iliad* and the epic cycle, see Griffin 1977. On the stability of the tradition, see Fenik 1968, 39, and Nagy 1979, 40, 81–82, esp. 81 n. 2. With respect to Sophoclean drama, Kirkwood (1958, 68) argues that "what the playwright tells us, he wants us to consider, and what he does not tell us (no matter how standard it is in the legend), he wants us to disregard." This provocative hypothesis might prove of great value in discussing the *Iliad*.

9. Typical sequences may also generate expectations of an outcome (see chap. 4).

10. Other terms have been used to describe the varieties of narrative anticipation. Genette ([1972] 1980, 73–76) prefers the terms *prolepsis, advance notice,* and *advance mention.*

11. On the predictive power of prayers, see Morrison 1991, 149–52.

12. Suspense is one of the three types of misdirection I discuss. See chap. 5.

13. The effect of such unpersuasive predictions as this is examined in chap. 3.

14. Block (1982, 9-10) remarks that in an oral performance the "narrator is expected to be reliable," and she believes Homer's narrator to be "straightforward and trustworthy." Dolezel (1980, 23-24) believes that the reliability of the narrator is not specific to epic but is the "basic norm of the narrative genre."

15. de Jong (1987) discusses the narrator's reliability (57, 178, 193) and that of the gods (170). On mortal characters' predictions, see Duckworth 1933, 18-21.

16. Nor does the narrator in exceptional cases—see chap. 6.

17. See de Jong 1987, 44.

18. Chap. 4 discusses at length the set of predictions anticipating the Greek defeat in book 1. Lewis (1942, 19-20) cites repeated predictions as one of the key differences between oral poetry and written literature. Although the story may be traditional, Lewis maintains it is more difficult for the audience to follow a rapid recitation. We infer then that the narrator repeats predictions (with variation) for the benefit of the audience. See Genette [1972] 1980, 72-75, on repeated *prolepsis;* cf. de Jong 1987, 85, and Duckworth 1933, 60-61.

19. See Genette [1972] 1980, 77-78. Duckworth (1933, 44) distinguishes "forecasts"—detailed announcements of future action accompanied by certainty—from vaguer "foreshadowing," which arouses curiosity but lacks specific detail. Cf. Wieniewski 1924, 120, 131.

20. An exception to the rule of incomplete predictions is the full and detailed network of predictions concerning Achilles' death and burial (see chap. 6). Still this exception possesses a rationale: the scene itself falls outside the scope of the *Iliad*.

21. See chap. 1, n. 13.

22. Todorov ([1971] 1977, 65) defines plot as "the thread of events followed within the story." This comes close to the story (*récit*) or succession of events analyzed by Genette ([1972] 1980, 24-29). De Jong (1985) contrasts Achilles' recapitulation at 1.366-92 with the actual preceding narrative (cf. 18.429-56). In general, recapitulation tells the plot alone (an exception is 1.376-77).

Chapter 3

1. This was also discussed in chap. 2.

2. See, e.g., Braswell 1971, 25: "The whole *Iliad* is a long catena of causes, so that at any stage of the action we can almost always find an immediate cause for a given event ... the poet constantly supplies reasons, because he has to tell a story and his audience will expect to know why a given character acts as he does in a particular situation. The source of Homer's causal reasoning lies then in the demands of his narrative art." Cf. de Jong 1987, 91-93.

3. The most explicit information comes from Nestor (*Od.* 3.130-328), Menelaus (*Od.* 4.441-592), and, of course, Odysseus (*Od.* 9-12). This picture is consistently presented throughout the epic (cf. the λυγρὸν νόστον of Phemius—1.325-27) and the cyclic *Nostoi*.

4. Cf. Agamemnon's feelings regarding Clytemnestra (1.113-15).

5. Naturally, not every possible alternative is explicitly stated. In the prayer scene, Chryses might have asked for any number of things. In response, Apollo might have refused rather than accepted the priest's prayer (cf. 6.311, e.g.). In the assembly, Agememnon could have continued to refuse to give up Chryses' daughter, even after Calchas' advice. I will be somewhat selective, highlighting those alternatives that the narrator explicitly expresses. For an analysis of this problem, see Barthes [1966] 1982, 265-67, which considers the development of a story in terms of alternatives.

6. Agamemnon could personally come to take Briseis: there would be no conflict with the tradition. Would the audience be expecting such a confrontation after the assembly episode?

7. Achilles and Agamemnon might have quarreled on another occasion, but this particular assembly would not have been called.

8. After the narrator notes the alternatives, the crisis is generally resolved by realizing the second (or last) alternative. This is parallel to the pattern of decision making, where the hero also invariably adopts the second of two alternative choices. Cf. the reasoning of Agenor (21.553-70) and Hector (22.99-130); see Lohmann 1970, 37-40. See also Arend [1933] 1975, 108 n. 1 (discussion at 106-15); Fenik 1968, 68 (discussion at 96-98).

9. On the relative numbers of Greeks and Trojans, see 2.123-30.

10. Fränkel ([1961] 1975, 18-19) remarks that Achilles' threat to go home relieves the "inflexible monolith" of the tradition. See chap. 5, where I discuss the possible alternative conclusions to the war.

11. Griffin (1980, 159 n. 29) calls the arrival of Athene "sudden and dramatic." That dramatic power derives in part from the irrevocability of an act that threatens the traditional story line.

12. At 4.169-82, Agememnon suggests that Menelaus' death would render their enterprise invalid.

13. For a discussion of this view, see de Jong 1987, 79-81. Schadewaldt (1938, 153, 153 n. 3) argues that the course of the work should not seem unalterably constrained.

14. Griffin (1980, 74) notes that if Achilles had a somewhat different character (more like Diomedes, e.g.), "there would be no *Iliad* at all."

15. For another example, consider the remarks on the proem: bT 1.1 ἔτι ζητεῖται, διὰ τί ἀπὸ δυσφήμου ὀνόματος τῆς μήνιδος ἄρχεται. ἐπιλύουσι δὲ αὐτὸ οἱ περὶ Ζηνόδοτον οὕτως ὅτι πρέπον ἐστὶ τῇ ποιήσει τὸ προοίμιον, τὸν νοῦν τῶν ἀκροατῶν διεγείρον καὶ προσεχεστέρους ποιοῦν, εἰ μέλλοι πολέμους καὶ θανάτους διηγεῖσθαι ἡρώων. "Problem: Why does the poet begin with an ill-omened word 'wrath'? Those following Zenodotus solve this as follows: the proem is suitable for the poem, in provoking the audience's concentration and making them more attentive, for the poet is about to tell of war and the deaths of heroes." On Alexandrian puzzle solving, see Slater 1982 and Combellack 1987.

16. This point is also made by Redfield (1975, 133), Nagy (1979, 40, 81-82), and Schein (1984, 64).

Chapter 4

1. Kirk 1985, 48-49. Rothe (1910, 198) calls books 3 and 4 a "retardation." Leaf (1900-1902, 1:154) complains of the delays in books 2-4, especially the review of troops (*epipolesis*) in book 4, which "prolongs beyond measure the delay in the opening of the battle, at a point where rapidity seems essential to the story." The speeches are "unreasonably prolix." See also Duckworth 1933, 66-68; Hellwig 1964, 16, 43 n. 44, 97-107.

2. Hellwig (1964, 21) describes this as "zig-zag" motion.

3. This often occurs in battle, as noted by Thornton (1984, 59-60): "A goal in the action is anticipated, but it is either retarded, or the reverse of what is expected takes place for a time: then events take a 'turn,' and anticipation is fulfilled." She argues that in books 2-4 there are three reversals and three expansions (59-62). See also Schadewaldt 1938, 15, 54-55; Reinhardt 1961, 26, 70-71; Hellwig 1964, 4-5.

4. My analysis here concerns only the audience's perspective. Of course, each prediction in book 1 is suited to the character speaking. Still smarting from the dishonor he received in front of the Greeks, Achilles mentions Agamemnon in each of his predictions (1.243-44, 1.342-44, 1.410-12); Thetis emphasizes the dishonor her son suffers (1.505-10); Hera expresses concern for the Greeks (1.558-59).

5. Except for the gifts promised by Athene at 1.212-14 (which are surely implied in the predictions that Achilles will be honored), each element of the Greek defeat is repeated at least once: Achilles' absence (1.240-41, 1.340-42), the Greek retreat (1.344, 1.409, 1.559; cf. 2.4), the death of many Greeks (1.242-43, 1.342-44, 1.409-10, 1.559; cf. 1.2-5), a Trojan victory (1.408, 1.509), regret and recognition (1.243-44, 1.410-12), and honoring Achilles (1.212-14, 1.508-10). The honor Achilles receives from Zeus is, in a way, coincident with the Greek defeat (1.558-59; cf. 1.353-54, 2.3-4, 9.607-10).

6. The narrator (1.1-7, 2.3-4); the gods (1.508-10, 1.522-30, 1.558-59).

7. Athene's promise is prefaced (1.212; cf. Zeus' nod of affirmation shaking Olympus at 1.525-27): ὧδε γὰρ ἐξερέω, τὸ δὲ καὶ τετελεσμένον ἔσται ("And this also will I tell you and it will be a thing brought to pass").

8. See discussion in chap. 2.

9. On νήπιος in this passage, see Duckworth 1933, 72. Cf. 12.113-15, 16.46-47, 16.685-87, 17.497-98, 18.311-13, 20.466. For a more general discussion, see Kraut 1863, 22-23; de Jong 1987, 86-87, with further bibliography.

10. For a discussion of the recurring theme of an early departure, see chap. 5.

11. As Fenik (1968, 39) remarks, frequently in the *Iliad* "a god prevents something that both the poem and, apparently, the tradition forbade." See Morrison (in press).

12. This has led the analyst Leaf (1900-1902, 1:47) to consider Agamemnon's dream and the four similes (2.1-50, 2.443-83) to be part of the original poem of Achilles' wrath, which—if attached to 11.56-309—would lead smoothly to

battle and the Greek defeat that the audience has been led to expect. For an excellent summary of this scholarly debate, see Neschke 1985, esp. n. 4, 10.

13. Note Agamemnon's exhortation (2.381-93) and the scholiast's response (Sch. bT 2.382): κινητικὰ τοῦ μελλόντος ἔσεσθαι πολέμου ταῦτα, καὶ τὴν πολεμικὴν παρασκευὴν διδάσκοντα τὸν ἀκροατήν ("These lines stimulate expectations of the coming battle, by showing the audience the preparations for battle").

14. The army (2.453-54, 2.542-44); Menelaus (2.588-90; cf. 3.28). ὦκα ("swiftly"—2.52, 2.444, 2.785, 3.14); cf. αἶψα ("immediately"—2.808). Presumably after the Greeks recognize their mistake, Achilles (and Philoctetes) will return "soon" (τάχα—2.694, 2.724; cf. 2.860-61, 2.873-75).

15. Cf. the similes that do lead to battle (4.275-82). See Krischer 1971, 43-49; Moulton 1975, 40-43.

16. Since the narrator does not indicate here which side will suffer defeat, he is able to present alternating success and failure for each side. Cf. 1.3-5, 11.54-55.

17. I have adopted Schadewaldt's (1938, 29-30) analysis with slight modifications.

18. The category of exhortation includes advice, criticism, or warning (cf. 2.381-93, 4.223-421, 19.408-17).

19. The prelude in books 2-4 is the longest: 1,700 lines. The other preludes (if we calculate from dawn until first combat) range from 59 lines (8.1-59) to over 700 lines (19.1-20.258); cf. 11.1-66, 16.1-283. No prelude after books 2-4 has the full complement of elements: sacrifice and exhortation are omitted in book 8; no meal is described in books 11 and 16. See Schadewaldt 1938, 29-40. The prelude to battle against the suitors in the *Odyssey* includes divine incitement (21.1-4), a decision to fight (21.188-241), a sacrifice and meal (20.276-83; cf. 21.265-68), arming (22.109-15, 22.142-45), a review of the suitors (16.235-57), and Odysseus' exhortation (21.234-41).

20. Not only is this prelude extremely elaborate, but several elements are repeated, partly due to the description of corresponding Trojan activities: divine incitement (2.156-11; cf. 2.786-807), gathering of troops (2.441-83; cf. 2.808-10), and a review (2.494-770; cf. 2.811-77).

21. See the discussion of book 19 below in chap. 4.

22. The scholiast notes that, at the end of this day of fighting, the proposal of the duel between Ajax and Hector is introduced by a scene where Athene descends to help the Greeks. This appears to signal further battle: cf. Sch. bT (7.29): ὁ μὲν ἀκροατὴς δεινὰ ἐλπίζει ἐπὶ τῇ παρόδῳ τῶν θεῶν, οἷα καὶ πρώην γέγονεν, ὁ δὲ ἀνακόπτει τὸ προσδοκώμενον ("The audience expects fearful battle at the entrance of the gods, such as happened before. The poet, however, thwarts this expectation"). In fact, the second duel puts an end to this day's fighting, neatly balancing the scene at the beginning of book 3 where the audience expects battle but the narrator presents a duel.

23. These two episodes—the troops' impulse to leave and the duel proposed by Paris—not only delay the start of battle (they are the means of effecting false

anticipation) but reverse the direction of the narrative. My focus here is on false anticipation; these untraditional episodes are further discussed in chap. 5.

24. In chap. 6, we will consider in a broader context Hector's eventual success at the Greek ships.

25. Athene recognizes that the Trojan success in book 8 is the wish (βουλαί) of Thetis (8.370-72). The narrator links Achilles' request with Trojan success several times (13.347-50, 15.592-600; cf. 15.72-77, 18.74-77). The relationship between honoring Achilles and Hector's victory is questioned by Poseidon (14.366-69, 14.374-75), but this plan prevails when Zeus awakens after Hera's seduction (cf. 15.57-77).

26. Cf. the use of κεῖμαι ("lie") to describe a hero who has withdrawn or been removed from battle (2.688, 2.694, 9.556).

27. On this use, see LSJ, s.v. ἔχω A.2.9. Cf. 9.300-306, where Odysseus promises great honor if Achilles slays Hector. On the limit of Hector's success, see chap. 6.

28. The narrator later remarks that the Greek wall will stand as long as Hector lives and Achilles is away in anger, then the best of the Trojans will die (12.10-18). This clearly refers to Hector, but the causal connection between Achilles' return and the death of Hector is not made explicit. Polydamas, too, expects that Achilles will not stay long from battle (13.744-47). Although Achilles is again unnamed in this passage, the reference is obvious.

29. The narrator, the dying Patroclus, and Achilles later reiterate that Hector will die at Achilles' hands. See 15.611-14, 16.851-54, 18.90-93, 18.114-15, 18.333-35. Hector's death is near, as we learn from the narrator (16.799-800), Zeus (17.201-8), and Thetis (18.131-33). Polydamas warns of Achilles' return (18.261-72), but Hector vows to meet him (18.305-9). The various predictions in this network are mutually reinforcing. Again authoritative predictions by Zeus and the narrator reinforce the words of the mortal characters Patroclus and Achilles.

30. Cf. Thetis' promise at 18.134-37.

31. Agamemnon's offer (19.139-44); Odysseus' counsel (19.155-83); Achilles' objections (19.148-53, 19.199-214).

32. Various themes occurring in book 19 later figure significantly. The offer of gifts (originally promised by Athene at 1.212-14) seems to have been realized, but Priam delivers more gifts in book 24. The importance of eating is also addressed there (cf. 24.601-19). Odysseus mentions burial of the dead, the focus of books 23 and 24. Achilles' recollection of his father and son (19.321-37) prefigures the scene with Priam (24.486-92, 24.511, e.g.). See Reinhardt 1961, 412-22.

33. Poseidon makes it clear that all Priam's sons will die (cf. 20.300-308).

34. The scholiast notes this interruption as a deliberate postponement of the ultimate encounter (Sch. Ab 20.443): πιθανῶς ἀναρτᾷ τὴν ἐπιθυμίαν τῶν ἀκροατῶν, εἰς τέλος τῶν ποιήσεων ἑαυτῷ ταμιευόμενος τὴν σφαγὴν Ἕκτορος ("The poet persuasively keeps the desire of the audience in suspense by shifting the slaying of Hector to the end of his poem").

35. The glory Achilles seeks—repeated in the next book at 21.542-43—is

interpreted there by the scholiast as killing Hector (Sch. bT 21.543): sc. τὸν Ἕκτορα. Cf. 21.296-97.

36. The name either precedes the phrase *son of Priam* (e.g., 3.314, 12.94-95), or the context makes the identity clear (e.g., 6.512, 21.97). At the very least, the name occurs in the same verse (e.g., 4.499, 20.81). The only exception is the pairs of sons at 5.159-60. Similarly, the patronymic follows the name (e.g., 4.490, 11.490, 13.157, 13.586, 20.408), or the context is unambiguous (3.356, 6.76, 13.433). Apollo, disguised as Lycaon, is also addressed as "Priamides" (20.87).

37. And examined in chap. 3.

38. Cf. Zeus' idea to save Sarpedon (16.435-38); also at 4.14-19, he ponders allowing victory to Menelaus in the duel. These possibilities are briefly articulated and soon rejected. The significance of these passages is addressed in chap. 8.

39. See my discussion in chap. 8, for the poet's possible motivations for explicitly raising these possibilities.

40. Even in book 21, Hector continues to be foremost in Achilles' thoughts (cf. 21.133-35, 21.224-26, 21.279-80, 21.294-97).

41. One might consider the capacity of the *aristeia* sequence to generate expectations: see, e.g., Krischer 1971, 23-28. Although Achilles follows the pattern of arming and breaking through the enemy lines, the Greek army is virtually nonexistent, Achilles is never wounded, and there are three duels: Aeneas, Agenor, and Hector. (Elements 1c, 2a, and 3a in Krischer's scheme are not suited to a one-man assault.) Certainly the audience cannot know in advance whether a particular element in a sequence will be deleted, substituted for, or repeated several times. As with the prelude sequence, great flexibility is the norm. It is safe to say that the audience may not expect the meeting of Hector and Achilles at the beginning of book 20; Achilles will presumably be involved in other episodes before he encounters Hector.

42. See Combellack 1976, 50, and A. Edwards 1984, on the postponement of their final meeting.

Chapter 5

1. Schiller ([1797] 1905, letter 378) argues that the epic poet does not work through suspense; this is the province of the dramatic poet. In the *Iliad,* we find a special sort of suspense: the audience knows a great deal, yet the narrator presents perplexing situations that challenge the audience's preconceptions.

2. A possible exception is Odysseus' prayer in mid-race to Athene (23.768-79); cf. 23.863-64, 23.872-73.

3. Booth 1961, 4-5.

4. See Fränkel [1961] 1975, 55 n. 7: "The auditors of an epic recitation must also have felt like the gods when with food and drink they enjoyed the spectacle which the poet's song spread before their minds."

5. Duckworth (1933, 10-11) considers this the narrator's most frequent type of anticipating the subsequent narrative. See Arend [1933] 1975, 64-78, 91 n. 2; Beckmann 1932, 85-88; Morrison 1991.

6. Cf., e.g., 1.43, 1.457, 5.121, 10.295, 16.527, 23.771. See Morrison 1991, 149-52.

7. Agamemnon's address begins as a prayer (3.275-80) but shifts toward stipulating the conditions (cf. 19.252-66).

8. Zeus' prediction (15.67); Sarpedon dies (16.502-3). As the heroes approach, Zeus and Hera discuss the fate of Sarpedon (16.419-30).

9. At first there are few details (8.475-76), but explicit preparation precedes the scene: cf. 15.64-67, 16.644-51, 16.685-93, 16.787.

10. I exclude the boxing and wrestling matches in book 23.

11. Beckmann (1932, 17 n. 1) calls this the only example of a disjunctive prayer. Although it is unique in the *Iliad,* Polyphemus' prayer takes a similar form in the *Odyssey* (9.526-35). The success of Polyphemus' prayer, however, is explicitly indicated. The duels in books 3 and 7 have been analyzed by Kirk (1978) and Whitman (1958, 268-69).

12. Two hundred lines later, Aphrodite attempts to save Aeneas but is wounded, and Apollo (who has not been mentioned) must intervene (5.311-448).

13. Throughout this day of battle, the gods are free to act and are watching (20.24-25, 20.136-37).

14. This has been discussed in chap. 4. Reinhardt (1961, 131) comments that, while Paris' rescue leads smoothly to another scene (with Helen), the rescue of Hector in book 20 seems less well integrated (*ein retardierendes Mittel*). I omit discussion of three short divine rescues (5.22-24, 13.554-55, 13.562-63).

15. Kakridis (1949, 80 n. 31) notes that this is the only instance of Iris conveying a message to anyone on her own initiative. M. Edwards (1987a, 192) calls her "the poet's messenger." Not only has the narrator's presence in book 3 receded, but the gods have virtually vanished. Kirk (1978, 21) feels that the duel in book 3 takes place "almost by accident," which is further explained in his commentary (1985, 279) as meaning that it is "a purely human arrangement."

16. While Menelaus expects one of them to die (3.101-2), Iris and Idaeus only mention a victor in their reports to Helen and Priam (3.138, 3.255).

17. Zeus notes that Paris was about to die (4.12). Helen, Paris, Agamemnon, Zeus, and, later, Antenor agree that Menelaus has won (3.403-5, 3.439, 3.457-60, 4.13, 7.350-53). M. Edwards (1987a, 191) says that the terms of the duel are altered by the poet when the oath is actually sworn (3.281-87) foreseeing the inconclusive ending it is bound to have. See also Postlethwaite 1985, 2-3.

18. Consider the ancient explanation (Sch. bT 3.95): καταπλήσσει δὲ αὐτοὺς τὸ ξένον, ὡς εἴ τις μοιχείας διωκόμενος προκαλοῖτο τὸν ἄνδρα τῆς γυναικὸς εἰς μάχην, ὡς μετὰ τῆς γυναίκης καὶ τὴν ψυχὴν ἀφελούμενος ("This stroke out of the blue startles the Greeks, since the man pursued for adultery now calls forth the husband of the woman to battle, risking his life as well as the woman"). Hector does not expect Paris to return to battle at all (cf. 3.45, 3.52). Silence is the usual response to a challenge from the opposing army (7.92-93, e.g.) or from someone on one's own side (10.218, 10.313, 23.676; cf. *Od.* 8.234), but these parallel passages are open challenges: anyone can respond, although no one does immediately. According to the scholiast, silence is appropriate to the situation in book 3 (Sch. bT 3.95): πρεπόντως οἱ πολλοὶ σιωπῶσιν. ἕνα γὰρ προὺ-

καλοῦντο εἰς μάχην ("The common soldiery appropriately keeps quiet, for a single man has been called forth to fight").

19. Cf. Priam's reaction on first hearing the news (3.259): ῥίγησεν δ' ὁ γέρων ("The old man shuddered"). Priam's presence represents some sort of guarantee that the truce will be observed. After the narrator's first hint that the truce will not be observed (3.302), Priam decides to leave. Menelaus' worry that the truce will be broken without Priam is well founded, but he is wrong to say that without Priam, Priam's sons are likely to violate the truce. Pandarus, who is an ally and not a Trojan (cf. 5.105), is the actual violator of the treaty.

20. Whitman (1958, 264-65) and others note that the duel is out of place in the tenth year of the war. He considers this episode a compressed reenactment of the original treachery that caused the war (267-68). See Owen 1946, 18-19; Kullman 1968, 18. Against this view, see Tsagarakis 1982, 61-72.

21. On Achilles' choice, see chap. 7.

22. On this topic, see recent discussion by S. Richardson (1990, 187-96).

23. Sch. bT 2.156: εἰς τοσοῦτον προάγει τὰς περιπετείας ὡς δύνασθαι θεὸν μόνον αὐτὰς μεταθεῖναι. πρῶτος δὲ καὶ τοῖς τραγικοῖς μηχανὰς εἰσηγήσατο ("The poet brings this reversal to such a limit that only a god is able to counteract it. He was the first to introduce devices to the tragedians"). See discussion in Griesinger 1907, 54-55.

24. See Willcock 1976, 19; de Jong 1987, 78-81. Welcker (1857, 1:192) calls the expression "hyperbolic" (ein hyperbolischer Ausdruck). Fenik (1968, 39) speaks of the gods preventing what the tradition forbids (cf. 81, 153-54, and 175-76). See also Nagy 1979, 40, 81 n. 2, 267-68.

25. Schadewaldt 1938, 153 n. 3. See also Fränkel [1961] 1975, 57-58, 65-66; Vivante 1970, 42-43.

26. 7.459-63, 15.70-71, 12.15. These authoritative predictions reinforce the words of Agamemnon (4.164-68) and Hector (6.447-65). Cf. 2.297-98, 9.48-49. For an excellent summary, see Haft 1990.

27. The strong desire to go home is acknowledged by Odysseus (2.292-94). Later, when Zeus inspires the Greeks to fight, "war became sweeter than going home" (11.13-14). Reinhardt (1961, 107) calls a premature homecoming "a real probability" (eine gewisse Wahrscheinlichkeit) that recurs as a motiv throughout the epic (ein immer wiederkehrendes Begleitmotiv). See his discussion of Agamemnon's test and similar passages (107-20).

28. Agamemnon (9.26-28, 14.75-81), Hector (6.526-29, 8.196-97, 8.510-11, 10.310-12, 15.497-99). Cf. Poseidon's concern at 15.212-17.

29. See discussion in chap. 6.

30. The Trojan elders independently consider sending Helen back (3.159-60).

31. See chap. 7.

32. Leaf (1900-1902, 1:117) argues from the internal consistency of this episode that the duel was a distinct poem, composed for its own sake. Gentili (1988) describes the "auditory memory" of Homer's audience as follows: "[It] may be said to be associative rather than symbolic. It lives and operates through a total but temporary immersion in one slice of mythic action before proceeding to the next."

33. The audience is not surprised in an absolute sense. At some level, it may

be "expecting" Aphrodite's rescue or some such intervention from outside this particular duel sequence. It may become accustomed to frequent divine intervention. Kirk (1978, 27) says that "Aphrodite naturally enough emerges to save Paris."

34. See Reinhardt 1961, 38-41.

35. Schadewaldt (1965, 213) calls Hector's meeting with Andromache the poet's goal of this episode. See also Rothe 1910, 206; Kirk 1978, 22.

36. On Hector's roles, see Schadewaldt 1965, 213. Compare the sequence of recognition scenes in the *Odyssey*, which expresses Odysseus' capacity as father, king, singer, warrior, husband, and son. This is discussed in Whitman 1958, 302-5; cf. Joyce's remarks on Odysseus, in Steiner and Fagles 1962, 156-57.

37. Contrast this with Priam's trip to Achilles' tent in book 24, where Zeus announces the sequence of episodes for that journey in advance (cf. 24.144-58 ≈ 24.171-87).

38. At one point, Hera states that the Trojans had never fought so far from the city of Troy when Achilles was fighting (5.788-91; cf. 9.352-54). This appears to contradict the Trojans' lack of success. Cf. Rothe 1910, 202-3. On the Alexandrians' views, see Griesinger 1907, 13-15.

39. The ancient commentators explain Hector's speech before the army (Sch. 6.114 bT): πιθανῶς δέ, ἵνα μὴ γυναῖκας μόνας ἐπὶ τοῦ στρατεύματος ὀνομάζῃ ("It is believable that he refuses to mention only women while on military business"). On his omission of Diomedes, see Sch. T 6.114: ὁ δὲ Ἕκτωρ τοῦ εὐπρεποῦς ἕνεκα προστίθησι μὲν τοὺς γέροντας, ἐκκλέπτει δὲ τὴν ὑπὲρ Διομήδους εὐχήν ("Hector appropriately hides away the prayer concerning Diomedes, instead inserting the mention of the elders"). He keeps the situation from appearing quite so desperate. Eustathius explains this (628.6-11): ψεύσεται ἄρα ἐν καιρῷ δεόντως ὁ στρατηγός ("A general will necessarily lie at the appropriate moment"). See Willcock 1977, 45-46.

40. At this point, a scholium provides a reason why Hector does not mention Andromache to his mother (Sch. AbT 6.280): ἵνα μὴ δι' Ἀνδρομάχην δοκῇ τῆς μητρὸς ὑπεξίστασθαι. καλῶς δὲ τὰ ἀναγκαῖα προκρίνει τῶν ἡδέων ("He rightly chooses necessity over pleasure so that he avoids the appearance of preferring Andromache to his mother"). This comment follows a logic similar to that explaining Hector's words to the army (see Sch. T 6.114 in the preceding note). He previously needed an official reason for his departure from battle; now he does not wish to appear to indulge his pleasure, but he appears to be considering the needs of the Trojan army.

41. LSJ defines πρηνής as "with the face downwards" and "falling forwards," but in the *Iliad*, it almost always refers to men dying in battle or to corpses lying on the plain (13 of 16 times). See, e.g., 2.418, 4.544, 12.396. The exceptions are 2.414, 6.43, and 24.11. For a discussion of Theano's prayer, see Morrison 1991, 152-56.

42. Athene need only stop the active support she provided in book 5, where she played healer, advisor, and charioteer.

43. After Aphrodite returns him to Troy in book 3, Paris finds his way into the battle narrative only at 5.93.

44. On Andromache's absence from home, cf. Sch. bT 6.371: ἐκκλίνων τὸ

ὁμοειδὴς πιθανῶς ἐποίησε τὴν Ἀνδρομάχην μὴ εὑρισκομένην ἔνδον ("The poet persuasively varies the monotony by having Andromache not discovered at home"). On the audience's expectations, see Sch. bT 6.371: ἐν δὲ τῷ τείχει παραδόξως συντυγχάνει αὐτοῖς ("Contrary to expectation, they happen to be on the walls").

45. Sch. bT 6.392: τοῦτο δέ φησιν ἵνα ἀγωνιώτερος ὁ ἀκροατὴς γένηται. Schadewaldt (1965, 215-16) notes the dramatic tension in this scene. See also M. Edwards 1987a, 209.

46. Andromache (6.407-13, 6.431); Hector (6.447-55, 6.456-65); death is preferable (6.410-11, 6.464-65). On the status of predictions in the voice of mortal characters, see Eustathius on Hector's earlier words to Helen at 6.367-68 (647.27-28): καὶ ἔστι καὶ τοῦτο εἶδός τι προαναφωνήσεως Ὁμηρικῆς, οὐχ' ὑπ' αὐτοῦ ῥηθὲν τοῦ ποιητοῦ, ἀλλὰ στοχαστικῶς ἀνατεθὲν ποικιλίας χάριν τῷ πεισομένῳ Ἕκτορι ("This too is a type of Homeric foreshadowing, not spoken by the poet himself, but skillfully transferred for the sake of variety to Hector, who will suffer").

47. The scholiast remarks on the change in Hector's mood (Sch. T 6.471): ἀπὸ τῆς πολλῆς λύπης ἐκ μικρᾶς αἰτίας γέλωτα κινεῖ ("From great trouble, a trifle can provoke laughter"). Also Sch. T 6.476: διαχυθεὶς δὲ ἐπιλέληπται τῶν πρώην ("Coming into good spirits, Hector forgets what has just been said"). On διαχυθείς, see LSJ, s.v. διαχέω 1.4. See Griffin 1980, 72. The ancient critics viewed his statement on fate as hopeful (Sch. bT 6.487): ὑποθεὶς αὐτὸν τῇ εἱμαρμένῃ ἴσον ἐποίησε τό τε κινδυνεύειν καὶ τὸ ἀσφαλῶς ζῆν ("By subordinating himself to fate, he equates taking risks with living safely"). Whitman (1958, 346 n. 86) characterizes this speech as having "more promise of life than foreknowledge of death." See also M. Edwards 1987a, 212.

48. The Alexandrian critics explained Athene's rejection of the prayer on these grounds (Sch. bT 6.311): τῇ γνώμῃ ἀνένευεν ἐπὶ τῇ ἀναιρέσει, ἐπεί τοι παύει Διομήδεα διὰ τῆς Αἴαντος πρὸς Ἕκτορα μονομαχίας ("The goddess rejects this proposition [the prayer by Theano] since she stops Diomedes by means of the duel of Ajax with Hector").

49. Cf. the coincidence of the audience's expectations with those of Achilles in book 19 (discussed in chap. 4).

50. On the omission of the divine reaction, Beckmann (1932, 88) attributes this to the fact that Astyanax is fated to die when the city is sacked. Since Hector prays for something that is contrary to fate, his request cannot be honored. Still this does not explain the omission of the narrator's comment. M. Edwards (1987a, 211) says that the usual indication of the gods' response is omitted because the audience knows it only too well. Another factor may be that the narrator does not usually foretell in his own voice events that occur after the end of the *Iliad* (there are two exceptions: 2.724 and 12.3-35).

51. Andromache's mood has not changed. She and the other Trojan women mourn Hector; they do not expect him to return from battle (6.495-502). Perhaps the ambivalency of the Trojan perspective (despair from war; hope for the future) is best captured by Andromache "laughing in her tears" (δακρυόεν γελάσασα—6.484).

Chapter 6

1. By *theme* I mean a recurrent issue or conflict that is developed throughout much of the work. This is different from the *theme* discussed by Lord (1960, 68–98).

2. On these limitations to Hector's success, see 1.508–10, 8.470–77, 11.191–94, 15.53–70. Contrast the immediate limits (8.236–52, 12.216–29, 15.370–78) with the Greeks' ultimate conquest (7.459–63, 12.10–16, 13.810–13). See Fenik 1968, 223–24.

3. Cf. Achilles' words at 9.352–55.

4. Hector is almost successful on the second day: 8.217–19, 8.498–501.

5. Trojan threat: 12.69–70, 12.245–46, 12.440–41, 13.778, 13.831–32, 15.347–51, 15.487–94, 15.693–95 (cf. the narrator's comments: 12.197–98, 12.417–20, 13.41–42, 15.603–4). The Greeks' concern: 10.43–45, 11.276–79, 11.314–15, 11.664–68, 11.823–24, 13.317–20, 13.628–29, 13.813–14, 14.44–47, 14.65–68, 15.295, 15.502–7, 15.370–78 (cf. the narrator's comments: 11.556–57, 11.569, 12.106–7, 12.122–26, 15.686–88, 15.699–700, 17.637–39).

6. Schadewaldt (1938, 68) notes that the threat to the ships ("*das Stichwort*" for the threatening disaster) becomes prominent before the ships are in immediate danger. See Whitman 1958, 132–37, on fire as a threat to the ships.

7. For the ships as an area of sovereignty, see, e.g., 1.26–28; for the ships as a harbor of safety, see 1.88–89, and *Od.* 4.253–55. The twofold capacity of the ships—locating a stationary camp and functioning as sea-going vessels—is brought out in book 2, where the ships' timbers are rotting, so long has it been since they sailed on the seas (2.135).

8. Other passages describe the peace at Troy before the Greeks came (9.401–3, 22.147–56, 24.543–48).

9. As Zeus predicts: 7.459–63 (cf. 15.70–71). Cf. 2.297–98, where Odysseus says it would be shameful to return home empty-handed.

10. The idea of dying far from home is first introduced by Agamemnon, when he thinks his brother is fatally wounded: Agamemnon would be the object of utter reproach (ἐλέγχιστος) if he were forced to leave Menelaus' bones behind (4.169–82). Cf. the similar fear of the Trojans' allies (4.101–3, 4.119–21, 5.212–26, 5.685–88); see discussion in Griffin 1976, 164–66.

11. See also 11.805–8. The ship of Protesilaus appears to be somewhere in the middle of the extended line (16.284–86).

12. Achilles must go to the trench beyond the wall in order to be seen by the armies (18.215–16; cf. 18.198).

13. 15.69–71 imply that the ships will not be safe until Achilles kills Hector. These lines are not so clearly false as 15.61–65. Although Patroclus appears to save the ships in book 16, Hector is promised success until sunset. See Reinhardt 1961, 217–18.

14. See Scodel 1989, 96.

15. For a full discussion of Achilles' decision in book 16, see Scodel 1989. In her view, Achilles sends Patroclus as a means of keeping his word that he will not return until his own camp is threatened. From the audience's perspective,

the possibility of a surrogate has already been raised by Nestor (11.794-803). Zeus also notes that he will send a surrogate (15.61-65). The question remains: How long will Achilles wait to send the Myrmidons? Zeus' prophecy appears to supply the answer.

16. Kirk (1985, 78) calls 1.240-44 a "riddling oath," for there is no mention of Achilles' not sailing. Of course, there is a difference between what the audience knows and what the Greeks realize. When Athene promises that Achilles will be compensated for Agamemnon's *hybris* (1.212-14), she appears to him alone (1.197-98); he is far from his men when he speaks with Thetis (1.348-50). Only the audience learns of these promises.

17. Sch. A 8.475-76: τό τε ἐπιφερόμενον ψεῦδός τι ἔχει. οὐ γὰρ ἐν τῷ στείνει αἰνοτάτῳ ("This contains a degree of falsity, for he is not in 'the most terrible straits'"). See Leaf 1900-1902, 1:363.

18. Sch. A 15.56: ἀθετοῦνται στίχοι εἴκοσι δύο, ὅτι οὐκ ἀναγκαίως παλιλλογεῖται περὶ τῶν ἑξῆς ἐπεισαχθησομένων καὶ κατὰ τὴν σύνθεσίν εἰσιν εὐτελεῖς "[The editors] have athetized 22 lines, because this recapitulates unnecessarily what has already been introduced; also the lines are of little value with respect to composition").

19. E.g., Thetis does not retell the story of Briareus to Zeus after it has been told by Achilles (1.393-407; cf. 1.508-528).

20. Other similar passages: 5.503-11, 11.73-83, 15.592-604, 15.610-14, and 16.685-91. It is worth comparing the recapitulation (*ripetizione*) of eighteenth-century Italian improvized poetry, as described by Gentili (1988, 9): "Its primary function was to impress firmly on the memory of those present the context of what they had heard, forcing them to look beyond the variety of themes to the subtle connecting thread that underlay them."

21. Even as Zeus honors Hector, the audience learns that he will soon die (15.611-14). Hector's moment of breaking through the wall at the end of book 12 is preceded by the prediction that the best of the Trojans will die and that Troy will be sacked (12.10-33). After Patroclus' death, Zeus guarantees a final period of success to Hector (17.201-8). Patroclus' *aristeia* is also filled with reminders that he will soon die. See Duckworth 1933, 78.

22. See Fenik's argument (1968, 54-55, 130).

23. Sch. A int. 15.63: ὅτι ψεῦδος. ("[The line is athetized] because it is false"). Cf. Eustathius 1006.1-3, and see the discussion in van der Valk 1964, 2:426; Kraut 1863, 17 n. 1; Wilamowitz 1918, 233 n. 1; Schadewaldt 1938, 111 n. 2.

24. See Schadewaldt 1938, 110 n. 3, 140, on the *Ungenauigkeitprinzip*. Lesky (1963, 33) labels the lines in book 15 an inconsistency. Wilamowitz (1918, 42) considers the god's prophecy to be only a general prediction. See also Rothe 1910, 226; Reinhardt 1961, 168.

25. On two middays, see Schadewaldt 1938, 44 n. 2. On inconsistency arising from this method of composition, see Fenik 1968, 69-72, 94, 103, et passim, and Willcock 1977.

26. Basset 1933; Segal 1971; Griffin 1976. See also Redfield 1975.

27. Agamemnon threatens his own troops and the Trojans (2.391-93, 4.235-37, 6.57-60); Sarpedon worries about himself (5.684-85).

28. In addition, Diomedes and Glaucus recognize their family ties and exchange armor (6.212-36); Ajax and Hector part in friendship (7.299-305).

29. Zeus prevents Athene, who has made this threat, from entering battle (8.397-437).

30. 8.491, 10.198-200. Bassett (1933, 46) sees the breaking of the truce in book 4 as the turning point, but this ignores the agreement before Hector's duel and the negotiations on the next day. The scholiast notes these two stages (bT 1.4d): ἐν μὲν τῇ πρώτῃ μάχῃ, ἐν ᾗ Τρώων ἐκράτουν, θάπτουσι τοὺς πεσόντας, τῇ δὲ μετ' αὐτὴν ἡττώμενοι, διὰ τὴν Διὸς βούλησιν, ἐπαυλιζομένων ταῖς ναυσὶ τῶν βαρβάρων, οὐκέτι περὶ τοῦ θάψαι τοὺς τεθνεῶτας, ἀλλὰ περὶ τῆς σφῶν αὐτῶν σωτηρίας φροντίζουσιν ("In the first battle, where the Greeks bested the Trojans, they buried those who had fallen. But in the next battle, they were defeated because of the will of Zeus. As the Trojans set up camp by the ships, [the Greeks] no longer thought of burying the dead, but rather of their own safety").

31. Threat and worry: 11.394-95, 11.452-55, 11.817-18 (cf. 11.161-62).

32. 20.481-83, 21.201-4, 22.395-404.

33. 16.544-47, 16.559-61, 16.836, 17.39-40, 17.125-27, 17.240-41, 17.254-55, 17.556-58, 17.666-67, 18.176-80, 18.270-72, 18.283; cf. 16.339-41, 17.268-73. In the battle over Patroclus' body, Hector and the Trojans are likened to dogs in similes: 17.110, 17.287, 17.658, and 17.722-26. See Faust 1970, 22-23.

34. See Segal 1971, 13, 27-28; Griffin 1976, 169-71; Griffin 1980, 44-49.

35. It is a common Homeric practice to predict the death of minor heroes as well: 2.859-61, 2.873-75, 10.336-37, 12.113-15, 21.47-48. See Kraut 1863, 19-20.

36. Sarpedon's death is first predicted at 15.64-67; it occurs at 16.502-3. His fate is reiterated by Zeus (16.433-34), Hera (15.450-52), and the narrator (16.458-61). Although Zeus contemplates saving Sarpedon, he yields when Hera objects (16.435-61).

37. Patroclus' death is first predicted at 8.476; it occurs at 16.855-57. Other predictions come from Zeus (15.64-67—specifying that Hector will be his slayer), Apollo (16.724-25), and the narrator (16.46-47, 16.247-52, 16.644-51, 16.684-93, 16.787). Apollo's later role is suggested in Achilles' warning to Patroclus that the gods—especially Apollo—love the Trojans (16.87-94).

38. Hector's death is first predicted at 15.68; it occurs at 22.361. Predictions are given by Zeus (15.68, 17.201-8), Thetis (18.96, 18.132-34), Poseidon (21.297; by inference 20.300-308), and Athene (22.216-23; cf. 12.10-18, 22.325). Mortal predictions come from the dying Patroclus (16.852-54), Achilles (18.91-93, 18.114-15, 18.334-35, 21.224-26), Priam (22.38-41, 22.54-58), and Hecuba (22.86-89). Even after recognizing Athene's trick, Hector goes to meet Achilles (22.299-311).

39. Patroclus (16.559-61); Glaucus (16.544-47). Segal (1971, 19) speaks of Zeus' calm certainty.

40. It first becomes clear that Patroclus will be buried at 18.165; for Hector

at 24.139-40. Euphorbus, a Trojan casualty in danger of mutilation by the Greeks, serves a parallel function in book 17.

41. See Fenik 1968, 203. We might note that Achilles' death is first foretold in book 18, that is, seven books (4,012 lines) before the *Iliad*'s close. The most striking feature of the anticipation of Achilles' death is that he himself realizes that his death is near (18.120-21, 21.110-13, 22.365-66). He acknowledges he will die far from home (18.89-90, 18.101, 18.329-32, 19.421-22, 23.150, 24.538-42). Further detail is found in the predictions of Thetis (18.59-60, 18.96, 18.440-41, 24.131-32), the divine horse Xanthus (19.416-17), the dying Hector (22.358-60), and the ghost of Patroclus (23.80-81). Renehan (1987, 113-14) notes that Achilles' death is always anticipated in speech, not in narrative: it is not mentioned by Zeus or the narrator (cf. 15.68-71, 12.10-18). Achilles' funeral is anticipated as well (23.82-92, 23.243-48).

42. The scholiast read this remark more optimistically (T 17.272): πιθανὴ ἡ προαναφώνησις, ἵνα μαθόντες τὸ πέρας ἀνεχώμεθα τῶν κινδύνων ("This announcement is persuasive; in learning the outcome, we are able to tolerate the danger").

43. Hera's secret act (18.168) may not oppose the sensibilities of Zeus, who has no desire for Patroclus' mutilation (cf. 17.268-73), yet until sundown, Zeus' promise of success to Hector still holds.

44. Achilles' threat against the twelve Trojans: 18.336-37, 23.22-23; his action: 23.175-76. Against Hector: 22.335-36, 22.352-54, 23.19-23, 23.182-83; cf. 18.334-35.

45. Even Achilles recognizes the change in himself (21.100-105). Bassett (1933, 47) notes that Achilles is the only one to bury a dead enemy. Cf. Odysseus' treatment of the suitors in the *Odyssey*: they are clearly not buried at 24.417-19.

46. See Segal's discussion of this passage (1971, 31).

47. Schadewaldt 1965, 332-34. Besides Achilles', four threats of violating a corpse are made in battle: Euphorbus (17.39-40), Patroclus (16.559-61), and Hector (13.828-32, 16.836; cf. 17.125-27, 18.175-80); none of them is fulfilled. Threats often are not carried out, and—except for Achilles—threats of mutilation never are. Duckworth (1933, 23 n. 63) finds that eleven threats in the *Iliad* and seven in the *Odyssey* fail to be realized. Wieniewski (1924, 125) puts the figure lower.

48. Of course, it is an act of mutilation to repeatedly stab Hector (22.369-75) and drag him around Troy. The issue I am addressing concerns the ultimate fate of the corpse. Will he receive burial rites or not? See Priam's concern and Achilles' response at 24.406-23.

49. Bassett (1933, 57) examines the motivations for Achilles' actions.

50. Apollo and Aphrodite protect Hector's body only provisionally (23.184-91). Zeus has already allowed mutilation (22.403-4), as Achilles' actions are described: ἀεικέα μήδετο ἔργα ("he planned shameful treatment"—22.395).

51. Priam first mentions ransom at 22.416-20, but this appears unlikely after Achilles' clear rejection of such an idea.

52. Rutherford (1982, 153) notes that there is no mention of Achilles' relenting

in Zeus' prophecy in book 15. Zeus emphasizes Troy's sack, not the issue of burial.

53. Whitman (1958, 209-10) says that in book 18 we find the "confrontation of [Hector's] delirious hope and [Achilles'] true tragic foresight." Schadewaldt (1965, 255-60) discusses Achilles' "prophetic certainty." Kullman (1968, 32-34) says that Achilles is free from mortal illusion by the end. Macleod (1982, 10) compares Achilles' reaction at 19.420-21 with Hector's response to Patroclus' dying words. See my discussion in chap. 7.

54. Bassett (1933, 57) says that the sacrifice of the twelve Trojans is more ruthless because, after letting them live for a day, it is more deliberate. McFarland (1955-56, 191-92) considers the slaying of Lycaon more savage due to Achilles' calm deliberation when he speaks to Lycaon.

55. See Redfield 1979, 109 n. 48.

56. Griffin 1976, 171. Although the proems of the *Iliad* and the *Odyssey* do not offer complete plot summaries, all the other events anticipated are later presented. Redfield (1979, 101 n. 18) notes that, while mutilation by birds and dogs is often threatened, it is never enacted. I follow Pfeiffer (1968, 111) and Redfield (1979, 95-110) in their reading of δαῖτα, but the important point for my argument is the prediction that bodies will be eaten by birds and dogs. (As Redfield argues, δαίς is always used of human meals except here; we can understand the change to πᾶσι, but the reverse is harder to explain.)

57. Renehan (1987, 115) notes that the anger of Achilles is said to bring death to many of his friends and countrymen, but there is no mention of Hector and the Trojans. Bassett (1923, 347) remarks that the climax in each epic (the slaying and burial of Hector, and Odysseus' revenge upon the suitors) is not found in the proems. The *Odyssey*'s proem (1.1-9) anticipates only books 1-13. See Duckworth 1933, 6-7; Wieniewski 1924, 115.

58. The invocation preceding the catalog of ships anticipates the naming of the leaders and numbers of ships (2.484-759; cf. 2.761-62, 11.218-47, 14.508-22, 16.112-24).

59. Redfield (1979, 103) says that we are prepared to learn about the fate of dead bodies. See Griffin 1976, 171. I will not enter the dispute about whether Homer or his audience found Achilles' threats outrageous, cruel, and savage. See Bassett 1933; Segal 1971; Redfield 1975.

60. Segal 1971, 71.

61. Macleod (1982, 28) sees further war and death implied in Hector's dying words. He calls the two burials that follow a "planned surprise." Thomson's speculations are recorded by Murray ([1907] 1961, 128-29).

62. Although the *Aeneid* does not highlight the theme of mutilation, reconciliation is absent in the final scene. The war is over—Turnus concedes victory to Aeneas—yet Aeneas slays his enemy as he lies wounded. Whatever the degree of completion of this epic, I believe this is the final scene Vergil intended for the *Aeneid*.

63. Although Achilles renounces his wrath in book 19, his energy is directed toward avenging Patroclus' death; after Hector is slain, Achilles has no interest

in sacking Troy—the Greeks' ultimate objective. In book 23, however, he appears more fully reconciled with Agamemnon and even entrusts his burial to the king of Mycenae (23.236-48; cf. 23.884-97).

64. Griffin 1976, 170.

65. The burials of Patroclus and Hector may not have been as central to earlier epics. We must also consider the alternative tradition of immortal heroes, found at *Odyssey* 4.561-69, at Hesiod *Works and Days,* 167-71, and in the epic cycle (see Griffin 1977, 40-43). Kullmann (1985, 16-17) considers the tragic death of heroes to be a Homeric invention. For further discussion, see West 1978, 192-94; Burkert 1977, 198; Nagy 1983, 204-6. However, Segal (1971, 2) believes that the mutilation of the corpse was "doubtless well-imbedded in epic tradition," as a way of intensifying battle scenes.

Chapter 7

1. The audience inhabits the narrator's level of the text, an intermediate one between the story's level and the external position of the real poet and his auditors.

2. Rutherford (1982, 146) cites *Il.* 5.440-42, 16.705-9, 24.525-26; *Od.* 18.129-42.

3. Griffin 1980, 169.

4. See Griffin 1978, 12-15. Scholes and Kellogg (1966, 52) say that the audience adopts the "narrator's god-like point of view." Todorov ([1971] 1977, 63-64) speaks of the certitude of the gods. See also Redfield 1975, 136.

5. In book 2, Agamemnon, following his dream, falsely assumes he will take Troy, yet this is merely false anticipation. The Greeks will take Troy eventually—this expectation is correct—but Agamemnon anticipates success prematurely. This is not unlike the audience's false anticipation that battle will begin in book 3 or that the Trojans will drive the Greeks to their ships in book 5.

6. Mueller (1978, 108-11) argues that by attacking the Greek fleet Hector abandons his role as defender of the city. Cf. Rutherford 1982, 157-58, on the differences in self-knowledge among Patroclus, Hector, and Achilles.

7. Mueller 1978, 113. Rutherford (1982, 146-47) calls this the "moment of revelation."

8. Mueller 1978, 116-18. On Achilles' choice, see Pestalozzi 1945, 40-41; Schadewaldt 1965, 260-63; Kullmann 1968, 25-26; Frontisi-DuCroux 1986, 57-58.

9. This was argued in chap. 6.

10. Cf. though Xanthus the horse at 19.407-24.

11. Mueller 1978, 120. Griffin (1980, 95) says "it is part of the greatness of Achilles that he is able to contemplate and accept his own death more fully and passionately than any other hero." Cf. Whitman 1958, 209-10; Schadewaldt 1965, 255-60; Kullmann 1968, 32-34; Macleod 1982, 10.

12. Putting this somewhat differently, Redfield (1975, 220) says that at times the heroes "share the perspective of poet and audience and look down upon themselves."

13. On the audience's sense of closure, see Roberts (1988, 193), who feels, however, that mortals other than Achilles are only capable of guessing.

14. Duckworth (1933, 93-96) limits the audience's sense of uncertainty to its vicarious experience of what characters feel. See Winkler 1985, 90.

15. Cf. de Jong 1987, 130-31.

16. Noted by Kullmann (1968, 36-37), though praise of seers is found (cf. 1.68-72, 6.76, 18.249-50).

17. Note how Priam distances himself from the soothsayers, priests, and diviners (24.220-22). In his foreword to Nagy 1979 (xi), Redfield argues that the successors of the Greek poets are the historians and the natural philosophers, a line of intellectual descent distinct from the prophets and priests connected with the mystery cults.

18. I owe this observation to William Grummel. Only in book 10 does one of Nestor's ideas—the night mission of Odysseus and Diomedes—meet with success.

19. Hellwig (1964, 21 n. 31) and Erbse (1986, 230) comment on the qualified nature of divine knowledge. On Delusion and heroes, see Nicolai 1987, 158-60.

20. See Griffin 1980, 95-102. On the poet's inadequacies, cf. 12.176.

21. Griffin (1980, 168-69) discusses the fate of men who compete with the gods.

22. I think the *Iliad*—in essence—was performed over a number of days by one singer. On the fixity of even the oral performance, see Thornton 1984, 17. The "plan" of the *Iliad*—with repeated delays and false leads—may be presented again and again, even if no performance exactly duplicates any other.

23. On a similar experience of the *Odyssey*'s audience, see Olson 1990, 70.

24. Members of Homer's actual audience may have wished to hear him sing many times, just as today devoted fans of the Grateful Dead follow the band from city to city. Similar devotion to the Sophists is described at Plato *Protagoras* 316C5-D2.

25. Nabokov 1980, 3-4.

26. See, e.g., Plato *Republic* 10.596C. Gould (1983, 41-42) discusses "the tragic moment" when the truth is realized. Rutherford (1982, 146-47) argues that epic is tragic both in emotions expressed and in the thematic significance of knowledge. He discusses recognition (*anagnorisis*) at 147-52.

27. Marg [1942] 1976, 18; Griffin 1980, 44, 76. Griffin says that Achilles' vision "possesses a depth and truth which transforms a mere narrative of killing into an insight into death itself" (1980, 55-56).

Chapter 8

1. See Notopoulos 1951; Lord 1960; Finnegan 1977; Thornton 1984. The accounts of singers performing in the *Odyssey* and Plato's *Ion* are valuable as well.

2. Lord (1960, 13-29) discusses the various arenas for a performance, including the thirty days of Ramazan. On the material rewards that a singer might win, see Thornton 1984, 30-31. At 47-48 and 47 n. 9, she judges the time

required for the *Iliad* to be three days (23-27 hours of singing). Bannert (1986) recounts a performance of a German translation of the *Iliad* that took 21½ hours. Cf. Lord 1948, 86-87 (33.5 hours for the *Iliad,* 25.9 hours for the *Odyssey*), and Notopoulos 1951, 81-86.

3. See Lord 1948, 88-91; Wyatt 1989, 251.

4. Walsh (1984, 136 n. 22) sees this passage as an explicit recognition that old epic songs once were young. See also Nicolai 1987, 145.

5. Fränkel ([1961] 1975, 18) uses the expression "inflexible monolith"; at 68-69, he sees Achilles' near murder of Agamemnon in book 1 as a means of lightening the weight of the tradition. Scholes and Kellogg (1966, 13) speak of the "tyranny of the traditional in story telling." Cf. Reinhardt 1961, 119-20, on "heroic monotony." Nagy (1979, 272) says that "generations after generations of audience [were] conditioned to expect from the performer the most extreme degrees of fixity in content, fixity in form."

6. See Morrison (in press). Flory (1988, 46-49) demonstrates that only Thucydides and Homer introduce such hypothetical scenarios with relatively high frequency.

7. Todorov ([1971] 1977, 63-64) argues that the gods' predictions express certainties, yet Homer allows Zeus to express the alternative. See Erbse 1986, 214-15, on Zeus' decision regarding Sarpedon; 284-92 on Zeus and the powers of destiny.

8. See Frontisi-DuCroux 1986, 58, on the motif of choice as a paradigm of the narrative process.

9. Achilles' role may approximate that of the singer in another way. Achilles, the greatest of the warriors at Troy, calls into question the heroic code (9.318-20, 9.401-9; cf. 1.152-57; for various formulations of the code itself, see 6.207-10, 6.441-46, 11.408-10, 11.782-84, 12.310-28). The hero, considering other modes of behavior, provides a model for Homer, a traditional poet in many ways, who contemplates alternatives to the traditional story line.

10. Martin (1989, 65-77) illuminates the competitive aspect of each Iliadic character's speech. This agonistic rhetoric culminates in the language of Achilles, which is "none other than that of the monumental composer" (222). The poet, Martin maintains, competes with previous generations of singer (227-30). On the agonistic aspect of Greek poetry, see Griffith 1990; on Homer's own competitiveness, see Wyatt 1989, 247-48, and M. Edwards 1990.

11. Whitman 1958, 82, on improvisation; 112-13, on skill in applying the compositional elements from an established tradition; cf. 258.

12. Silk (1987, 25-26) compares the improvisational features of jazz with oral poetry. See also Havelock 1963, 147.

13. See Lord 1960, 13-29. Mingus (1971, 25-26) describes his early training on cello as "listen[ing] to the sounds [his teacher is] producing rather than making an intellectual transference from the score paper to the fingering process." He learned by ear, "knowing only how it sounded."

14. Dizzy Gillespie describes improvisation as "a gathering together of all the evidence you have of how to resolve going from here to here to here." See Balliett 1990, 54.

15. See Hellwig 1964, 13-19; Fenik 1974, 5-130; Rose 1976, esp. 406; Olson 1990. Pedrick (in press, 59) argues that innovation by storytellers in the *Odyssey* is generally met by criticism or indifference.

16. This may be one reason that Herodotus was considered the "most Homeric" of all Greek authors (Ὁμηρικώτατος—Longinus *On the Sublime* 13.3). Perhaps this development reaches its apex in the pairs of speeches in Thucydides, where again the dichotomy of choice is introduced. See Flory 1988.

17. Erbse 1984.

18. O'Hara 1990.

19. For examples, see Griesinger 1907, 33-35, 53-54, and von Franz 1943, 15-17.

Appendix

1. See Rothe 1910, 339-42; Schadewaldt 1938, 139-40; Kakridis 1949, 25-33; Page 1959, 312-13; Willcock 1964, 147-53; and Rosner 1976. On the general topic of mythological adaptation and innovation, see also Braswell 1971 and Lang 1983.

2. Meleager's stay by Cleopatra is verbally reminiscent of Achilles' wait by the ships (9.556; cf. 2.688, 2.694, 7.230).

3. Willcock (1964, 147) says that paradigms are usually meant to show that the person addressed should act in a similar manner: that is, most paradigms present positive exempla. Phoenix uses Meleager as a negative exemplum, although the words introducing the story give no clue of this. See Schadewaldt 1938, 140; Rosner 1976, 324; Alden 1983, 5-6; and Lang 1983, 161-62. Page (1959, 312-13) believes a paradigm should inform the audience of what to expect. He tells us that Achilles—like Meleager—should be forced to fight, and then find out that it is too late to receive the gifts. The parable "loses all color and significance if it is addressed to a man to whom it does not apply." Achilles' compensation in book 19, Page argues, contradicts the expectation generated in the story of Meleager that Achilles would be compelled to fight without compensation. Page's goal is to emphasize the narrative problems in book 9, but his argument presupposes a simplistic fit between paradigm and narrative.

4. Homer provides a linguistic clue: Cleo-patra and Patro-clus are etymological mirror images of each other. The evidence we have is subject to several interpretations, but Homer may well have given Meleager's wife the name Cleopatra in order to anticipate the scene in book 16 when Patroclus successfully pleads with Achilles. On her two names—Halycone and Cleopatra—see 9.556-64. Willcock (1964, 150) feels that the character of Patroclus led to the invention of Cleopatra. See Schadewaldt 1938, 139-40; Kakridis 1949, 28; and Rosner 1976, 323 n. 22.

5. See Kakridis 1949, 25-26, on how danger to the town prefigures the threat to the ships.

Bibliography

Alden, M. 1983. "When did Achilles come back?" In *Mélanges Edouard Delebecque*, ed. J. Laffitte, 1-9. Marseilles.
Allen, T.W. 1963. *Homeri Opera*. Vol. 1-4. Oxford.
Arend, W.A. [1933] 1975. *Die Typischen Szenen bei Homer*. Vol. 4 of *Problemata*. Berlin.
Arieti, J.A. 1983. "Achilles' Inquiry About Machaon: The Critical Moment in the *Iliad*." *CJ* 79:125-30.
Armstrong, J. 1958. "The Arming Motif in the *Iliad*." *AJP* 79:337-54.
Auerbach, E. 1946. *Mimesis: Dargestellte Wirklichkeit in der abendländischen Literatur*. Bern.
Bachmann, W. 1902. *Die aesthetischen Anschauungen Aristarchs in der Exegese und Kritik der homerische Gedichte*. Nürenburg.
Balliett, W. 1990. "Profiles (Dizzy Gillespie)." *New Yorker*, September 17, 48-58.
Bannert, H. 1986. "Die Ilias ganz." *Weiner humanistische Blätter* 28:37-39.
———. 1987. "Versammlungsszenen bei Homer." In *Homer: Beyond Oral Poetry*, 15-29. *See* Bremer et al. 1987.
Barnouw, D. 1980. "Critics in the Act of Reading." *Poetics Today* 1 (4): 213-22.
Barthes, R. [1966] 1982. "Introduction to the Structural Analysis of Narratives." In *A Barthes Reader*, ed. S. Sonntag, 251-95. New York.
Bassett, S.E. 1923. "The Proems of the *Iliad* and *Odyssey*." *TAPA* 54:339-48.
———. 1933. "Achilles' Treatment of Hector's Body." *TAPA* 64:41-65.
Beckmann, P.J.B. 1932. *Das Gebet bei Homer*. Ph.D. diss., Würzburg.
Bergren, A.L.T. 1980. "Helen's Web—Time and Tableau in the *Iliad*." *Helios* 7 (1): 19-34.
———. 1983. "Odyssean Temporality: Many (Re)Turns." In *Approaches to Homer*, 38-73. *See* Rubino and Shermerdine 1983.
Block, E. 1982. "The Narrator Speaks: Apostrophe in Homer and Vergil." *TAPA* 112:7-22.
———. 1986. "Narrative Judgement and Audience Response in Homer and Vergil." *Arethusa* 19:155-69.
Booth, W. 1961. *The Rhetoric of Fiction*. Chicago.

Braswell, B.K. 1971. "Mythological Innovation in the *Iliad*." *CQ* 21 (1): 6-26.
Bremer, J.M., I.J.F. de Jong, and J. Kalff, eds. 1987. *Homer, Beyond Oral Poetry: Recent Trends in Homeric Interpretation.* Amsterdam.
Brinker, M. 1980. "Two Phenomenologies of Reading: Ingarden and Iser on Textual Indeterminacy." *Poetics Today* 1 (4): 203-12.
Burkert, W. 1977. *Greek Religion.* Stuttgart.
Clarke, H.H.C. 1981. *Homer's Readers: A Historical Introduction to the "Iliad" and "Odyssey."* Newark.
Combellack, F. 1965. "Some Formulaic Illogicalities in Homer." *TAPA* 96:41-56.
———. 1976. "Homer the Innovator." *CP* 71:44-55.
———. 1981. "The Wish without Desire." *AJP* 102:115-19.
———. 1987. "The λύσις ἐκ τῆς λέξεως." *AJP* 108:202-9.
Dacier, Mme. A.L. 1714. *Des Causes de la Corruption du Goust.* Paris.
Daniele, A. 1985. "Remarques sur le chant IX du *l'Iliade*." *BAGB* ser. 4:257-79.
Davidson, J.A. 1955. "Peisistratus and Homer." *TAPA* 86:1-21.
de Jong, J.F. 1985. "*Iliad* 1.366-392: A Mirror Story." *Arethusa* 18:5-22.
———. 1987. *Narrators and Focalizers: The Presentation of the Story in the Iliad.* Amsterdam.
Dolezel, L. 1980. "Truth and Authenticity in Narrative." *Poetics Today* 1 (3): 7-25.
Doyle, R.E. 1984. *Ate: Its use and meaning: A study in the Greek poetic tradition from Homer to Euripides.* New York.
Duckworth, G.E.D. 1931. "Προαναφώνησις in the Scholia to Homer." *AJP* 52:320-28.
———. 1933. *Foreshadowing and Suspense in the Epics of Homer, Apollonius, and Vergil.* Ph.D. diss., Princeton.
Easterling, P.E. 1984. "The Tragic Homer." *BICS* 31:1-8.
Edwards, A. 1984. "*Aristos Achaion*: Heroic Death and Dramatic Structure in the *Iliad*." *QUCC*, n.s., 17 (2): 61-80.
Edwards, M. 1987a. *Homer: Poet of the "Iliad."* Baltimore.
———. 1987b. "Topos and Transformation in Homer." In *Homer: Beyond Oral Poetry*, 47-60. See Bremer et al. 1987.
———. 1990. "Neoanalysis and Beyond." *ClAnt* 9 (2): 311-25.
Else, G.F. 1967. *Aristotle's Poetics: The Argument.* Cambridge, Mass.
Emlyn-Jones, C. 1984. "The Reunion of Penelope and Odysseus." *G and R* 31: 1-18.
Erbse, H.E. 1969-83. *Scholia Graeca in Homeri Iliadem I-V.* Berlin.
———. 1983. "Ilias und Patroclie." *Hermes* 111:1-15.
———. 1984. *Studien zum Prolog der euripideischen Tragödie.* Berlin.
———. 1986. *Untersuchungen zur Funktion der Götter im homerischer Epos.* Berlin.
Faust, M. 1970. "Die kunsterische Verwendung von κύων 'Hund' in den homerischen Epen." *Glotta* 48:8-31.
Fenik, B.F. 1968. "Typical Battle Scenes in the *Iliad*: Studies in the Narrative Techniques of Homeric Battle Description." *Hermes*, Einzelschriften Heft 21. Wiesbaden.
———. 1974. *Studies in the Odyssey.* Wiesbaden.

Finnegan, R. 1977. *Oral Poetry: Its Nature, Significance, and Social Context*. Cambridge.
Flory, S.F. 1988. "Thucydides' Hypotheses about the Peloponnesian War." *TAPA* 118:43–56.
Fränkel, H. [1961] 1975. *Early Greek Poetry and Philosophy*. Trans. M. Hadas and J. Willis. Oxford.
Frazer, R.M. 1989. "The Return of Achilleus as a Climactic Parallel to Patroklos Entering Battle." *Hermes* 117:381–90.
Frontisi-DuCroux, F. 1986. *La Cithare d'Achille: Essai sur la poétique de l'Iliade*. Rome.
Frye, N. 1957. *Anatomy of Criticism: Four Essays*. Princeton.
Genette, G. [1972] 1980. *Narrative Discourse: An Essay in Method*. Trans. J.E. Lewin. Ithaca, N.Y.
Gentili, B. 1988. *Poetry and Its Public in Ancient Greece from Homer to the Fifth Century*. Trans. A. Thomas Cole. Baltimore.
Goold, G.P. 1977. "The Nature of Homeric Composition." *Ill. Class. St.* 2:1–34.
Gould, J. 1983. "Homeric Epic and the Tragic Moment." In *Aspects of the Epic*, ed. T. Winnifrith, P. Murray, and K.W. Gransden, 32–45. London.
Griesinger, R. 1907. *Die aesthetischen Anschauungen der alten Homererklärer*. Ph.D. diss., Tübingen.
Griffin, J. 1976. "Homeric Pathos and Objectivity." *CQ*, n.s., 26:161–87.
———. 1977. "The Epic Cycle and the Uniqueness of Homer." *JHS* 97:39–53.
———. 1978. "The Divine Audience and the Religion of the *Iliad*." *CQ* 28:1–22.
———. 1980. *Homer on Life and Death*. Oxford.
Griffith, M. 1990. "Contest and Contradiction in Early Greek Poetry." In *Cabinet of the Muses: Essays on Classical and Comparative Literature in Honor of Thomas G. Rosenmeyer*, ed. M. Griffith and D. Mastronarde, 185–207. Atlanta.
Gunn, D.M. 1971. "Thematic Composition and Homeric Authorship." *HSCP* 75:1–31.
Haft, A. 1990. "'The City-Sacker Odysseus' in Iliad 2 and 10." *TAPA* 120:37–56.
Haüssler, R. 1976. *Das historische Epos der Griechen und Römer bis Vergil*. Vol. 1. Heidelberg.
Havelock, E.A. 1963. *Preface to Plato*. Cambridge, Mass.
Heitsch, E. 1968. "Der Anfang unserer *Ilias* und Homer." *Gymnasium* 87:38–56.
———. 1980. *Epische Kunstsprache und Homerische Chronologie*. Heidelberg.
Hellwig, B. 1964. *Raum und Zeit im homerischen Epos*. Hildesheim.
Hogan, J.C. 1973. "Aristotle's Criticism of Homer in the *Poetics*." *CP* 68:95–108.
Howald, E. 1946. *Der Dichter der Ilias*. Erlenbach-Zürich.
Iser, W.I. 1974. *The Implied Reader*. Baltimore.
Kakridis, J.Th.K. 1949. *Homeric Researches*. Humanistiska Vetenskapssamfundet 1. Skrifter 40. Lund.
Kirk, G.S. 1978. "Formal Duels in Books 3 and 7 of the *Iliad*." In *Homer: Tradition and Invention*, ed. B. Fenik, 18–40. Leiden.

———.1983. "The *Iliad*: The Style of Books 5 and 6." In *Aspects of the Epic*, ed. T. Winnifrith, P. Murray, and K.W. Gransden, 16-31. London.
———. 1985. *The "Iliad"; A Commentary Vol. I: Books 1-4.* Cambridge.
Kirkwood, G.M. 1958. *A Study of Sophoclean Drama.* Ithaca, N.Y.
Knox, M.O. 1971. "Huts and Farm Buildings in Homer." *CQ* 21:7-31.
Köhnken, A. 1976. "Die Narbe des Odysseus: Ein Beitrag zur homerische-epische Erzähltechnik." *A und A* 22:101-14.
Kraut, K.B. 1863. *Die epische prolepsis nachgewiesen in der "Ilias," ein Beitrag zur Kenntnis des epischen Stils.* Tübingen.
Krischer, T. 1971. "Formale Konventionen der homerischen Epik." *Zetemata* 56. München.
Kullmann, W. 1960. *Die Quellen der Ilias.* Wiesbaden.
———. 1968. "Vergangenheit und Zukunft in der *Ilias*." *Poetica* 2:15-37.
———. 1985. "Gods and Men in the *Iliad* and *Odyssey*." *HSCP* 89:1-23.
Lang, M.L. 1975. "Reason and Purpose in Homeric Prayers." *CW* 68:309-14.
———. 1983. "Reverberation and Mythology in the *Iliad*." In *Approaches to Homer*, 140-64. *See* Rubino and Shermerdine 1983.
Lattimore, R. 1951. *The "Iliad" of Homer.* Chicago.
Leaf, W. 1900-1902. *The "Iliad."* 2 vols. 2d ed. London.
Lesky, A. 1963. *A History of Greek Literature.* Trans. J. Willis and C. de Heer. 2d ed. London.
Levine, D.B. 1983. "Theoclymenos and the Apocalypse." *CJ* 79:1-7.
Lewis, C.S. 1942. *A Preface to "Paradise Lost."* London.
Lohmann, D. 1970. *Die Komposition der Reden in der Ilias.* Berlin.
Lord, A.B. 1948. "Homer, Parry, and Huso." *AJP* 52:81-94.
———. 1953. "Homer's Originality: Oral Dictated Texts." *TAPA* 84:124-34.
———. 1960. *Singer of Tales.* Cambridge, Mass.
Lucas, D.W. 1962. "Pity, Terror, and *Peripeteia*." *CQ*, n.s., 12:52-60.
McFarland, T. 1955-56. "Lycaon and Achilles." *Yale Review*, n.s., 45:191-213.
Macleod, C.W. 1982. *Homer "Iliad" Book XXIV.* Cambridge.
Marg, W. [1942] 1976. "Kampf und Tod in der Ilias." *Die Antike* 18:167-87. Reprint. *Würzburger Jahrbücher* 2:7-19.
Martin, R.P. 1989. *The Language of Heroes: Speech and Performance in the "Iliad."* Ithaca, N.Y.
Merkelbach, R. 1948. "Zum Y der *Ilias*." *Philologus* 97:303-11.
Mingus, C. 1971. *Beneath the Underdog: His World as Composed by Mingus.* New York.
Morrison, J.V. 1991. "The Function and Context of Homeric Prayers: A Narrative Perspective." *Hermes* 119:145-57.
———. In press. "Alternatives to the Epic Tradition: Homer's Challenges in the *Iliad*." *TAPA*.
Moulton, C. 1975. "Similes in the Homeric Poems." *Hypomnemata* 49:11-155.
Mueller, M. 1978. "Knowledge and Delusion in the *Iliad*." In *Essays on the "Iliad": Selected Modern Criticism*, ed. J. Wright, 105-23, 149-50. Bloomington, Ind.
Muellner, L.C. 1976. *The Meaning of Homeric εὔχομαι Through its Formulas.* Innsbruck.

Murray, G. [1907] 1961. *The Rise of the Greek Epic*. 4th ed. Oxford.
Nabokov, V. 1980. *Lectures on Literature*. New York.
Nagy, G. 1979. *The Best of the Achaeans*. Baltimore.
———. 1983. "On the Death of Sarpedon." In *Approaches to Homer*, 189–217. See Rubino and Shelmerdine 1983.
Neschke, A.B. 1985. "βουληφόρος ἀνήρ—Zur Bedeutung der sogenannten Diapeira im 2. Buch der Ilias (B, 1–483)." *A und A* 31:24–34.
Nicolai, W. 1983. "Rezeptionssteuerung in der Ilias." *Philologus* 127:1–12.
———. 1987. "Zum Welt- und Geschichtsbild der Ilias." In *Homer: Beyond Oral Poetry*, 145–64. See Bremer et al. 1987.
Notopoulos, J.A. 1951. "Continuity and Interconnexion in Homeric Oral Composition." *TAPA* 82:81–101.
O'Hara, J.J. 1990. *Death and the Optimistic Prophecy in Vergil's "Aeneid."* Princeton.
Olson, S.D. 1990. "The Stories of Agamemnon in Homer's *Odyssey*." *TAPA* 120:57–71.
Owen, E.T. 1946. *The Story of the "Iliad" as told in the "Iliad."* Toronto.
Parry, A. 1972. "Language and Characterization in Homer." *HSCP* 76:1–22.
———. 1966. "Have We Homer's *Iliad*?" *YCS* 20:175–216.
Parry, M. 1971. *The Making of Homeric Verse: The Collected Papers of Milman Parry*. Oxford.
Pedrick, V. 1982. "Supplication in the *Iliad* and *Odyssey*." *TAPA* 112:125–40.
———. 1983. "The Paradigmatic Nature of Nestor's Speech in *Iliad* 11." *TAPA* 113:55–68.
———. In press. "The Muse Corrects: The Opening of the *Odyssey*." In "Beginnings in Classical Literature," ed. F.M. Dunn, *YCS* 29:39–61.
Pestalozzi, H. 1945. *Die Achilleis als Quelle der Ilias*. Erlenbach-Zürich.
Pfeiffer, R. 1968. *History of Classical Scholarship*. Oxford.
Postlethwaite, N. 1985. "The Duel of Paris and Menelaos and the Teichoskopia in *Iliad* 3." *Antichthon* 19:1–6.
Pucci, P. 1982. "The Proem of the *Odyssey*." *Arethusa* 15:39–62.
Redfield, J.M. 1975. *Nature and Culture in the "Iliad": The Tragedy of Hector*. Chicago.
———. 1979. "The Proem of the *Iliad*: Homer's Art." *CP* 74:95–110.
Reinhardt, K. 1960. *Tradition und Geist: Gesammelte Essays zur Dichtung*. Ed. C. Becker. Göttingen.
———. 1961. *Die Ilias und ihr Dichter*. Göttingen.
Renehan, R. 1987. "The Heldentod in Homer: One Heroic Ideal." *CP* 82:99–116.
Richardson, N.J. 1980. "Literary Criticism in the Exegetical Scholia to the *Iliad*: A Sketch." *CQ* 30:265–87.
———. 1983. "Recognition Scenes in the *Odyssey* and Ancient Literary Criticism." In *Arca II Papers of the Liverpool Latin Seminar*, vol. 4, ed. F. Cairns, 219–35. Liverpool.
Richardson, S. 1990. *The Homeric Narrator*. Nashville, Tenn.
Roberts, D. 1988. "Sophoclean Endings: Another Story (for Helen North)." *Arethusa* 21:177–96.

———. 1989. "Different Stories: Sophoclean Narrative(s) in the *Philoctetes*." *TAPA* 119:161-76.
Rose, J. 1976. "The Unfriendly Phaeacians." *TAPA* 100:387-406.
Rosner, J. 1976. "The Speech of Phoenix: *Iliad* 9.434-605." *Phoenix* 30:314-27.
Rothe, C. 1910. *Die Ilias als Dichtung*. Paderborn.
Rubino, C.A. and C.W. Shermerdine. 1983. *Approaches to Homer*. Austin.
Rutherford, R.B. 1982. "Tragic Form and Feeling in the *Iliad*." *JHS* 102:145-60.
Sale, W.M. 1987. "The Formularity of the Place Phrases of the *Iliad*." *TAPA* 117:24-50.
Schadewaldt, W. 1938. *Iliasstudien*. Abh. Sachs. Ak. d. Wiss., vol. 43.6. Leipzig.
———. 1958. "Prologue of the *Odyssey*." *HSCP* 63:15-32.
———. 1965. *Von Homers Welt und Werk*. Stuttgart.
Schein, S.L. 1984. *The Mortal Hero: An Introduction to Homer's "Iliad."* Berkeley.
Schenkeveld, D.M. 1982. "The Structure of Plutarch's *De Audiendis Poetis*." *Mnemosyne* 35:60-71.
Schiller, J.C.F. [1797] 1905. *Der Briefwechsel zwischen Schiller und Goethe*. Intro. H.S. Chamberlin. Jena.
Scodel, R. 1982. "The Achaean Wall and the Myth of Destruction." *HSCP* 86:33-50.
———. 1984. "Epic Doublets and Polynices' Two Burials." *TAPA* 114:49-58.
———. 1989. "The Word of Achilles." *CP* 84:91-99.
Scholes, R. and R. Kellogg. 1966. *The Nature of Narrative*. Oxford.
Scully, S.P. 1986. "Studies of Narrative and Speech in the *Iliad*." *Arethusa* 19:135-53.
Segal, C. 1971. "The Theme of the Mutilation of the Corpse in the *Iliad*." *Mnemosyne*, suppl. 17. Leiden.
Severyns, A. 1948. *Homère*. 3 vols. Brussels.
Silk, M.S. 1987. *The "Iliad."* Cambridge.
Slater, W.J. 1982. "Aristophanes of Byzantium and Problem-Solving in the Museum." *CQ* 32:336-49.
Smith, P.M. 1981. "Aineidai as Patrons of *Iliad* XX and the Homeric Hymn to Aphrodite." *HSCP* 85:17-58.
Snell, B. 1953. *The Discovery of the Mind*. Trans. T.G. Rosenmeyer. Cambridge, Mass.
Steiner, G., and F. Fagles. 1962. *Homer: A Collection of Critical Essays*. Englewood Cliffs, N.J.
Suleiman, S.R., and I. Crosman. 1980. *The Reader in the Text: Essays on Audience and Interpretation*. Princeton.
Svenbro, J. 1976. *La Parole et le marble: Aux origines de la poètique grecque*. Lund.
Thalmann, W.G. 1984. *Conventions of Form and Thought in Early Greek Poetry*. Baltimore.
Thornton, A. 1984. "Homer's *Iliad*: Its Composition and the Motif of Supplication." *Hypomnemata* 81. Göttingen.

Todorov, T. [1971] 1977. *The Poetics of Prose*. Trans. Richard Howard. Ithaca, N.Y.
Tompkins, D. 1986. "Response." *Arethusa* 19:211-18.
Tsagarakis, O. 1979. "Oral Composition, Type-Scenes, and Narrative Inconsistencies in Homer." *GB* 8:23-48.
———. 1982. "The Teichoskopia Cannot Belong to the Beginning of the Trojan War." *QUCC* 41:61-72.
van der Valk, M.H.A.L.H. 1964. *Researches on the Text and Scholia of the "Iliad."* Vols. 1-2. Leiden.
Verdenius, W.J. 1983. "The Principles of Greek Literary Criticism." *Mnemosyne* 36:14-59.
Vivante, P. 1970. *The Homeric Imagination*. Bloomington, Ind.
von Franz, M.L. 1943. *Die aesthetischen Anschauungen der Ilias-Scholien*. Ph.D. diss., Zürich.
Walsh, G.B. 1984. *The Varieties of Enchantment: Early Greek Views of the Nature and Function of Poetry*. Chapel Hill, N.C.
Weil, S. 1940. *The "Iliad," or the Poem of Force*. Trans. M. McCarthy. Lebanon, Pa.
Welcker, F.W. 1857. *Götterlehre*. Vols. 1-2. Göttingen.
West, M.L., ed. 1978. *Hesiod: "Works and Days."* Oxford.
White, J.B. 1984. *When Words Lose Their Meaning*. Chicago.
Whitman, C. 1958. *Homer and the Heroic Tradition*. New York.
Whitman, C., and R. Scodel. 1981. "Sequence and Simultaneity in *Iliad* N, Ξ, and O." *HSCP* 85:1-15.
Wieniewski, I. 1924. "La technique d'annoncer les événements futurs chez Homère." *Eos* 27:113-33.
Wilamowitz, U. 1918. *Die Ilias und Homer*. Berlin.
Willcock, M.M. 1964. "Mythological Paradeigma in the *Iliad*." *CQ*, n.s., 14:144-54.
———. 1976. *A Companion to the "Iliad."* Chicago.
———. 1977. "Ad Hoc Invention in the *Iliad*." *HSCP* 81:41-53.
Winkler, J.J. 1985. *Auctor & Actor: A Narratological Reading of Apuleius' "Golden Ass."* Berkeley.
Wolf, F.A. 1795. *Prolegomena ad Homerum*. Halle.
Wyatt, W.F., Jr. 1989. "The Intermezzo of Odyssey 11 and the Poets Homer and Odysseus." *Studi Micenei ed Egeo-Anatolici*, Fasc. 27. Rome.
Zielinski, T. 1901. "Die Behandlung gleichzeitiger Ereignisse im Antiken Epos." *Philologus*, Suppl. 8, Heft 3:407-49.

Index of Passages

Aristotle
  Poetics
    1451B19–26: 128n.8
    1453B22–26: 126n.14
Bacchylides
  5.94–154: 120
Eustathius
  628.6–11: 137n.39
  647.27–28: 138n.46
  1006.1–3: 140n.23
Hesiod
  Works and Days 167–71: 144n.65
Homer
  Iliad
    1.1: 127n.6
    1.1–5: 90
    1.1–7: 37–38, 131n.6, 143n.56
    1.2–5: 131n.5
    1.3: 32
    1.3–4: 126n.10
    1.3–5: 132n.16
    1.4: 131n.5, 141n.30
    1.6–12: 31
    1.8–11: 54
    1.9–12: 26
    1.12–33: 25
    1.17–19: 24–25
    1.22–23: 25
    1.26–28: 139n.7
    1.29–31: 18, 26
    1.43: 15, 54, 135n.6
    1.44–67: 28
    1.59–61: 17, 27–28, 30, 60
    1.68–72: 128n.8, 145n.16
    1.88–89: 139n.7
    1.94–117; 28
    1.101–247: 29
    1.106–8: 13, 128n.7
    1.113–15: 129n.4
    1.116: 26
    1.116–17: 18
    1.152–57: 146n.9
    1.169–71: 18, 30, 60, 80
    1.194–221: 30–31, 130n.11
    1.197–98: 140n.16
    1.202–5: 28–29
    1.212: 131n.7
    1.212–14: 17, 19, 30, 38, 80, 122, 131n.5, 133n.32, 140n.16
    1.233–39: 18
    1.240–41: 131n.5
    1.240–44: 18, 38, 39, 140n.16
    1.242–43: 131n.5
    1.243–44: 131nn.4, 5
    1.247–52: 128n.8
    1.247–348: 29
    1.298–303: 28
    1.338–39: 18
    1.338–44: 18, 38, 39, 75
    1.340–42: 131n.5
    1.342–44: 131nn.4, 5
    1.344: 131n.5
    1.348–50: 140n.16
    1.352: 101
    1.353–54: 131n.5
    1.366–92: 129n.22
    1.376–77: 129n.22
    1.393–407: 140n.19
    1.408: 131n.5
    1.408–12: 38
    1.409: 131n.5
    1.409–10: 131n.5

158 / Index of Passages

Homer, *Iliad (continued)*
  1.410-12: 131nn.4, 5
  1.416: 101
  1.421-22: 18, 30, 80
  1.423-27: 82
  1.427-29: 19
  1.457: 54, 135n.6
  1.488-92: 18, 30
  1.505: 32
  1.505-10: 38, 101, 131n.4
  1.508-10: 131nn.5, 6, 139n.2
  1.508-28: 140n.19
  1.508-30: 2, 19, 74, 122
  1.509: 131n.5
  1.522-30: 15, 17, 38, 131n.6
  1.525-27: 131n.7
  1.558-59: 38, 131nn.4, 5, 6
  1.559: 131n.5
  2.1-50: 131n.12
  2.1-72: 39-40
  2.3-4: 39, 131nn.5, 6
  2.35-36: 18
  2.35-38: 39-40
  2.39-40: 42
  2.52: 132n.14
  2.73-141: 40
  2.75: 40
  2.123-24: 61
  2.123-30: 130n.9
  2.135: 139n.7
  2.149-56: 60
  2.155: 113
  2.155-56: 40, 66
  2.156-211: 132n.20
  2.212-78: 41
  2.216-3.15: 41, 43
  2.279-368: 41
  2.292-94: 136n.27
  2.297-98: 136n.26, 139n.9
  2.303-30: 128n.7
  2.328-38: 43
  2.381-93: 132nn.13, 18
  2.382-84: 42
  2.391-93: 141n.27
  2.414: 137n.41
  2.418: 137n.41
  2.435-40: 41
  2.441-83: 132n.20
  2.443-83: 131n.12
  2.444: 132n.14
  2.453-54: 132n.14

  2.484-93: 105
  2.484-759: 143n.58
  2.493-760: 75
  2.494-770: 132n.20
  2.542-44: 132n.14
  2.588-90: 132n.14
  2.688: 133n.26, 147n.2
  2.694: 5, 13, 18, 44, 80, 132n.14, 133n.26, 147n.2
  2.724: 132n.14, 138n.50
  2.761-62: 143n.58
  2.785: 132n.14
  2.786-807: 132n.20
  2.808: 132n.14
  2.808-10: 132n.20
  2.811-77: 132n.20
  2.858-61: 104
  2.859-61: 80, 141n.35
  2.860-61: 132n.14
  2.873-75: 80, 132n.14, 141n.35
  3.14: 132n.14
  3.28: 132n.14
  3.30-37: 58
  3.45: 135n.18
  3.52: 135n.18
  3.67-120: 41
  3.71-72: 57
  3.71-75: 57
  3.92-93: 57
  3.95: 2, 58
  3.101-2: 135n.16
  3.105-11: 58
  3.111-12: 58
  3.121-40: 56
  3.138: 135n.16
  3.159-60: 136n.30
  3.255: 135n.16
  3.259: 136n.19
  3.264-324: 61
  3.275-80: 135n.7
  3.276-87: 57
  3.281-87: 135n.17
  3.302: 55, 136n.19
  3.303-13: 58
  3.314: 134n.36
  3.318-24: 55
  3.324: 55
  3.349-55: 55
  3.349-56: 16
  3.351-54: 13

Index of Passages / 159

3.355: 55
3.356: 134n.36
3.373-82: 56
3.403-5: 135n.17
3.439: 135n.17
3.456-60: 58
3.457-60: 135n.17
4.12: 135n.17
4.13: 135n.17
4.13-29: 113
4.14-19: 134n.38
4.30-67: 128n.7
4.101-3: 139n.10
4.119-21: 139n.10
4.164-68: 136n.26
4.169-82: 130n.12, 139n.10
4.170-82: 60
4.221-22: 42
4.221-445: 42
4.223-421: 132n.18
4.235-37: 141n.27
4.275-82: 132n.15
4.446: 39, 42
4.461: 125n.2
4.490: 134n.36
4.499: 134n.36
4.503: 125n.2
4.526: 125n.2
4.543-44: 42
4.544: 137n.41
5.22-24: 135n.14
5.93: 137n.43
5.105: 136n.19
5.121: 135n.6
5.129-32: 56
5.159-60: 134n.36
5.212-26: 139n.10
5.309-10: 125n.2
5.311-13: 60
5.311-448: 135n.12
5.440-42: 144n.2
5.503-11: 140n.20
5.553: 125n.2
5.659: 125n.2
5.684-85: 141n.27
5.685-88: 139n.10
5.788-91: 75, 137n.38
6.11: 125n.2
6.43: 137n.41
6.57-60: 141n.27
6.73-76: 3, 64

6.76: 134n.36, 145n.16
6.86-101: 65
6.90-97: 65
6.93-98: 64
6.97-98: 66
6.111-15: 65
6.113-14: 65
6.207-10: 146n.9
6.212-36: 141n.28
6.271-78: 65
6.277-78: 66
6.280: 63, 65
6.280-85: 65
6.305-11: 66
6.311: 130n.5
6.313-42: 67
6.363-68: 67
6.365: 63
6.367-68: 138n.46
6.386-89: 67
6.392-95: 67
6.407-13: 138n.46
6.410-11: 138n.46
6.414-28: 88
6.431: 138n.46
6.441-46: 146n.9
6.447-55: 138n.46
6.447-65: 98, 136n.26
6.456-65: 138n.46
6.464-65: 138n.46
6.466-71: 68
6.471-74: 68
6.476-81: 68, 138n.50
6.484: 138n.57
6.488: 32
6.495-502: 138n.51
6.503-14: 69
6.512: 134n.36
6.526-29: 68, 136n.28
7.1-7: 69
7.17-22: 69
7.24-27: 69
7.29-30: 55
7.29-36: 69
7.52-53: 55
7.76-91: 84
7.92-93: 135n.18
7.104-8: 60
7.204-5: 55-56
7.230: 147n.2
7.299-305: 141n.28

Homer, *Iliad (continued)*
7.324-436: 84
7.350-53: 61, 135n.17
7.459-63: 136n.26, 139nn.2, 9
8.1-59: 132n.19
8.5-17: 17
8.90-91: 60
8.178-83: 75
8.196-97: 136n.28
8.217-19: 60, 139n.4
8.222-26: 77
8.236-52: 139n.2
8.370-72: 133n.25
8.397-437: 141n.29
8.470-77: 2, 5, 74, 139n.2
8.473-76: 4, 5
8.473-77: 80, 123
8.474: 44
8.475-76: 78, 80, 135n.9, 140n.17
8.476: 141n.37
8.488-501: 139n.4
8.491: 141n.30
8.510-11: 136n.28
8.526-41: 75
8.535-41: 98-99
9.14-15: 4
9.26-28: 61, 136n.28
9.48-49: 136n.26
9.144-48: 128n.7
9.230-46: 75
9.244-46: 76
9.286-90: 128n.7
9.300-306: 133n.27
9.318-20: 146n.9
9.352-54: 137n.38
9.352-55: 139n.3
9.356-63: 60, 80
9.393-400: 101
9.393-429: 60
9.401-3: 139n.8
9.401-9: 146n.9
9.410-16: 101
9.412-13: 76
9.417-20: 61
9.434: 76
9.434-38: 75
9.519-32: 120
9.524-26: 120
9.550-52: 120
9.553-60: 120
9.556: 133n.26, 147n.2

9.556-64: 147n.4
9.574-87: 120
9.585-87: 121
9.588-89: 121
9.590-94: 121
9.595-98: 121
9.598-99: 121
9.601-2: 75
9.607-10: 131n.5
9.618-19: 80
9.622: 76
9.649-55: 5
9.650-55: 76, 80, 122-23
9.655: 44
9.673-75: 75
9.677-92: 80
10.43-45: 139n.5
10.198-200: 141n.30
10.218: 135n.18
10.295: 135n.6
10.297-98: 84
10.310-12: 136n.28
10.313: 135n.18
10.336-37: 141n.35
10.454-57: 84
11.1-66: 132n.19
11.5-9: 77
11.13-14: 136n.27
11.54-55: 126n.10, 132n.16
11.73-83: 140n.20
11.84-91: 82
11.104-6: 88
11.146-47: 84
11.161-62: 141n.31
11.163-64: 125n.3
11.181ff.: 1, 125n.3
11.191-94: 1, 2, 74, 139n.2
11.206-9: 1, 2, 74, 139n.2
11.218-47: 143n.58
11.261: 84
11.276-79: 139n.5
11.284ff.: 2
11.288-89: 125n.1
11.299-300: 2
11.314-15: 139n.5
11.354-56: 2, 125n.2
11.369-400: 125n.3
11.394-95: 141n.31
11.408-10: 146n.9
11.452-55: 144n.31
11.490: 134n.36

11.497–507: 126n.3
11.556–57: 139n.5
11.569: 139n.5
11.604: 19
11.664–68: 139n.5
11.782–84: 146n.9
11.790–803: 122
11.794–803: 139n.15
11.805–8: 139n.11
11.817–18: 141n.31
11.823–24: 139n.5
12.3–35: 138n.50
12.10–16: 139n.2
12.10–18: 13, 133n.28, 141n.38, 142n.41
12.10–33: 140n.21
12.15: 136n.26
12.56–309: 131n.12
12.69–70: 139n.5
12.94–95: 134n.36
12.106–7: 139n.5
12.113–15: 131n.9, 141n.35
12.122–26: 139n.5
12.173–74: 125n.3
12.176: 145n.20
12.197–98: 139n.5
12.216–29: 139n.2
12.233–36: 125n.1
12.245–46: 139n.5
12.254–55: 125n.3
12.290–93: 125n.3
12.310–28: 146n.9
12.396: 137n.41
12.417–20: 139n.5
12.436–38: 125n.3
12.440–41: 139n.5
13.41–42: 139n.5
13.157: 134n.36
13.225–27: 76
13.317–20: 139n.5
13.347–50: 133n.25
13.433: 134n.36
13.453–54: 78
13.554–55: 135n.14
13.562–63: 135n.14
13.575: 125n.2
13.580: 125n.2
13.586: 134n.36
13.620–27: 13
13.628–29: 139n.5
13.744–47: 133n.28

13.778: 139n.5
13.810–13: 139n.2
13.813–14: 139n.5
13.828–32: 142n.47
13.831–32: 139n.5
14.44–47: 139n.5
14.65–68: 139n.5
14.69–70: 76
14.74–81: 61
14.75–81: 136n.28
14.366–69: 133n.25
14.374–75: 133n.25
14.438–39: 125n.2
14.508–22: 143n.58
14.519: 125n.2
15.4–217: 17
15.53–70: 139n.2
15.53–77: 78
15.56: 140n.18
15.56–77: 80
15.57–77: 133n.25
15.60–65: 3
15.61–65: 5, 19, 78, 123, 139nn.13, 15
15.63: 140n.23
15.64–65: 122
15.64–67: 135n.9, 141nn.36, 37
15.64–68: 19
15.64–77: 80
15.67: 135n.8
15.68: 18, 44, 141n.38
15.68–71: 142n.41
15.69–71: 139n.13
15.70–71: 136n.26, 139n.9
15.72–77: 133n.25
15.212–17: 136n.28
15.295: 139n.5
15.347–51: 139n.5
15.370–78: 139nn.2, 5
15.487–94: 139n.5
15.490–93: 125n.1
15.497–99: 136n.28
15.502–7: 139n.5
15.504–5: 76
15.592–600: 133n.25
15.592–604: 140n.20
15.596–600: 79
15.603–4: 139n.5
15.610–14: 140n.20
15.611–14: 133n.29, 140n.21
15.685–91: 140n.20
15.686–88: 139n.5

Homer, *Iliad (continued)*
15.693-95: 139n.5
15.699-700: 76, 139n.5
15.719-25: 125n.1
16.1-283: 132n.19
16.3-4: 4
16.46-47: 4, 13, 131n.9, 141n.37
16.60-63: 77
16.87-94: 141n.37
16.97-100: 101
16.112-24: 143n.58
16.247-52: 141n.37
16.284-86: 139n.11
16.316: 125n.2
16.325: 125n.2
16.339-41: 141n.33
16.419-30: 135n.8
16.433-34: 141n.36
16.433-38: 113
16.435-38: 134n.38
16.435-61: 141n.36
16.450-52: 141n.36
16.450-57: 85
16.458-61: 141n.36
16.502: 125n.2
16.502-3: 135n.8, 141n.36
16.527: 135n.6
16.544-57: 141nn.33, 39
16.559-61: 141nn.33, 39, 47
16.644-51: 135n.9, 141n.37
16.684-93: 141n.37
16.685-87: 131n.9
16.685-93: 135n.9
16.692-93: 12, 15
16.698-701: 60
16.705-9: 144n.2
16.724-25: 141n.37
16.777-80: 82
16.787: 135n.9, 141n.37
16.799-800: 133n.29
16.836: 86, 141n.33, 142n.47
16.851-54: 133n.29
16.852-54: 141n.38
16.855: 125n.2
16.855-57: 141n.37
17.39-40: 141n.33, 142n.47
17.110: 141n.33
17.125-27: 86, 141n.33, 142n.47
17.201-8: 18, 99-100, 133n.29, 140n.21, 141n.38
17.240-41: 141n.33

17.254-55: 141n.33
17.268-73: 86, 141n.33, 142n.43
17.287: 141n.33
17.497-98: 131n.9
17.556-58: 141n.33
17.637-39: 139n.5
17.658: 141n.33
17.666-67: 141n.33
17.711-14: 86
17.722-26: 141n.33
18.59-60: 142n.41
18.74-77: 133n.25
18.89-90: 142n.41
18.90-93: 133n.29
18.91-93: 141n.38
18.96: 141n.38, 142n.41
18.101: 142n.41
18.114-15: 133n.29, 141n.38
18.120-21: 142n.41
18.131-33: 133n.29
18.132-34: 141n.38
18.134-37: 133n.30
18.151-68: 86
18.165: 141n.40
18.165-68: 86-87
18.168: 142n.43
18.175-80: 142n.47
18.176-80: 141n.33
18.198: 139n.12
18.203-33: 87
18.215-16: 139n.12
18.249-50: 145n.16
18.261-72: 133n.29
18.270-72: 141n.33
18.283: 141n.33
18.293-95: 125n.1
18.305-9: 18, 100, 133n.29
18.310-13: 79
18.311-13: 131n.9
18.329-32: 142n.41
18.333-35: 133n.29
18.334-35: 141n.38, 142n.44
18.334-37: 88
18.336-37: 142n.44
18.429-56: 129n.22
18.440-41: 142n.41
19.1-20.258: 132n.19
19.86-138: 105
19.139-44: 133n.31
19.148-53: 133n.31
19.155-83: 133n.31

Index of Passages / 163

19.199–214: 133n.31
19.252–66: 135n.7
19.321–37: 133n.32
19.407–24: 144n.10
19.408–17: 132n.18
19.416–17: 142n.41
19.420–21: 143n.53
19.421–22: 142n.41
20.24–25: 135n.13
20.29–30: 60
20.75–78: 45
20.81: 134n.36
20.87: 134n.36
20.104–7: 56
20.136–37: 135n.13
20.288–91: 60
20.300–308: 133n.33, 141n.38
20.301–8: 56
20.313–17: 128n.7
20.351–64: 45
20.371–72: 45
20.375–80: 45
20.393: 125n.2
20.408: 134n.36
20.419–37: 45
20.441–43: 45–46
20.443–44: 46
20.452–54: 46
20.466: 131n.9
20.471: 125n.2
20.481–83: 141n.32
20.502–3: 46
21.4–5: 47
21.26–32: 88
21.34–35: 46–47
21.35: 46
21.40–43: 88
21.46–48: 16
21.47–48: 141n.35
21.97: 134n.36
21.100–105: 142n.45
21.110–13: 141n.41
21.122–25: 87, 88
21.133–35: 134n.40
21.181: 125n.2
21.200–204: 87
21.201–4: 88, 141n.32
21.224–26: 134n.40, 141n.38
21.273–83: 47
21.279–80: 134n.40
21.284–98: 47

21.294–97: 134n.40
21.296–97: 133n.35
21.297: 141n.38
21.316–23: 47
21.395–404: 141n.32
21.515–17: 60
21.542–43: 133n.35
21.544–46: 60
21.544–49: 56
21.553–70: 130n.8
22.37–91: 47
22.38–41: 141n.38
22.54–58: 141n.38
22.78: 48
22.86–89: 85, 141n.38
22.91: 48
22.99–130: 130n.8
22.99–131: 100
22.111–21: 47
22.122–30: 48
22.147–56: 139n.8
22.174–76: 47–48
22.174–81: 113
22.177–247: 48
22.209–13: 48
22.216–23: 141n.38
22.250–72: 85
22.297–305: 100
22.299–311: 141n.38
22.306–63: 48
22.325: 141n.38
22.335–36: 15, 88, 142n.44
22.338–60: 85
22.352–54: 15, 88–89, 142n.44
22.358–60: 142n.41
22.361: 125n.2, 141n.38
22.365–66: 142n.41
22.369–75: 142n.48
22.395: 142n.50
22.403–4: 142n.50
22.416–20: 142n.51
22.466–67: 125n.2
22.508–14: 85
23.19–23: 142n.44
23.22–23: 142n.44
23.80–81: 142n.41
23.82–92: 142n.41
23.150: 142n.41
23.175–76: 142n.44
23.179–83: 90
23.182–83: 142n.44

Homer, *Iliad (continued)*
  23.184-91: 142n.50
  23.236-48: 143n.63
  23.243-48: 142n.41
  23.676: 135n.18
  23.768-79: 134n.2
  23.771: 135n.6
  23.863-64: 134n.2
  23.872-73: 134n.2
  23.884-97: 144n.63
  24.11: 137n.41
  24.15-18: 89
  24.27-30: 13, 128n.7
  24.131-32: 142n.41
  24.139-40: 89, 141n.40
  24.144-58: 137n.37
  24.171-87: 137n.37
  24.220-22: 145n.17
  24.406-23: 142n.48
  24.486-92: 133n.32
  24.511: 133n.32
  24.525-26: 144n.2
  24.538-42: 142n.41
  24.543-48: 139n.8
  24.601-19: 119, 133n.32
  24.650-55: 91
  24.660-70: 102
  24.751-53: 88
  24.778-803: 102
Odyssey
  1.1-9: 143n.57
  1.325-27: 129n.3
  1.351-52: 112
  3.109: 128n.7
  3.130-328: 129n.3
  4.253-55: 139n.7
  4.259-89: 128n.7
  4.441-592: 129n.3
  4.561-69: 144n.65
  8.234: 135n.18
  books 9-12: 129n.3
  9.526-35: 135n.11
  11.333-34: 110
  11.339-41: 110
  11.543-65: 128n.7
  13.1-2: 110
  16.235-57: 132n.19
  18.129-42: 144n.2
  20.276-83: 132n.9
  21.1-4: 132n.9
  21.188-241: 132n.9
  21.234-241: 132n.9
  21.265-68: 132n.9
  22.109-15: 132n.9
  22.142-45: 132n.9
  24.417-19: 142n.45
Homeric scholia
  Il. 1.1: 130n.15
  Il. 1.3: 32
  Il. 1.4: 141n.30
  Il. 1.106: 128n.7
  Il. 1.108-9: 128n.7
  Il. 2.156: 136n.23
  Il. 2.382: 132n.13
  Il. 3.95: 135n.18
  Il. 6.114: 137n.39, 139n.40
  Il. 6.280: 137n.40
  Il. 6.311: 138n.48
  Il. 6.371: 137n.44
  Il. 6.392: 67, 138n.45
  Il. 6.471: 138n.47
  Il. 6.476: 138n.47
  Il. 6.487: 138n.47
  Il. 7.29: 132n.22
  Il. 8.475-76: 140n.17
  Il. 11.356: 125n.2
  Il. 15.56: 140n.18
  Il. 15.63: 140n.23
  Il. 17.272: 142n.42
  Il. 20.443: 133n.34
  Il. 21.543: 133n.35
Longinus
  On the Sublime 13.3: 147n.16
Ovid
  Metamorphoses 8.270-525: 120
Plato
  Protagoras
    316C5-D2: 145n.24
  Republic
    596C: 145n.26
Vergil
  Aeneid 12.940-52: 91

General Index

Achilles, 8, 38-39, 44-45; character of, 79-80; choice of, 101, 113-14; foresight of, 89-90, 101-3, 144n.11; suggestions of, 17, 27-28; threats of, 15, 87-91; vows of, 18-19
Alexandrian scholars, 3, 8-9, 32, 60, 80-81, 106, 126n.5, 127n.19, 127n.20, 130n.15. *See also* Homeric scholia *in Index of Passages*
Alternatives. *See* Innovation
Analysts, 3, 126n.5
Aristotle, 126n.14, 128n.8
Athetesis, 3, 80-81, 126n.5, 128n.8, 140n.18
Audience: ancient listening, 5-6, 14, 105-6; expectations of, 1-8, 13-14, 23-24, 25-26, 35-37, 85-86; implied, 12-13, 95-105, 127nn.4, 5; knowledge of, 7-8, 13, 20-21, 31, 36, 48-49, 52, 58-59, 92; and miscalculation, 8, 98-105, 107-8; modern reading, 6, 14, 106-7, 127n.6; perspective of, 21-22, 52-53, 54-57, 58-62, 69-71, 95-108, 127n.20, 134n.4, 144nn.4, 12

Delay: types of, 36-37, 62; and interruption, 36-37; and reversal, 36-37, 131n.3, 132n.23; and retardation, 7, 35-49, 131n.1

Expectations. *See* Achilles; Audience; Hector

Foreshadowing, 4-6, 13, 111-12; effects of, 6, 95-97, 103; mechanism of, 19-20; and paradigms, 121-22; relationship of, to misdirection, 6, 21-22, 102-3, 111-12; scholarship on, 126n.13

Hector: boasts of, 18; expectations of, 2, 98-101, 103, 125n.1

Iliad. See Innovation; Narrative; Tradition
Innovation: alternatives, 32-33, 130n.5, 130n.8; alternatives to the plot, 23-33, 37, 47-48, 91-92, 134n.38; alternatives to the tradition, 7-8, 22, 23, 30-31, 37, 82-83, 127n.17; untraditional episodes, 6, 37, 51-54, 59-62

Misdirection, 1-3; defined, 3-4, 6, 14, 20; effects of, 4-5, 6-7, 14, 73, 95-108; and false anticipation, 35-49; influence of, on later literature, 116-17; mechanism of, 14, 20; and miscalculation, 22; and paradigms, 121-24; relationship of, to foreshadowing, 6, 11, 21-22, 111-12; and suspense, 16, 51-71, 86-87, 134n.1; thematic, 73-93
Mutilation, 83-93

Narrative: analysis of, 12; and plot, 21, 24, 129n.22; structure of, 4, 127n.18
Narrator: characteristics of, 12; choices of, 15; and poet, 12, 127n.3; reliability of, 79, 102, 126n.6, 129nn.14, 15; strategy of, 21-22. *See also* Poet

Oral theorists, 3, 126n.5

Paradigms, 119-24
Performance, 7-8, 11-12, 81-82, 105-6,

165

Performance *(continued)*
    109-12, 127n.2, 129n.14, 145nn.1, 2, 22, 24; oral, and jazz, 114-16
Poet: attitude of, toward the tradition, 32-33, 109-10, 112-16; and composition, 4; historical situation of, 5-6, 105-6; motivations of, 1, 3-4, 7-8, 14, 109-18; and narrator, 12, 109. *See also* Narrator
Predictions: absence of, 16; accuracy of, 19; authoritative, 16-18, 23-24, 31, 37-39, 73-74, 90-91; completeness of, 19; correction of, 18, 80; defined, 14-15; false, 1-3, 6-8, 19; fulfillment of, 6-7, 19, 23, 36-37; hierarchy of, 17-18, 22, 129n.15; inexactitude of, 81-83, 140n.24; network of, 18-19, 74-75, 78, 129n.18; postponed fulfillment of, 35-49; precision of, 74, 129nn.19, 20; reinforcement of, 19, 79-80
Prophecy, 104, 145nn.16, 17

Retardation. *See* Delay

Ships, 73-83, 139nn.6, 7
Suspense. *See* Misdirection

Tradition: orality, 127nn.1, 6, 129n.14, 18; relationship of, to fate, 21, 32-33, 60-62, 67-69, 130n.16, 146n.5; in story of Trojan War and Homecomings (Nostoi), 5, 11, 12-13, 26-27, 31, 75-76, 92-93, 128nn.7, 8, 129n.3, 130n.10. *See also* Innovation
Typical scenes: "A if not B," 60, 64, 136nn.23, 24, 25; aristeia, 134n.41; divine rescue, 56-57, 135nn.12, 13, 14; duel, 55-56; prayer, 15-16, 54-55, 65-66, 128nn.4, 134nn.2, 5, 138n.50; prelude, 39-43, 132n.19

Zeus, predictions of, 1-3, 15, 17, 19, 22, 38-39, 78-79, 126n.4